Integrated Project
Support Environments

The Aspect Project

This is volume 33 in the A.P.I.C. Series

General Editors: M.J.R. Shave *and* I.C. Wand

A complete list of titles in this series appears at the end of this volume

The A.P.I.C. Series
No 33

Integrated Project Support Environments

The Aspect Project

Edited by

ALAN W. BROWN

*Department of Computer Science,
University of York, Heslington, England*

ACADEMIC PRESS

Harcourt Brace Jovanovich, Publishers
London   San Diego   New York   Boston
Sydney   Tokyo   Toronto

ACADEMIC PRESS LIMITED
24/28 Oval Road,
London NW1 7DX

United States Edition published by
ACADEMIC PRESS INC.
San Diego, CA 92101

British Library Cataloguing in Publication Data

Is available

ISBN 0–12–136740–1

Printed in Great Britain by
T. J. Press (Padstow) Ltd., Padstow, Cornwall

Contents

Foreword

An important plank of the Alvey Programme on IT Research and Development was the proposition that the use of Software Engineering Tools and Methods would be advanced by producing a series of Integrated Project Support Environments. These would provide integrated support throughout the software life-cycle for the designers, implementors and eventually for the systems maintainers. Three generations of IPSEs were planned, respectively to be file based, data based, and knowledge based systems, and it was expected that full development of these projects would need up to ten years to come to fruition.

The eventual outcome was that three major projects were launched, each of four years duration; Aspect, Eclipse, and IPSE 2.5. Each investigated different approaches to the issue of building a useful IPSE; in the case of Aspect the central design choice was to base the system around a relational database.

We are now in the post-Alvey era and it is time to evaluate what has been achieved in order to derive the maximum possible benefit from the substantial investments made in the Alvey Programme. It is important to publish the results as widely as possible.

I welcome this book as a substantial contribution to this task. Publication as a book gives a valuable opportunity to study the project as a whole in a coherent way which separate papers would not achieve. The co-operation necessary to produce it demonstrates the continuing benefits of the style of co-operative working between partners both from industry and academia which was brought about in large measure by the Alvey programme. It is, in my opinion, well worth study by all concerned with the development of large software systems.

Professor J.N. Buxton

Director, Systems Engineering
Information Technology Division
Department of Trade and Industry

Preface

Over the past twenty years many large scale software development projects have been notorious for being behind schedule, over-budget, and producing a low quality end-product. Indeed, it has been suggested [14, 42] that:

- at least 15 per cent of all software projects never deliver anything; that is, they fail utterly to achieve their established goals;
- overruns of 100 and 200 per cent are common in software projects;
- the cost of maintaining a software system is typically more than twice the original development cost.

Given the large amounts of money which are being spent on software development (for example, it is estimated that in the USA over 50 billion dollars were spent on software development and maintenance in 1987), there is clearly a need for a better approach to building such systems.

One approach which seems to offer hope to large scale software developers is to provide automated support for the development process whenever possible. The aim of this approach is to develop an **Integrated Project Support Environment (IPSE)** which helps control and coordinate the many tasks which must take place within a large software project.

The **Aspect** project, started in 1984, was directly concerned with investigating issues involved in realising a practical, cooperative IPSE. This book provides an overview of the work carried out on the Aspect project, with particular attention focussed on a prototype IPSE implementation which was developed in order to evaluate some of the Aspect concepts.

The Organisation of the Book

The book starts with a discussion of the software crisis, and introduces IPSE technology in general as a possible solution. This is followed by an overview of the approach taken by the Aspect project to building an IPSE, illustrated by a demonstration of a prototype Aspect IPSE. Each technical area studied by the Aspect project is then discussed in depth. Finally, the achievements of Aspect are put into a wider software engineering context by comparing them with other work in the IPSE area.

Due to the large, diverse, and collaborative nature of the Aspect project, the book is organised as a collection of individual papers describing many of the specialised areas which were examined in the project. Note that the use of a large number of authors in writing the chapters of this book has inevitably resulted in a variation in the styles and approaches used for each chapter. However, far from being a drawback of the multi-author approach, we believe that this has encouraged the use of a style which is most appropriate to the material being discussed. Hence, each chapter conveys its subject matter in the most the suitable format, ranging from high-level descriptions in Chapters 1, 2 and 3, to formal definition in the Z specification language in the case of Chapter 10.

The Structure of the Book

The book divides into five main parts.

Part 1

The first part comprises Chapters 1, 2, 3 and 4 and provides an introduction and overview of IPSE technology in general, and the work carried out by Aspect in particular.

- **Chapter 1** is a general introduction to the Aspect project, describing the background, funding and organisation of the project.

- **Chapter 2** argues the need for an IPSE, and describes the basic architectural principles of current work on IPSEs. The basic requirements for an IPSE are reviewed, and previous attempts at tool development are briefly discussed. The issue of tool integration is then developed in more detail.

- **Chapter 3** provides an overview of the main aims and approach of the Aspect project, and describes the architecture adopted for the Aspect IPSE.

- **Chapter 4** gives details of the demonstration example which is used to illustrate some of the later descriptions of the Aspect IPSE technology.

Part 2

The next three parts of the book deal with the technology of building an Aspect IPSE. Each part concentrates on the details of the conceptual design and implementation of the component Aspect technologies. Part 2 is concerned with the central database, or information base, which forms the heart of an Aspect IPSE.

- **Chapter 5**, the Information Base Engine, describes how the information base is built on top of a relational database using Codd's extended relational model RM/T to provide the enhanced semantic features required.

- **Chapter 6**, the Information Base Superstructure, describes facilities to support the software development process which we believe will be common to any IPSE that might be configured within the Aspect framework. These include task (or, activity) definition and planning, the view mechanism which provides an object-oriented abstract environment, the rule mechanism, the publication mechanism, configuration management, and version control.

Part 3

In the third part of the book, the important user interface work of the Aspect project is discussed in detail.

- **Chapter 7**, Human Computer Interface Perspectives, describes the overall philosophy of that part of the architecture which handles the interface to users.
- **Chapter 8** describes in detail the user interface component of the Aspect IPSE known as the Presenter.
- **Chapter 9** describes the Doubleview tool. This is an interactive tool for quickly developing user interfaces using the Aspect Presenter.

Part 4

The fourth part of the book examines the work on supporting host/target software development which was an important component of the Aspect project.

- **Chapter 10** describes the work on host/target debugging of distributed Ada programs. The development of real-time application software (such as avionics systems) is a major driving force of much of the current work in IPSEs.

Part 5

The final part of the book summarises the achievements of the Aspect project, and attempts to place the Aspect work in the context of current IPSE developments.

- **Chapter 11** examines work on PCTE, CAIS and ATIS, relating it to the work that was carried out in the Aspect Project.
- **Chapter 12** summarises the achievements of the Aspect project, and draws comparisons with other Alvey-funded IPSE projects.

Acknowledgements

As a large collaborative project, there have been many people who have had a direct influence on the Aspect Project. In addition to the contributors to this book, we acknowledge the work of a number of others:

- At SD-Scicon, Anthony Hall (now with Praxis Ltd.) and Dave Robinson were particularly influential. Both acted as technical architects for the project, and as such made major contributions to the success of the Aspect project. Peter Rusling (now with Systematica) smoothed the running of the project by dealing with much of the administration, and was responsible for overseeing much of the work on Perspective Kernel.
- At MARI, work on the distribution of the information base was carried out by a large number of people over the lifetime of the project. These included Phil Fisher, Anirban Bhattacharyya, Rachel Wilmer, Anthony Davies, and Sidney Burness.
- At York, Ben Dillistone (now with Praxis Ltd.) was responsible for much of the early work on the Aspect version control and configuration management system.

- Ian Wand was in overall charge of the work carried out at York, and Brian Randell performed a similar role at Newcastle.

The work described in this book was supported by the Science and Engineering Research Council (SERC) through the Alvey Software Engineering Directorate under a number of grants, including:

GR/C/98092 - Research and Development Leading to a Distributed Integrated Project Support Environment (1st July 1984 to 31st October 1987).

GR/E/05353 and GR/E/06398 - Aspect Two: Centrally procured equipment (1st November 1986 to 31st October 1987).

GR/D/86041 - SE Computing Facilities to Support Additional Research in IPSE's (1st February 1986 to 31st January 1987).

GR/E/42303 and GR/E/42082 - SE/170 Aspect Change II (1st July 1987 to 31st March 1989).

Finally, my thanks to Alison Pearcy and Robert Stroud who were particularly active in providing me with help during the editing process for this book. The final form of the book has been greatly enhanced by their work, particularly Robert's diligent reviewing of the final drafts of the book.

Alan W. Brown
University of York

List of Contributors

Ian D. Benest	University of York
Alan W. Brown	University of York
Anthony N. Earl	Hewlett-Packard Laboratories
Peter Hitchcock	University of York
Sylvia J. Holmes	University of York
Andy D. Hutcheon	University of York
Alison Pearcy	University of York
Ann Petrie	University of Newcastle upon Tyne
David S. Snowden	University of York
Robert J. Stroud	University of Newcastle upon Tyne
Roger K. Took	University of York
Ray A. Weedon	Open University
Andy J. Wellings	University of York
Richard P. Whittington	Hand, Whittington and Associates

The work reported in this book was carried out while the above contributors were employed by the Universities of York and/or Newcastle upon Tyne.

Chapter 1

Introduction

P. Hitchcock and A.W. Brown

1.1 Project History

The Aspect project had its origins in March 1982, when Mr. Kenneth Baker, the Minister for information technology in the United Kingdom, set up a committee to advise on the scope of a collaborative research programme in Information Technology (IT). This committee was formed as a direct result of the unveiling, in October 1981, of the Japanese Fifth Generation Computer Programme, which was seen to pose a major competitive threat to the UK IT industry. The Committee, chaired by John Alvey, produced its report in the summer of 1982, which became known as the *Alvey Report.*

The Alvey report recommended a five-year programme to mobilise the UK's technical strengths in IT by setting up collaborative projects between industry, the academic sector and other research organisations. The cost would be 350 million pounds with the Government contributing two-thirds of the direct cost of the programme. Four areas of work were identified: software engineering, man-machine interfaces, intelligent knowledge based systems and very large scale integration. Within these areas of work the emphasis was to be on the core enabling technologies. For software engineering this was the concept of the **Information Systems Factory (ISF)**. The ISF would provide an integrated set of tools for producing IT systems using software engineering techniques and would be developed from successive generations of **Integrated Project Support Environments (IPSEs)**, starting with a consolidated set of the tools that were currently available.

The Alvey Report identified three generations of project support environment:

1. The first generation IPSEs consisted of separate tools which interacted at the file level. The Unix operating system and its associated tools was a good example of this approach.

2. Second generation IPSEs were to be developed around suitable database systems. Information would be shared at a finer granularity than was possible with the file based technology used by first generation IPSEs. In addition, it would be possible to hold in the database descriptions of the data as well as the actual data itself.

3. The third generation IPSE was the Information Systems Factory which would introduce the more powerful facilities of a knowledge base to a second generation IPSE.

The time-scale was that the ISF should be available by year 6 of the programme.

The Alvey Report was accepted by the Government and three IPSE projects were started. These were Aspect, Eclipse [17], and IPSE 2.5 [93]. Both Aspect and Eclipse are examples of second generation IPSEs. Eclipse was developed using the Portable Common Tool Environment (PCTE) [27], an Esprit project funded by the European Economic Commission. IPSE 2.5, as its name suggests, is a further stepping stone along the route towards an ISF, in this case investigating support for formal methods and the incorporation of knowledge based system techniques.

The **Aspect** project itself started in January 1984. It was a collaborative venture between four industrial companies and two Universities, and was the first contract to be awarded by the Alvey Software Engineering Directorate. The proposed work plan for the first three years of Aspect amounted to 80 person years, for which an initial grant of over two million pounds was awarded.* System Designers PLC (now SD-Scicon) led the Aspect project as the prime contractor during its primary three year term. The other industrial partners were International Computers Limited (ICL), GEC Computers Limited, and MARI Advanced Electronics Limited. The academic partners were the Universities of York and Newcastle upon Tyne.

1.2 The Aim of the Aspect Project

The aim of Aspect was to carry out research into second generation IPSE technology, and to demonstrate and evaluate the results of the research through a number of prototype IPSEs supporting the distributed development of large scale software systems. Aspect was particularly interested in support for multi-language programming, host-target working, and any prototype would give support to all stages of the software development process.

Aspect has produced two such environments. The first is a prototype IPSE framework embodying advanced research in key areas. This is the prototype which forms the basis for discussion in this book, and is subsequently referred to as ''the Aspect IPSE''. The second is an exploitable commercial IPSE framework, called

---

* The Alvey funding rules were that the Universities received all of their direct costs, and the industrial partners, one half.

Perspective Kernel (PK), which was developed from current technology by extending an existing Systems Designers product called Perspective. Results from the research thread of the project were fed directly into PK which acted as a vehicle for the commercial exploitation of those research results. Details of the PK system can be found elsewhere [68].

Following a successful demonstration of an early research prototype at the Alvey Conference in July 1987, the project was funded for an additional year to continue development and provide more analysis of the Aspect IPSE.

1.3 Achievements of the Aspect Project

The major achievement of the Aspect project was an increased understanding of *integrated* support for large scale software development. This was a direct consequence of the development of a prototype Aspect IPSE which brought together much of the work which had been carried out in the various component technologies.

In addition, however, many secondary benefits have come from the project besides the research results described in this book. In particular, collaboration between academic and industrial partners of the project was very successful, notwithstanding the early withdrawal of GEC from the project. Essential to the smooth running of the project was co-ordination of the development effort of more than fifteen people, distributed on five sites, over a period of four years. This success can be attributed to three main factors:

1. There was a clear technical direction for the project provided by a full-time technical architect. The importance of this role in coordinating the development effort cannot be overstated.

2. The formal notation **Z** [95] (developed by the Programming Research Group at the University of Oxford) was used throughout the first three years of the project for the specification of the Aspect facilities. While the formal specification of Aspect IPSE services was a major achievement in itself [84], the use of a formal notation, although requiring a significant amount of effort to learn in the early stages of the project, proved to be an important common basis for the integration of the individual design efforts. During technical discussions it also provided a common language, understood by all project members.

3. All the project partners had an effective means of electronic communication. While this might seem to be a trivial requirement, the infrastructure which we constructed to allow technical documents to be quickly and uniformly communicated between all sites proved to be vital to the smooth running of the project.

As a result, close ties have been built between the project partners which have continued beyond the life-time of the project.

Chapter 2

Basic IPSE Principles

A.W. Brown, P. Hitchcock and R.J. Stroud

2.1 Introduction

Improving the quality and productivity of computer software development has long been the aim of the software engineering community. Initially, programming productivity was increased when high-level languages were used in place of assembler languages. This gave a big boost to the production of computer-based systems. Since then, however, systems have become more complex, and programming forms less and less of the total system development effort. Typically, more than eighty per cent of the resources required by a software project are used in areas of the project such as requirements analysis, design, testing, and maintenance [14]. Thus, it has been recognised that the next major increases in productivity will come from integrating all these development activities into a well-planned and controlled structure, with automated support through an IPSE.

Evidence for this is beginning to emerge. For example, British Aerospace used one of the first support environments when they produced the avionics software for the Experimental Aircraft Project. They found that for an investment of thirty thousand pounds per person they were able to increase productivity by a factor of six [108]. Furthermore, it was possible to add extra staff to the project when it was running late and to successfully bring it back to schedule. Contrary to most previous experience, this could be achieved because use of an IPSE ensured that the interfaces and specifications were under such tight control that people could be brought in to build part of the system to a sound specification in isolation from the others. The IPSE enforced a measure of consistency between the resultant components.

The problem of maintaining consistency between the components of a system is relatively straightforward for a small project. For example, if a program is conceived, designed and implemented by one person, it is easy to keep track of the interaction between the design and the code, and to find the latest versions of modules when the system is built. (Even so, many of us run into problems if a certain amount of self-discipline is not maintained.) Introducing an IPSE would probably not be cost effective for such a small project. However, a typical large software development project will involve not just one person, but perhaps a hundred developers responsible for eight thousand source files scattered across eight machines [86]. When the problems of maintaining consistency are scaled up to such a project, they become much more serious. Clearly, some form of computer-based support is required simply to administer the development process and to control access to source code. It is this scale of project that IPSEs are intended to benefit.

2.2 History and Development of IPSEs

2.2.1 Individual tools

Over the years, numerous languages, notations and methodologies have been defined to help understand software development during each phase of the software life-cycle. Individual software tools that automate some aspect of these methods and techniques can greatly increase their usefulness [19].

As an example, consider the project which produced the IBM operating system, OS/360. That project involved about five thousand person years of effort between 1963 and 1966, and required many individual tools to be developed to bring it to fruition. Brooks [18] considers that one of the most useful aspects of the OS/360 development environment was the control of program libraries. Each development group had a 'playpen' area where they could develop and test new versions of programs without affecting anybody else. When a private version had been tested, it was integrated into the next larger component of the system. This *system integration library* was under the control of the system manager and the original programmer could not change it. It could now be used by others working in the subsystem to build and test their components without the fear that it would be changed underneath them. If a new version was introduced, then the users of the old version could be informed. When a system version was ready for wider use it could be promoted to the *current version sublibrary*. Brooks claims that two important lessons were learned: formal control of versions was taken away from the programmer, and versions were formally moved between separate sublibraries.

Another example of the individual tool approach comes from the Unix development environment. A large measure of the success of Unix has been because of its library of tools. For example, *Make* is a program for maintaining computer programs [49]. Programs may be built from modules which are dependent on each other. For example, two source programs may each use the same library of definitions at compile time, with run-time libraries included at load-time to obtain an executable program. These libraries are themselves liable to change and, hence, a lot of work will be wasted if everything is recompiled to rebuild the system following a single change to these libraries. To overcome these problems using *Make*, the dependencies between files are captured in a *Makefile*, together with the commands necessary to recreate a dependent file if any of the files it depends upon are changed. When a system build is requested, *Make* examines the *Makefile* to determine which components need to be re-built to create the system. During a system build only those components which have changed, or depend on some component that has changed, will be recreated.

While very useful in its own right as an individual tool, we can use the *Make* tool to highlight some of the problems that may come from using individual, but not integrated, tools. The first point is that the *Makefile* for *Make* essentially contains a description of the system design. Such a design is often most naturally represented by some form of design diagram, as diagrammatic notations are often easier to both construct and to understand. *Makefiles* for large systems are notoriously difficult to write, and even more difficult to maintain. One way to provide this would be to integrate the system design phase with the generation of the *Makefile* in such a way that the *Makefile* could be automatically generated.

The second point is that the format of the *Makefile* is peculiar to *Make*. If, for example, you wanted to carry out some impact analysis and see what components must be re-built if a particular sub-component is changed, it would be most easily achieved by querying the *Makefile*. The complex format of the *Makefile* notation does not facilitate this. If, however, if *Makefiles* were represented in a database according to a well known schema, then the integration of *Make* information with other tasks would be much easier.

In many ways, the set of tools available on Unix provide a software developer's workbench [78]. Other tools in the workbench include SCCS [85] a tool which manages versions of files by means of a naming convention and changes to a base version of the file. Other tools include Build [48] that is an extension to *Make* which allows the *Makefile* to be shared between members of a programming team in such a way that it builds the system using an individual's private files in preference to common shared files. Hence, it achieves the separation of private and public libraries referred to earlier. However, it is up to other tools to establish the control over the promotion of versions from private to public areas.

2.2.2 Integration of construction tools

Individual tools become much more powerful when linked to other tools which support different phases of the software development life-cycle. Initial attempts at tool integration produced a customised development environment by linking together an existing set of individual tools. Due to the original construction of the individual tools, attempts to bind tools together usually required a great deal of effort. The principle exception to this was within the Unix development environment, which provided a number of simple mechanisms for aggregating the individual tools it provided. For example, The Software Development System [86] is an example of the construction of a set of tools to manage some aspects of software development. It consists of four distinct software administration and generation systems:

1.   The Modification Request database system identifies requests and links them

to changes in the source programs. This enables the appropriate tracking and status reports to be generated.

2.   The Change Management System uses SCCS and its own database system to relate source file changes to a Modification Request.

3.   The Software Generation System constructs executable software for three different software environments.

4.   The Build tool is used in conjunction with the Software Generation System to control private, test and released versions through a mechanism of software views.

Using this approach a *closed* environment is provided; i.e. a fixed set of tools are fitted together to provide a development environment which cannot be changed, extended, or customised by the environment users. Other examples include CADES [67] developed by ICL, and Clear/Caster [26] developed by IBM.

2.2.3 Integration of design tools

Earlier we alluded to linking the design objects to the implementation. Recently, some stages of the design phase have been incorporated into support environments. For example, Mascot [9] is a diagrammatic notation which identifies system components and the interfaces which interconnect them. These diagrams can be expressed in an extended Pascal programming language notation which allows them to be machine checked for consistency. This forms the basis of the Perspective programming environment [100] which automates many of the tasks necessary to design systems in MASCOT for subsequent implementation in Pascal.

Although environments such as Perspective extend the range of the software life-cycle that is automated, they still provide a closed set of tools. It would be better to build *open* environments that allowed support for new methods and techniques to be added in the form of new tools. Such environments could themselves evolve throughout the life of the project.

An early example of this open approach can be found within the data processing community. *Data Dictionaries* were invented out of necessity when users of early database systems found it necessary to keep track of the dependencies between the database structures and their use by application programs. In the mid 1970s data dictionaries began to hold design information about databases. The *conceptual* model expressed in terms of entities, relationships and attributes was held in the dictionary together with its mapping onto the *implementation* in terms of records, fields and sets. (More details about these ideas can be found in the report of the British Computer Society Data Dictionary Systems Working Party [10].)

The data dictionary has now become the focus for generic tools such as report writers, query processors and very high level languages, which all work together in a very integrated fashion. Hence, a set of tools for database application development are integrated around the data dictionary information.

The advantage of this approach is that the data dictionary information is stored in a way that is amenable to (privileged) users with a general query language available to obtain the information. Thus, new tools can be integrated more easily. Database manufacturers have been continually extending the range of tools which they provide, centred on the data dictionary. For example, database systems are now often equipped with graphical query languages, screen painters, fourth generation languages (4GLs), and entity-relationship design tools.

2.2.4 Project support

The tools and environments described so far have concentrated on the production process. However, it has been recognised that many other factors are critical to the success of a project. In particular, *managerial* aspects of the project can be as influential as *technical* considerations. Thus, support environments must also provide support for project planning and organisation, allow management visibility and control, task allocation, and many other functions. Good communications are essential. Electronic mail, query languages, support tools for critical paths methods and resource allocation are essential for an integrated *project* support environment.

2.3 Architectural Principles*

One of the most important architectural principles governing the design of an IPSE is its approach towards integration. Indeed, the whole history of the development of IPSEs may be portrayed as a quest for greater degrees of tool integration. It is integration that binds the tools provided by the environment together to form a coherent whole, and it is this property of coherence that distinguishes an integrated environment from an arbitrary collection of incompatible tools. However, to achieve a truly integrated environment requires a revolutionary approach which is not pragmatic in a world that is already populated with large collections of incompatible tools. The only pragmatic alternative is to adopt a more evolutionary approach and recognise different degrees of integration.

The facilities provided by the IPSE infrastructure are described by an interface that is used by tools. Thus, it is these facilities which control the degree of integration that is possible between tools constructed to use the same interface. By layering the infrastructure and not insisting that tools can only use the top-level interface, it is possible to achieve different degrees of integration. Tools using a lower level of the infrastructure will be less well integrated than tools using a higher level of the infrastructure. However, the use of de-facto (or even official) standards such as Unix and PCTE for the lower levels of the infrastructure will make it easier to port foreign tools to the environment, even though they will not be able to take advantage of the facilities provided by the higher levels of the infrastructure without being rewritten. Hopefully, as IPSE technology matures and becomes more widely accepted by industry, the degree of standardisation and commonality at higher levels of IPSE infrastructure will increase, thus encouraging tool vendors to rewrite their tools to use these higher level interfaces and hence achieve a greater degree of integration with native tools provided by the IPSE supplier.

---

* This section was written by R.J.Stroud while he was employed by MARI Applied Technologies Ltd. on the RACE funded ARISE project. It has previously been published as part of RACE deliverable 21/IPS/RD1/DS/B/009/B1 and appears here by kind permission of MARI Ltd. and IPSYS Software Plc.

2.3.1 Integrating principles

At least three kinds of integration have been identified and are commonly accepted. These are integration by user interface, integration by data and integration by control. Each will now be discussed in turn.

Integration by user interface

At a superficial level there is integration by user interface. The way in which the functions offered by a given tool are invoked should be based on some kind of easily learned common metaphor shared by all tools such as a control panel interface or a pulldown menu bar. All tools should share the same "look and feel" so that a user can interact with an unfamiliar tool without difficulty. Of course, it will still be necessary for a user to understand what each function of the tool does and this may require very detailed technical knowledge for a complex tool or toolset. Even so, the use of meta-tools such as generic editors makes it possible to construct a whole family of tools that share a great deal of functionality at an abstract level and only differ in the details of the notation they support. This is a more sophisticated form of integration. In much the same way that the layers of the infrastructure allow different levels of integration, different degrees of customisation of a meta-tool can provide families of related toolsets, integrated to a greater or lesser extent.

Integration by data

Another kind of integration is integration by data. An important service that the infrastructure of an IPSE provides to its tools is a repository for persistent data. Several technologies are possible for implementing this repository: a conventional file system, a database (relational, network, object-oriented or whatever), or a knowledge base.

Even if two tools are integrated in the sense that they use the same kind of repository, they still need to agree a common representation if they are to share data. Data modelling languages make it possible for the semantics of a data model to be expressed independently of the technology which will be used to represent that schema. Thus, Entity-Relationship models may be implemented by relational databases or object management systems [32].

If tools which share a common data model access their persistent data in terms of that model rather than in terms of the implementation-dependent database schema that is used to represent that model, then integration is possible, even if the tools do not share the same underlying database technology. Furthermore, even if it is not possible for every tool in the IPSE to share the same universal data model of the entire project, it should still be possible for clusters of tools to share common data models that are perhaps overlapping subsets of an idealised whole.

Integration within such groups of tools is possible because of the common data model; integration across such groups requires mapping between two different representations of the same information with possibly different semantics, a problem which is intractable in general but may be soluble in specific cases. Again, the use of meta-tools can produce a family of tools, integrated around a common data model shared by all the customisations of a given tool, and differing only in the refinements of the customisations. Thus, a generic design editor may specify the way in which diagrams are to be stored as graphs of nodes and arcs but allow this representation to be extended to allow different kinds of arcs and nodes with method-specific attributes. A software metric tool that measured the complexity of diagrams could thus be applied to a diagram produced by any method-specific customisation of the generic design editor provided that its complexity measures were only expressed in terms of the abstract node/arc model supported by the generic editor.

The information base component of an IPSE which provides the repository for persistent data is used to model as much as possible of the real-world project that the IPSE is supporting. This will include both information about the artifacts that the project is developing and information about the process by which those artifacts are developed. Although artifacts such as software and design documents will be constructed using specific tools and methodologies and will thus contain method-specific information, there will still be a need to store management information about the process by which these artifacts were developed which will be method-independent (or at least independent of the technical method employed, if not the method of management).

This separation into method-independent and method-specific information affords another opportunity for tool integration. Tools that are only concerned with a particular technical method should not be concerned with the management of the process in which that method is employed. Similarly, tools that are concerned with the management of a process, should not need to be aware of the technical details of the tools employed during that process. By maintaining a clean separation between management information and technical information in the information base, it should be possible to develop tools and methods to support change management and project management procedures which can then be applied to any of the artifacts in the environment, irrespective of the technical information represented by those artifacts.

For example, such a separation would make it possible for tools to operate without considering configuration management (CM) issues in a context set separately by a CM tool. Rather than achieving integration by agreeing a common view of CM, CM would be abstracted away altogether, thus freeing a technical tool writer from these management concerns and ensuring a uniform treatment of these management issues by specialised tools. The alternative approach, that of making the developer of a technical tool responsible for interfacing his/her tool to the CM system, has been shown to be undesirable by past experience because it adds an unnecessary burden to the tool writer and risks an inconsistent treatment of CM issues across the system.

Database technologies which can help to achieve the necessary separation between management and technical information are the ability to define two different views of the attributes and relationships associated with a given object (perhaps by the use of multiple inheritance), and the use of fine-structured objects within a coarse-grained object management system such as PCTE to separate management information common to all objects from the internal details of any particular object.

Integration by control

Information about the process by which artifacts are developed can be used for management purposes to monitor and control the progress of the project. However, such information can also be used to guide the progress of the project and provide active support for the software developer. In particular, knowledge about the sequence in which tools must be applied to particular objects can be used to guide the user through a complex sequence of tool invocations. Similarly, knowledge about the tasks which have been assigned to a particular user and the resources they require in the way of information and tools can be used to set up a working context for a given task in which only those things which are relevant to the task in hand are available.

This kind of integration is called integration by control because it controls the manner in which tools are invoked. Control can take many forms and again there are various degrees of integration possible. A flexible approach in this area is more likely to be acceptable to software developers who will probably not appreciate being overly constrained. Control at one level may provide guidance in the use of a particular method-specific toolset; control at another level may take the form of generic browsing tool for locating objects in the database and invoking appropriate tools on them.

2.3.2 A layered model of integration

If an IPSE is to support integration by user interface, integration by data and integration by control with the degree of flexibility described above, then it cannot impose a rigorous, inflexible structure on the tool builder. Paradoxically, although IPSEs are intended to promote a degree of openness that makes them attractive to foreign tool suppliers, the more integrated they are, the more inflexible and closed their structure becomes. What is needed is a loosely coupled, flexible structure supporting different levels of integration.

The traditional picture of the structure of an IPSE, proposed in the Stoneman model [29] is circular, showing a central database surrounded by a family of tools and enclosed by a user interface layer. This implies a very tight degree of coupling between the tools and the centralised database. An alternative way of viewing this circular structure is as a series of layers with the database at the bottom, the user interface at the top and a collection of tools in between. This picture may also be applied to a subset of an IPSE such as an integrated toolset that supported a particular method. Such a toolset may be integrated in each of the three senses discussed above. In other words, the tools share a common user interface, are built upon a common data model and have their invocation controlled from above.

The degree of integration possible between different toolsets is governed by the degree of commonality between their data models and the extent to which a mapping can be defined between these data models that provides some common semantic ground. Ultimately, the data model used by each toolset will be implemented using the underlying database technology on which the IPSE is built. However, this is not a useful level of integration unless common meaning can be ascribed to the representations at this level.

2.4 Summary

The development of large software systems requires the control of a large number of people producing many documents, pieces of code, designs, and so on. While individual software tools can help, there is a clear need to *integrate* tools to support the wide spectrum of activities which take place throughout the software life-cycle.

In addition, any such environment must be concerned with more than just the technical aspects of the project. True *project* support implies support for the management functions which are vital to the success of any large software project.

Chapter 3

An Overview of Aspect

I.D. Benest, A.W. Brown, A.N. Earl,
A. Pearcy, A. Petrie, R.J. Stroud,
A.J. Wellings and R.P. Whittington

3.1 Introduction

This chapter presents in abstract the principles and concepts that underlie an Aspect IPSE. It aims to provide the reader with an overall appreciation of Aspect which is substantiated in the following, more specifically targeted writings.

The first section presents the architecture of an Aspect IPSE, identifying specific areas of IPSE technology which the Aspect project has studied. These are the central information base, the human-computer interface, and the support required for developing distributed target systems.

Following this discussion of the general services provided by an Aspect IPSE, the chapter continues by describing the role of *customisation* in the development of a specific Aspect IPSE aimed at the needs of a particular project or organisation. This leads into a discussion of a high-level view of the services that are provided in such a customisation, relating the facilities of an Aspect system through a model of software development that is centred on the notion of project personnel performing tasks to develop software products.

3.2 The Aspect Infrastructure Services

An Aspect system is defined as a set of services for software development control. The overall architecture of an Aspect IPSE (see Figure 3.1) is little different from other IPSEs. The provision of a logically centralised information base which contains all data relevant to the project enables data independence and communication between tools. Further advantages of a central repository for data are that recovery, security and integrity of the data can be handled centrally and do not have to be embedded in the tools. Unnecessary duplication of data is avoided, the data can always be manipulated using the same language, and views of the data can be presented which are more suitable for particular tools (indeed, all of the advantages that are now well understood from the use of database management systems in the development of business and administrative systems).

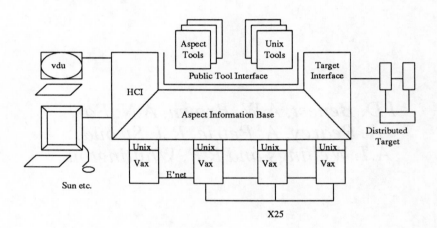

Fig. 3.1 The Aspect architecture

The human-computer interface (HCI) component of Aspect provides some equivalent advantages by isolating tools from the underlying interface device, offering a set of interaction primitives based on a logical structure of the display, and enabling productive interfaces to be quickly generated through the power of such primitives.

It was not possible for the target interface to provide the same sort of isolation for tools from the underlying target architecture because no single model of a distributed target architecture was found to exist. Instead, work on particular architectures and the communication between their elements was carried out.

The concept of a Public Tool Interface (PTI) is central to Aspect. The PTI offers a collection of services, in the areas described above, for use in IPSE customisation and tool building. These services are themselves integrated through their common basis on the Aspect information base.

In addition to supporting Aspect-specific tools, the PTI also supports an Open Tool Interface (OTI) to accommodate existing tools that are not written to use the facilities provided by Aspect but which can be integrated into the Aspect IPSE and still maintain the integrity of the whole system.

We now briefly examine the services provided by Aspect at its PTI.

3.3 The Information Base Facilities

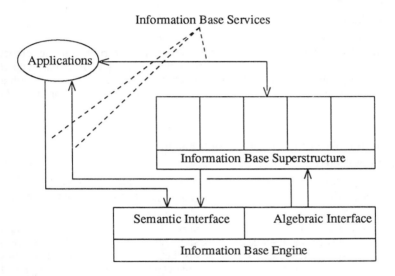

Fig. 3.2 The structure of the Aspect information base facilities

The Aspect IB facilities divide into two components (as illustrated in Figure 3.2):

1. Information Base Engine (IBE) – the raw data object manipulation capabilities, offering a secure basis for development; and

2. Information Base Superstructure (IBS) – the generic application layer constructed upon the IBE, supporting general models applicable to the development process.

The IBE is comparable functionally to a conventional database management system (DBMS), except that its basis on a semantic data model results in the existence of two quite different interfaces:

1. The *semantic* interface, which supports updating through a complex checking

process based on the IBE's understanding of the semantics of the data objects.

2.   The *algebraic* interface, which supports retrieval through an extended relational algebra.

The IBS is comparable to a certain class of application-development facility offered with some conventional DBMSs through 4GLs and CASE tools. It offers support in the following areas:

- information sharing using a publication-based notion,
- integrity by means of application-specific rules and their evaluation,
- the definition and exploitation of abstractions (or views) of data and operations,
- configuration and version management,
- a model of process (i.e. tasks).

These various facilities are integrated through their basis on the object management facilities of the IBE. They augment the PTI with facilities based upon its lowest-level primitives (i.e. the IBE), in order to provide the IPSE users with a more powerful base on which to work. These facilities are described in detail in Chapter 6.

3.4 The Human-Computer Interaction Facilities

These comprise two components:

1.   A graphical interaction management service (Presenter), and

2.   A rapid prototyping tool for designing graphical user interfaces (Doubleview).

The Presenter is a constituent part of the public tool interface; at the program level, and at the lowest interface level, it handles the graphical interaction and output graphics of the application, and as such it is the outer layer of software that lies between the user and the functionality of the application. The Presenter is designed to take the place of a conventional window manager, but instead of the window, it provides the more generalised concept of a screen region. Regions can logically contain other regions and such containment may occur, in principle, to any depth and complexity. Regions that are logically contained within another region are not necessarily constrained to lie within the visual boundary of the parent region. The resulting hierarchical structure of the screen presentation can be made to persist, between invocations of the application, and indeed it is this structure that both the user and the application manipulate during interaction. Regions have attributes that govern their presentation and dynamic behaviour. Many of the lower level forms of interaction can be designed to be handled directly by the Presenter. For example, when a button is selected, the Presenter can invert the button presentation on behalf of the application, or the designer can specify that the Presenter merely report the fact that the button has been selected and leave the application to supply (via the Presenter) the necessary feedback. However, the Presenter also provides higher level interaction; in particular, text within regions can be editable, providing the lowest (and most dynamic) editing functions on behalf of the application. The Presenter imposes little overt style on any user interface, making it possible for software houses to adopt their own 'designer label' for their products.

Doubleview is a rapid prototyping tool designed to enable persistent Presenter structures to be specified and viewed by the software designer. As its name suggests, Doubleview provides both a view of the Presenter tree, and a view of its physical realisation as it would appear on the screen when fronting its application. Doubleview can be used to design low-level interface objects (i.e. a menu, or a slider control) or complete application interfaces containing many instantiations of the low-level interface objects. Through the persistence of the presenter structure, libraries of basic low-level interface objects may be produced and re-used in a variety of applications.

3.5 The Target Development Facilities

The availability of cheap microprocessors and the advent of local-area network technology has brought about an increasing interest in distributed computer systems. For *embedded* (target) computer systems, distribution allows not only geographical distribution and the potential for improved performance but also the promise of improved reliability through the use of redundant components. The support for programming and debugging distributed target systems is provided by a set of tools which make use of both the database and the HCI facilities. It is this set of tools along with their underlying philosophy which is the subject of Chapter 9.

Although the Ada programming language is becoming increasingly popular for programming embedded computer systems, there are (and will continue to be) other languages which are extensively used. For this reason Aspect provides a set of tools whose underlying philosophy is language independent. The intention is that the approach should be applicable to C, variants of Pascal (such as Perspective Pascal), Modula-1 and Modula-2, as well as Ada.

3.6 IPSE Customisation

The set of services provided by Aspect can be considered as a kit of parts. The kit is designed to be as generic as possible, because there are many management methods, specification techniques, and classes of IPSE user. For example, using an IPSE kit is should be possible to build an IPSE which provides little more than a traditional operating system with a good interface and configuration management, and yet the same kit should be able to be used to build an environment to support a very restrictive and secure formal development method.

The design and development of an Aspect IPSE from the facilities available in the Aspect IPSE kit is known as *customisation*. The large number of design decisions that can be made combined with their potentially great impact on the IPSE, its qualities, performance, and productivity, imply two important points. The first is the question of *who* does the customisation, and the next section describes the various roles which are implied by the term *IPSE user*. The second question is *how* the customisation should be achieved.

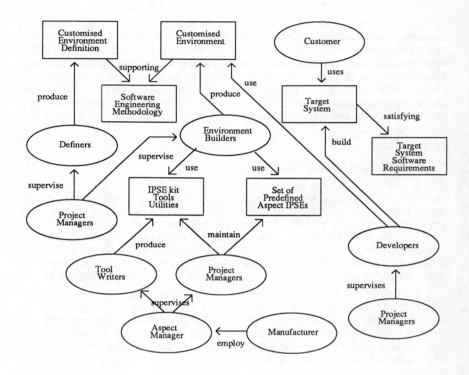

Fig. 3.3 Roles associated with an IPSE

3.6.1 IPSE users and usage

Figure 3.3 shows the roles (ellipses) associated with IPSE development, management, maintenance and customisation. Relationships (arrows) between roles and other elements (boxes) are also shown.

The *Developers* are those who build target systems according to a *Customer's* software requirements. Such developers use a customised environment which will have been produced according to a customised environment definition (produced by *Definers*) to support a software engineering methodology. Such production may form a project in its own right and require management supervision.

The work of producing a customised environment is carried out by *Environment Builders*. At any stage in the history of an IPSE's development and use, parts of the IPSE may be modified; this implies that the customisation process, just as the development of any large system, continues throughout the life of the IPSE. It thus follows that any of the roles described may perform customisation. Clearly, the major responsibility for customisation lies in the early parts of the IPSE's development. Note that any systematic method of customisation will have to account for development loops.

The management of customisation is further complicated since it is likely that the various roles would be carried out by different types of companies. The expertise required to develop a powerful, efficient IPSE kit may well not reside alongside that required to produce a complex management tool.

3.6.2 A customisation methodology

An IPSE with sufficient facilities for its own self-description could support its own customisation. The problems noted above associated with the management of customisation would then be addressed by the facilities provided by the IPSE, and thus be addressed in an integrated, coherent fashion.

The recognition that customisation is a complex development process has led the Aspect project to start an investigation into the process. There appear to be two important preconditions for starting such an investigation. The first is a good understanding of the environment in which an IPSE is developed and used. The second is the availability of at least a prototype IPSE kit which can be used experimentally.

The starting point for customising an Aspect IPSE kit is the set of Aspect invariants which are embedded in the primitives provided by the kit. Examples of these would be the integrity rules of RM/T++, or the application of pre- or post-rules at the start and end of tasks. Such rules are clearly bound into the final IPSE from the start.

The customisation process consists of constructing a sequence of bindings to the generic facilities provided by the IPSE kit. This sequence may start with a system definition stage in which the hardware, communication, host and target facilities are modelled within the IPSE. This would be followed by an organisation definition phase concerning the roles, users or teams involved at corporate, quality assurance, and project level. Finally, there is a method definition phase during which decisions are made concerning the choice of tools, how they are to be used and by whom. There will certainly be iteration of any such sequence to allow for errors, or changes in the environment or requirements.

The work in the area of an IPSE customisation methodology described here has only been treated superficially; it will become increasingly important as customisable IPSEs become more widely available and used. What follows is a description of a possible customisation methodology based on the concepts provided by the Aspect IPSE kit.

3.7 The Aspect Process Model

Having presented the basic architecture of the Aspect IPSE infrastructure and discussed the notion of IPSE customisation, we now describe the Aspect Process Model. This was developed in order to provide a top-level view of the facilities provided by an Aspect IPSE, and to guide the process of customising the Aspect IPSE kit. The model describes software development in terms of project personnel defining and carrying out tasks within the development process.

3.7.1 The top-level view

The facilities of Aspect are designed to support a simple, generic model of software development control, illustrated in Figure 3.4. Support for software development in Aspect focuses on three main areas:

- products,
- project plans, and
- project organisation.

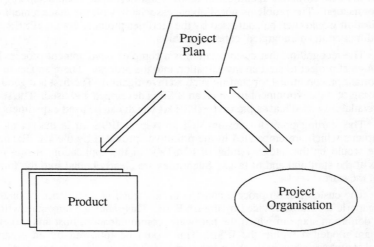

Fig. 3.4 Top-level view of Aspect

The main goal of a software project is to develop a *product*. It is, therefore, important that support for software development represents and controls the components that make up a software product: version control and configuration management facilities for the identification of product components; maintenance of relationships between versions of components; and the controlled assembly of configurations of component versions into larger components.

A fundamental principle of Aspect is that effective support for software development can only be provided through modelling the development process itself within an IPSE [22]. Hence, although mechanisms must be provided within an IPSE for representing and controlling the product under development, of equal importance is the need to represent and control the development process that is being used to produce the product. This manifests itself in the *project plan*, which is a description of how the product is to be produced and maintained.

Representing a project plan in an IPSE would be of little value without recognition that a fundamental part of a project is the large group of people (programmers, designers, managers, and so on) who carry out the project plan. Collectively, this aspect of the project can be called the *project organisation*. Vital to the effective operation of an IPSE is the ability to model and control the numerous facets of the project organisation, such as individual users, the roles they perform, and so on.

Essentially: a project organisation functions under the guidance of a project plan to produce the desired product.

Current environments for supporting software development concentrate almost exclusively on providing tools for the generation and maintenance of a software product. The best of these provide a measure of tool integration which allows for more consistent support of product development.

Research in the IPSE field is now beginning to realise that support for the software product alone is not sufficient. Effective support can only be provided through representing and controlling the development process itself as an integral part of IPSE data. In recognition of these developments, Aspect provides an environment in which the product, the project plan, and the project organisation can be modelled and controlled in a flexible, integrated way. The following sections examine these areas in more detail.

3.7.2 Controlling development through a project plan

The information base (IB) at the heart of an Aspect IPSE is used to model both the product under development and the development process itself. The state of the product at any particular stage in its life-cycle is represented in the IB as a collection of objects. In addition, every action which is performed to develop the product during the project is modelled in the IB by a task object. Tasks may be grouped together to form a plan which can then be performed to develop one part of the product. The project plan consists of all the tasks and plans that must be performed in order to build the product in its entirety.

A project plan has two functions. It describes what must be done and it describes what has been done to further a project. As a project develops, so does its plan. It is unlikely that a plan can describe a project in its entirety and in sufficient detail before a project begins. Consequently, beginning with an initial plan (which may simply be to develop a better plan), a project progresses by completing part of the plan and extending and detailing that plan. There is a sense in which a plan is a picture which is slowly coloured in (executed) except that as some parts of the picture are completed, other parts reveal themselves, so that the task may be unending. However, this analogy does not capture the self-referential nature of the Aspect model. Developing a project plan is itself a task which must be captured by the model. Such a task, instead of modifying an object in the IB which represents part of an end-product, modifies an object in the IB which represents another task or part of an overall project plan.

Task descriptions

A task models a piece of work that is carried out as part of a project. Since everything in a project is represented by an object in the IB, it follows that a task may be described in terms of those objects in the IB which it manipulates or accesses in some way. In general, a task requires some input and uses some tools on this input to produce some output. Consequently, a task description may be modelled in the IB by the database relations *uses, produces* and *requires*.

For example, a task to write a piece of program *requires* a specification, *uses* an editor and *produces* some program text. By recording these relationships in the IB, it is possible to track how an object was derived, where it came from originally and on which other objects it depends. Thus, if it is subsequently necessary to change a specification, the impact of the change can be traced through the IB, and tasks to deal with the problem can be defined, added to the project plan and initiated. Naturally, tracing the impact of a change and defining new tasks to deal with the problem are themselves tasks with their own *uses, produces* and *requires* relationships.

Constraints

A task description purely in terms of *uses, produces* and *requires* is not in general sufficient to capture the semantics of a task. There must also be some additional constraints to ensure that what the task produces meets certain criteria. For example, a task to *produce* a piece of program text must ensure that the program meets the specification that the task *requires* in order to begin. Any additional tools or data that are needed to verify the constraints should appear in the *uses* and *requires* relations describing the task. Constraints describing the purpose of a task, therefore, take the form of expressions in a formal language which only involve objects *used, produced* or *required* by the task.

Under certain circumstances, it may be possible to ensure that something produced by a task conforms to certain standards by using tools to produce the task's output from its input which enforce a particular development methodology. For example, if the compiler used by the task was a Pascal compiler, and the task description constrained the output to be something that compiled without error, then obviously the output would have to be a program written in Pascal. Perhaps more usefully, if the specification was written in a formal language, then it might be possible to ensure that the program conformed to the specification automatically by using an editor which only allowed the program to be produced by applying correctness-preserving transformations to the specification. In this way, the need to enforce certain constraints can be relaxed by using sufficiently powerful tools, but within the limits of current technology and for the foreseeable future, there will always be a practical need to check constraints which cannot be automatically enforced.

Parameterised tasks

Task descriptions are complex objects and need to be created and manipulated by specialised tools. However, there is a degree of commonality between the descriptions of similar tasks. For example, writing one program is very like writing another. The same compiler and editor are *used* and only the specification *required* and the program *produced* changes between two such tasks. Consequently, it should be possible to construct a library of reusable generic task descriptions. These will be partially specified in the sense that some parts of the description are already supplied whereas other parts are as yet incomplete. The incomplete parts of the description serve to parameterise the task description and these parameters must be instantiated before the task description can be used to carry out a task.

For example, a task library may contain a generic task description for writing Pascal programs which specifies that a particular Pascal compiler and editor should be *used* to *produce* a program that compiles without error. However, such a task *requires* a specification of the program that is to be *produced* and this specification may be a parameter to the description. Such a parameter must be supplied before the task is performed in order to ensure that the task description describes the task of writing a particular Pascal program rather than just any program.

Task descriptions and configuration management

A task description specifies that a task *uses*, *produces* and *requires* certain objects in the IB. Every object in the IB may potentially exist in several versions tracked by the configuration management (CM) system. The CM system distinguishes between logical objects and physical versions of those objects. Although the task description should be written in terms of logical objects, at some stage during the instantiation of a generic task description or perhaps as a separate phase before the task is executed, these logical objects must be associated with (i.e. bound to) physical versions. Thus, a generic task description may be both instantiated (by supplying the values of parameters) and configured (by supplying the versions of objects).

Before a task description can be executed it must be fully bound. In other words, all parameter values must be supplied together with a configuration which binds the logical objects referred to by the description to physical versions of those objects. This will ensure that by the time a task starts executing, all the objects in the IB which it *uses*, *produces* or *requires* have been fully defined and are guaranteed not to change while the task is being executed. This property guarantees that task executions are atomic with respect to the rest of the IB, an important property which is required in order to ensure that the history of a task execution is reproducible.

Task executions

Since a task execution may take some time, it is necessary to establish a context in which the execution takes place. This context is a part of the IB, and is private to the task execution. If a task is suspended for some reason, then the context records whatever is necessary to continue the task at a later date. The existence of such a context (modelled, as usual, as an object in the IB) makes it possible to pass work-in-progress from one individual to another, should this become necessary.

The representation of tasks in the IB

It should be noted that the term *task* is used in at least three senses: as a generic description of a piece of work, as a description of a particular piece of work, and as a piece of work in progress. It is important to understand this distinction and to realise that each form of task is modelled within the IB. It is also necessary to appreciate the self-referential nature of the model; task descriptions are like any object in the IB and may therefore have versions or be *used*, *required* or *produced* by other task descriptions.

Tasks and plans

Tasks may be grouped together to form plans. A plan is a higher-level task description – which describes the combined effect of the constituent tasks – together with a decomposition of the higher-level task into sub-tasks which must be performed in a certain order. The *uses*, *produces* and *requires* relations in the task description provide a natural way of decomposing higher-level tasks (or joining sub-tasks together). For example, if a task *produces* several objects, it may be decomposed into a collection of sub-tasks which produce each object individually. These sub-tasks may then be executed in parallel. Similarly, if one task *produces* something that another task *requires*, then the two tasks may be joined together in sequence to form a bigger task.

In this way, the decomposition of abstract tasks into sequences of sub-tasks that may be executed in parallel in accordance with some plan arises naturally out of the *uses*, *produces* and *requires* parts of a task description. The logical expressions that act as additional constraints on a task description may also be used as a structuring mechanism. One possibility might be to allow a task to be decomposed into the repetition of some simpler task until an additional constraint is met. This construct would be particularly useful if the simpler task was in fact a group of related tasks. For example, such a task description could be used to describe a compile-edit-test cycle with the additional constraint being the requirement that the test results must be correct for the task to be complete. Note that such an iteration is not just a grouping of tasks which must be repeated, but it is also a constraint which must be met before the repetition can terminate.

As another example of this kind of constraint-oriented decomposition, suppose that the constraint on a task is expressed as a disjunction of sub-conditions (so that the constraint is met if any one of the sub-conditions is met). Then, the task may be decomposed into a choice between sub-tasks, each one of which seeks to fulfill one of the sub-conditions that forms part of the constraint on the parent task. Similarly, a task whose constraint is expressed as a conjunction of sub-conditions (all of which must be satisfied to fulfill the constraint) may also be decomposed into sub-tasks, except that in this case, all rather than just one of these sub-tasks must be executed in order to complete the parent task.

Summary

To summarise the Aspect model of a project plan, all actions to be performed during a project are modelled in the IB as tasks. Tasks are described in terms of the inputs they *require*, the tools they *use* and the outputs they *produce*. Task descriptions may be generic but need to have all their parameters resolved, not just to logical objects but to physical versions of those objects, before the task they represent can be executed. Task descriptions may also require additional constraints to be satisfied before a task is terminated. Finally, tasks may be grouped together into a hierarchy to form a plan, using their constraints and the objects they *use*, *produce* and *require* as the basis for this structure. Because everything, including a task description and a plan, is represented within the IPSE in the same way (as an object in the IB), the model is self-referential and tasks may be used to manipulate other tasks.

3.7.3 Project organisation

In the course of developing the product that a software engineering project is trying to build, a certain number of tasks (parcels of work that need to be done) need to be performed. As well as recording the creation of these tasks and controlling the progress of their execution, the IPSE must also model the project organisation responsible for carrying out the work in order to associate tasks with the individuals responsible for their management and execution.

As with any project, any work that is required to be done in the course of a software engineering project is, ultimately, carried out by people. Nevertheless, the organisation of such a project will usually be conceived and structured in terms of roles such as Manager, Specifier, Designer, Programmer, Tester, Quality Assurer and Maintainer. A role is related to particular skills and abilities which, in addition to technical expertise, might include such things as experience of working in a particular application area or seniority.

Each project will construct a set of roles that it regards as appropriate to the job that needs to be done and to the sort of organisational structure that it wants. These roles may represent a broad or narrow range of skills, and the granularity of the roles used in the project organisation will reflect this. For example, each software engineering project will have a role structure for programmers. However, one project may choose to have a coarse granularity of roles and have a single Programmer role while another might choose to have two Programmer roles, Junior Programmer and Senior Programmer or several programmer roles such as View_Programmer, CM_Programmer and Activities_Programmer. Yet another might choose to have several Senior Programmer and several Junior Programmer roles and so on.

Aspect supports each of these levels of granularity by allowing a project to choose a set of roles which reflect its organisational requirements. Some, if not all, of the roles required will be created at the beginning of the project when the IPSE is configured, but, subject to appropriate permissions, it will be possible to extend or change the set of roles during the lifetime of the project.

These roles, in a sense, stand as place holders for the people who will eventually fill them. The qualification, "in a sense", is made because, in the situation where a role may be filled by more than one person, although each of the role's jobs will be carried out by one person, the whole role function will be performed by several people.

Each person working on the project will be expected to be able to fill at least one of the project roles. This gives rise to an association between roles and people based on the suitability of each person for carrying out each role, taking account of their abilities and experience. A particular person working on a project may well be able to assume more than one role and, if this is the case they will be associated with more than one role. In a similar way, several people may be able to assume the same role, in which case the role will be associated with more than one person.

The set of roles chosen by a project might well form a partial or full hierarchy in which some roles such as, for example, C_Programmer are specialisations of a parent role such as Programmer. In this case one would expect that anyone who could be associated with a particular role could also, if necessary, be associated with an ancestor of that role. However, one would not expect the reverse to be true.

Although Aspect does not explicitly support such an hierarchy, the flexible mechanisms provided for rule definition and enforcement would allow such relationships to be defined and controlled on a per project basis. Such a hierarchy would be defined during the customisation of the IPSE.

The separation of roles and people has the advantage that the organisation of a project can be established without knowing who will be available to work on it. As people join the project they will be associated with an appropriate role or roles and as the project progresses the association between roles and people can be changed as and when necessary. Someone who acquires a new skill can be associated with an additional or different role. For example, if someone is promoted to being a Manager, say, then their previous association with the role of Programmer can be deleted if they are no longer required to write programs.

It must be emphasised that, as part of the initial customisation of an Aspect IPSE to suit a particular project, it is necessary to establish the role structure that the project wishes to have. This involves choosing a set of roles of the type and granularity appropriate to the project and defining any hierarchical or other relationships between them.

Tasks and roles

In order to carry out a task, particular skills and abilities are needed and, consequently, any task that the project has to do will be associated with some particular role such as Programmer, Designer, Manager etc. Note that this is a technical rather than a managerial decision and in order that this can be done the role structure of the project must have already been set up. When a task is defined, part of the definition will state which role, or type of role, should carry out the task and should therefore be associated with the task.

Assignment – tasks and people

Although project tasks are associated with roles they will actually be carried out by people. A task will consequently be assigned to a person who is able to carry out the role that is associated with that task. In other words, tasks are assigned to people acting in particular roles and it is on the basis of the roles that a person can assume that they are given responsibility for the tasks that need to be done.

Assigning a task to a person is largely a managerial task. The technical information as to who has the required skills to perform the task can be derived from the associations of people and tasks with roles. If more than one person is able to perform the task, the choice of a particular person will be made by taking account of the availability of those who are able and, possibly, the availability of other resources.

Although Aspect can provide some help and assistance in making the association of a task to a role, or the assignment of a task to a person, by, for example, providing information to task designers on the skills pertaining to the various roles or by allowing managers to discover who is both competent and available to do a particular piece of work, ultimately these associations will, in part, be based on human judgement.

Summary

The relationships between roles, people and tasks can be summarised as follows:

- *Each project has a set of roles.* Roles reflect the sort of skills and abilities required by people working on the project. These roles may be of any desired degree of granularity and may be involved in one or more hierarchies or organised into sets by role type.

- *Roles are associated with people.* This association is determined by matching abilities and experience with those expected in someone performing the role. This matching is possibly done by the personnel department.

- *Tasks are associated with roles.* This association is determined on the basis of the abilities and experience required to perform the task and matches these to the role structure that the project has chosen. This is a technical decision that can be performed independently of any decisions relating to roles and people.

- *Tasks are assigned to people acting in a particular role.* This is a managerial decision separate from the two previous ones which will take into account availability of people and resources in addition to suitability.

3.7.4 Product management

One of the major headaches of large project organisation is controlling the many documents, source code modules and executable programs which are created during the life-time of a software system.

Even one person working alone needs some system to keep track of the results of their creative activities, to answer such questions as "If I want to give a copy of my program to Fred, what else will he need to be able to run it?" "How did I create that version which worked last week?" and "What happens if I delete *temp*?"

As soon as more than one person is involved, sharing of data adds to the already considerable problems of multiple versions. The classic sign that things are out of control is the modification that mysteriously vanishes the week after going live, overwritten by an older version. Slips like this can be very embarrassing, and are hard to avoid when everyone needs access to the same things, every item of work is needed as soon as possible, and people cannot easily find out what repercussions their actions may have on the rest of the system.

There are several distinct problems involved in this area of data control, although they are all closely related. We have distinguished three main areas of concern – version control, configuration management and concurrency control. This section introduces the aims, concepts and terminology of the IB structures that support these Aspect components, and the interrelations between them.

Concurrency control applies to all objects in the IB, whether or not regarded as part of a *product,* whereas version control and configuration management, although technically independent of each other, both apply only to that subset of IB objects representing a product. Concurrency control is therefore treated separately in the technical discussion of Chapter 6.

Stepping back, the aims of product control may be summarised as follows:

- storage – to keep copies of, or the means to recreate, all versions of components of the system being developed/maintained,

- retrieval and/or rebuilding – to be able to pick up the correct version from the many, or the correct versions of sub-components and the instructions for rebuilding,
- freezing – protection against overwriting of recent modifications by later versions,
- locking – protection against any changes of versions in use,
- parallel development – should be allowed, while preserving the protection of shared data in the previous two aims.

The Aspect approach to satisfying these aims is described below.

The product concept

This is the system being developed or maintained, regarded in Aspect as IB objects to be identified, protected from loss or corruption, and built into larger objects. The Aspect product controls are intended to cover more than just a deliverable system (the executables, user documentation and possibly source code). The product includes objects produced at every stage of the software life-cycle including all supporting information. The exact scope is set during customisation and a particular Aspect IPSE may or may not include, for instance, fault reports, project time sheets or sales performance figures in the product. Objects not defined as part of a product would, of course, be subject to other IPSE controls, including concurrency control, as mentioned above.

Components – the logical analysis of a product

Earlier work on this area in Aspect (see, for example [43]) set the basic framework for the current model by distinguishing between the logical and physical levels of analysis of a product. At the logical level, a software system is made up of *components*. Components can be further analysed as a set of sub-components, and so on, to any required level of granularity using the configuration management system.

To Aspect, a product covers the whole system throughout its life-cycle. Components, therefore, include documentation (from requirements analysis through to test results), as well as the more usual source code modules and executable programs. Component types are defined in customisation to suit the project methodology, and are typed accordingly. Figure 3.5 shows the types that might be required in a simplified view of the life-cycle.

Versions – the physical instantiations of the product

Each component may go through several changes during its development, and there may be several in use on different sites or machines at any one time. The component exists, therefore, as a set of *versions*.

Versions are the various physical instantiations of their component and hold the *contents* – text, source code, and so on – of the component. The contents and any other features of a version must be appropriate to the typing of its component. Features of a version, other than its physical contents, are the relationships into which it can enter with other versions in the IB.

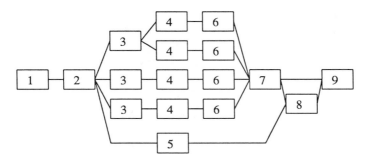

Key to component types (stages of the life-cycle):

1 Requirements analysis	5 System test
2 Functional specification	6 Object code module
3 Design Specifications	7 Executable program
4 Source code module	8 Test results
	9 Deliverable system

Fig. 3.5 Component types in a simplified software life-cycle

Revisions

One version is a *revision* of another if it is the next step in its chronological development. Revisions are versions in a sequence, with the last in the sequence being the "latest version".

Three such sequences are shown in Figure 3.6. Version A.2 is, for instance, a revision of A.1, and version A.4.C.1 has not yet been revised.

Variants

Variants are parallel development paths of the component. Variants are typically developed for different machine architectures or operating systems, and also for application-specific cases.

Each variant is a sequence of versions, storing the modifications made along that development path. New variants may branch off from any version, i.e. at any point during the development of the source variant. Thus trees of versions may be created to any depth. Figure 3.6 shows such a tree, where the original line of development (A) has, after some time, spawned a variant (B). Work continues on both the main and the new variant until another line of development (C) branches off, again from the main variant.

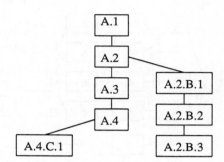

Fig. 3.6 Tree of versions and variants

Naming schemes for versions and variants

No particular numbering or naming scheme has been imposed on customisable Aspect IPSEs. The relevant features of the version control system provided by Aspect are that revisions have a sequence number, and that variants must have a unique identifier. One possible naming scheme which simply combines these two features is shown in the version/variant tree in Figure 3.6. Using this scheme, names take the form:

<component name>{.<variant name>.<version number>}

and can identify any version and its position in the tree, in a tree of any depth of nesting of variants. (Note that in Figure 3.6 the component name has been left out for clarity). This is not the only possible naming schema.

Constraints on updating

The version control system ensures that only the latest version of a variant may be updated. In the example tree (Figure 3.6), this means versions A.4.C.1, A.4 and A.2.B.3.

Additionally, concurrency control limits such updating to the person who currently has *development permission* on that variant. Only one person at a time may have such permission. If the variant (i.e. the latest version) is frozen and cannot be modified, an attempt to update it causes a new version to be created and added to the end of the sequence.

The point at which freezing occurs is a matter for customisation. There could exist a customised Aspect IPSE where a new version is automatically created on every invocation of an editor. This would be very safe, but saving all intermediate versions, some of which may never be used, would consume a great deal of storage, even if the differences between versions ("deltas") were stored, as in some existing systems (for example, Gandalf [55]), rather than the versions themselves.

Another approach is to allow the latest version to be updated at any time, within general Aspect constraints, until given some formal acceptance by Quality

Assurance. If this looser form of control were adopted in a particular customisation, the person with development permission could re-invoke the editor, or re-run the steps to build the latest version, several times until satisfied.

Any updating can only take place within general Aspect concurrency control constraints, which provide a *freezing point* that is built into any Aspect system. Briefly, an object may not be modified while visible to more than one person. Each person only has access to objects in their own *domain*, and permission to access objects is passed on by the mechanism of *publishing* between domains. Once an object has been published from the domain of its creation, it cannot be modified, unless subsequently *withdrawn*. Aspect concurrency control, therefore, places conditions on updating of objects in the IB (whether a version control system is in operation or not), and the version control system places further conditions on the updating of versions of components. The constraint of development permission, as described above, is a specialisation of concurrency control adapted to be more effective in conjunction with version control. Further constraints could be added during customisation by the mechanism of user-defined rules (see Section 6.7).

Configuration management

So far, components and their versions have been treated as if each component existed in isolation. The version control system can indeed be implemented and used in this way, without introducing any means of expressing relationships between components. In an Aspect IPSE, customised to include version control without configuration management, the logical analysis of a product is no more than a list of the components involved, and the concept of component is just a way of grouping versions of the same thing.

Full product control requires an IPSE with configuration management facilities. These record how components (and their versions) are produced from other components (and their versions). In the example of different types of components (Figure 3.5), executable programs are built from several object modules, and a deliverable system (in this idealised example) is made up of the executable program and test results.

Note that in Aspect, the term configuration does not only refer to the building of larger objects from smaller ones, but is generalised to include the dependencies which result from all processes of software development. Configurations (both logical and physical, as explained below) therefore cover the case of the specification which is the source of several module designs, as well as the examples just given. Thus, the overall configuration of the entire life-cycle fans out from the initial input, through the central modular phase of development, and the various parts come together in the final phase of development to form the released system. The information held by configuration management facilities is used to:

- reproduce given versions of components,
- produce new components and versions from existing designs,
- track dependencies between components and repercussions of impending changes.

Logical designs

The logical analysis of a product is extended from the simple list of components necessary for version control. Each component has one or more *logical designs*, meaning the set(s) of components required for its construction. In Figure 3.5, for instance, the logical design of the deliverable system includes two components – one of type *executable program* and one of type *test results*. If the version control system is not installed in a particular IPSE, then the logical design provides all the information necessary to fulfill the above aims of a configuration management system. In this case, each component would be limited to one design.

If the components exist in more than one version, additional information must be recorded. For example, later versions of a deliverable system may also include a user documentation component. In this case at least two logical designs for the deliverable system component would be needed, as indicated in Figure 3.7.

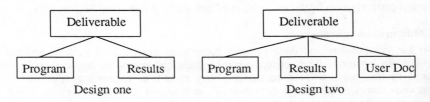

Fig. 3.7 Two logical designs for one component

There may be several versions of the deliverable system produced from each of these designs. They may also be used as prototypes for versions of new components of type *deliverable system*.

Physical configurations

The configuration of a particular version of a component must not only specify a valid logical design for that component, but also select a version for each component of that design. This is the information required to work out the consequences of a modification to the component (i.e. to a version of a component, as constrained by the version control system).

If the functional specification is to be altered, for instance, the configuration will indicate which module design documents depend on the latest version of that specification. These may then be examined for any changes required, and the consequences of these changes for the source code checked, and so on. Conversely, if an error is discovered in a version of the executable program, the possible source of the error can be traced back to any earlier step in the development.

Rebuilding

The logical design of component X records which other components are required to build a sub-set of versions of X. The physical configuration records the versions required to build particular versions of X and the full details of how these are then used to build a specific version are held as a task description. The physical configuration holds a pointer to the task which produced that version. Where the task can be automatically re-run, e.g. compilation, the results of building that version need not of course be stored, thus saving space in the IB.

Summary

The controls over the product in Aspect are designed for flexibility, so that they can be customised to form a wide range of systems. The version control and configuration management systems can be implemented separately or together. In addition, the constraints of concurrency control over the whole of the IB have particular implications for the product, and provide a minimum level of protection from the dangers of unconstrained data sharing.

3.8 Summary

In this chapter we have presented an overview of the Aspect project. An Aspect IPSE is defined by a set of services for controlling software development. This set of services may be thought of as an IPSE kit which may be customised to build an IPSE tailored to meet the needs of a particular organisation or project. The Aspect IPSE kit includes an Information Base based on a semantic data model and supported by a superstructure providing additional software engineering support facilities for tool builders, powerful HCI facilities and a target interface for developing distributed applications.

The Aspect Process Model which may be used to guide the customisation process was also described. This models the software development process in terms of an organisation performing a plan to develop a product.

Chapter 4

Demonstrating Aspect

S.J. Holmes and A. Pearcy

4.1 Introduction

Aspect, as defined in the PTI specification and as implemented in the corresponding set of C programming language functions, is an IPSE kit. The kit has been designed for flexibility in customisation, allowing a wide range of software development methods and project management styles in the final IPSE.

One such customisation, though a simple and partial one, has been implemented. The customised IPSE is shown in use in a typical part of the software life-cycle, supporting maintenance of a particular product within an imaginary company. The company in our demonstration markets software for controlling and operating lift systems. The software, which resides in the IB along with other data about our imaginary company, is an Ada program which has been developed as part of the Targets work in Aspect and is described in detail in Chapter 10.

In this chapter we set out our reasons for attempting this implementation, the criteria which guided its design, and some notes on how the information base and user interface facilities were used in its development.

The reader is then taken through a screen-by-screen description. The intention is to give an impression of what it feels like to use the Aspect demonstration software, but of course this is difficult to convey in a series of screens with textual explanations.

4.2 The Design and Development of the Demonstration

4.2.1 Aims

Work on this example of a customised IPSE was undertaken in order to demonstrate the following features of Aspect:

- The integration of the individual facilities provided in the IPSE kit (the superstructure of the IB).
- The ease of development of tools to support specific areas of software engineering, using elements of the IPSE kit.
- The flexibility of the Aspect user interface facilities, creating a variety of styles of interaction with the IB and tools.
- The use of the above structures, tools and user interface in solving a real, though much simplified, software problem. This would provide concrete examples of the use of parts of the IPSE kit, to be used in Chapter 6 (the Information Base Superstructure) to help the reader visualise how Aspect theory operates in practice.

This does NOT mean that we intended to create a complete IPSE, fully-populated with tools and data to support a life-size software development problem. The functionality provided in the demonstration IPSE is at best restricted, and in some areas has been omitted. The intention was, rather, to create the skeleton Aspect IPSE with some parts more fully developed than others, to give a flavour of the potential of the Aspect kit.

4.2.2 Criteria guiding our design decisions

1. The software which is the object of work carried out in the IPSE had to be complex enough to demonstrate the advantages gained from using an IPSE, but not so complex that the task of understanding it might distract from the task of understanding Aspect.

2. A wide enough section of the software life-cycle had to be covered to demonstrate the integration of tools though a common information base.

3. The project management style had to include examples of tight control, as well as loose guidance, so that we could demonstrate IPSE support given to a range of styles.

4. The tools developed were to illustrate Aspect rather than some particular software engineering methodology. The methodology used therefore had to be typical, though a simplification, of existing standards.

5. The demonstration had to cover the implementation and integration of the major parts of the IB superstructure. We therefore needed to:

   a. show several tasks being assigned and carried out;

   b. show several users of the system, and the control and communication of data shared between them;

   c. show work on software and accompanying documentation whose components are built into configurations, exist in more than one version, and appear differently to different users.

The underlying mechanisms supporting these events in the demonstration are described in detail in the appropriate sections of Chapter 6.

4.2.3 Information base superstructure: using the IPSE kit

The building of the demonstration provided much valuable feedback to the designers of parts of the kit. Attention was focussed on practical issues rather than the theoretical problems of the various kit elements of task definition, version control, and so on. The initial stage of integration proved more difficult than anticipated, and was only achieved through the addition of many refinements to the model.

Tool building, our second aim, took a lower priority as a result. General tools for browsing and manipulating the IB were built specifically for the demonstration. Some method-specific tools were developed separately under the Targets work. The attempt to incorporate one of the latter into the demonstration raised interesting questions about how much modification would be required to any reasonably complex tool before it could be said to be fully integrated. In this case, the tool in question (the Distribution tool) records information in files which it creates. For true integration this information would need to be recorded in the IB instead, and so the tool would require extensive rewriting.

A third area of valuable experience was the method adopted for co-ordinating development work on the user interface and the underlying IB. Our intention was to separate out the two levels by interposing a third layer of data structures and operations, to be accessible to both. In this we were, on the whole, successful. Development of the user interface did not require knowledge of relational algebra, and the design of the IB operations and structures of the Aspect kit did not depend on the user model of the IB. The concept of a flexible, re-usable kit was therefore proved viable in practice, although our experience pointed to the possible need for a higher level of data structures and operations than are currently provided by the IB superstructure.

4.2.4 The user interface to the demonstration IPSE

For the demonstration IPSE, the user interface was charged with illustrating one of the many ways in which the IB can integrate high-level project management and software engineering concepts such as tasks, publication, and configuration management to form a practical working environment. A usable but very flexible user interface was required, so that different ways of expressing underlying functionality could be tried out easily and cheaply by the system developers.

Rapid prototyping was the development route chosen; several different stand-alone versions of the demonstration user interface were developed, before arriving at the present format. Further changes, some of them quite radical, were requested later by the IB developers during the integration process. Presenter (Aspect's Display Manager, described in Chapter 8) and Doubleview (a user interface design tool, described in Chapter 9) were used, and proved to be invaluable tools for this kind of iterative, rapid prototype development cycle, because they promote a strong separation between application and user interface concerns.

In the demonstration user interface, a consistent working environment has been provided for all users whatever their current role or task. Lists of data objects or operations obtained from the IB are displayed using a general purpose menu generation package, which provides a consistent appearance while still flexible enough to allow variations in presentation where necessary.

The left-hand portion of each task environment (the Browse area) is dedicated to the display of data, i.e. the contents of the IB as seen by users carrying out particular roles and tasks. Control objects within this area permit display and navigation of the file contents of IB objects. No updates to the IB are carried out by operations within the Browse panel.

The Task Execution panel on the right of the screen displays function buttons which may change the content of the IB. These functions may be grouped together to form task-specific tools such as document formatters, debuggers etc. On invocation, such tools may contain a different or more detailed view of the piece of data currently selected in the Browse area.

Interaction objects displayed on the screen form a simple hierarchy of object types, and distinctions between object types are expressed visually where appropriate through the use of layout, font and line-weight conventions. Operations are invoked on data by the end-user via simple data/function selection sequences. The design and implementation of the demonstration user interface is described in more detail in Chapter 8.

4.3 Brief Overview of the Scenario

4.3.1 The lift-system software

The lift systems are controlled by distributed computers consisting of one processor per lift shaft plus one processor to handle requests and scheduling. Although components of the Ada program are in fact distributed among the processors and communicate by remote procedure call, the Aspect distribution work has developed a programming environment where the software is written as a single Ada program. A set of tools then handle program partitioning and inter-processor communication.

This work is fully described in Chapter 10. For the purposes of understanding the demonstration, we only need to appreciate why the configuration graphs of the software appear to build just one program, rather than several.

The configuration of the whole system, for a program controlling two lift shafts, is shown below as it appears in the demonstration Browse panel. Lower-level components (carA_package, parallel_package etc.) could be further queried to display the configuration in more detail.

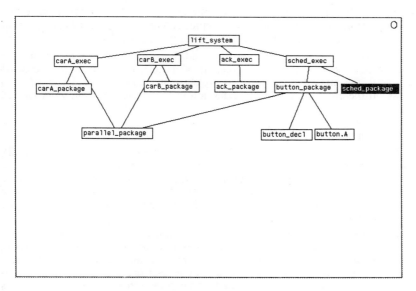

Fig. 4.1 The lift-system configuration

4.3.2 The demonstration story

In our scenario the existing program controls two lift shafts, and the company receives a request from a customer to extend this to cover four. We follow the progress of the requested enhancement from its initiation with Customer Services, the production of an estimate for costs by the Project Team, and the update being carried out on acceptance of the estimate.

In detail, the demonstration goes through the following stages.

- Step 1: Logging on.

- Step 2: Selection of role and task-list.

- Step 3: The logging of the customer's request – taking the place of the detailed requirements capture which would be necessary in a real project.

- Step 4: The production of an estimate – an investigation of the work involved in fulfilling the customer's request. In a real project this would be the design stage, but we have assumed that this particular extension to the software had been planned for and that there are already tasks set up to deal with it.

- Step 5: Customer acceptance of the estimate – the authorisation for assignment of tasks for the next step.

- Step 6: The production of the new variant – the coding stage.

We have not continued beyond the production of new software to demonstrate the process of testing and the feedback to appropriate earlier stages in design or coding, as this would result in a long and repetitive demonstration. We believe that the general principles of the Aspect IPSE kit – the specialised task environments, either pre-defined or individually tailored, and controlled communication of data – would provide the basic building blocks for tools for feedback channels.

The task of developing such tools would, however, be far from trivial. We need a deeper understanding of the support which can be given by low-level IB structures to the high-level concepts of project management. The design of such tools would therefore be a valuable extension to the implementation work carried out so far.

Step 1: Logging on

After entering a password user "freda" selects the *Role List* operation (Figure 4.2). The mouse is used for all selection of objects and operations. The choice of roles for this user is read from the IB. A user may be assigned more than one role in the project, as the user's tasks may relate to very different areas of work; e.g. one Analyst/Programmer may also be responsible for internal training courses, and be given the additional role of Training Officer.

The user in our demonstration has a choice of three roles – Senior Programmer, Project Leader and Customer Services. In a real situation, of course, one user probably wouldn't have such diverse roles within the company. We have chosen to operate the demonstration through one user only, as if this were a one-person company and our user had chosen to keep the three roles distinct. This is partly to show the Aspect user-role relationship and partly for the purely practical reason that this approach saves having to log on as different users during a run through of the demonstration.

Step 2: Selecting roles and task lists

To carry out tasks the user must be in the appropriate role, selected from the role list. Within each role, different tasks are available on the task list, as tasks are assigned to roles, not users. The *Task List* operation retrieves from the IB the list of tasks currently ready for execution. On completion, tasks disappear from the task list.

Users may perform more than one role at once if they wish, as shown in Figure 4.3. By default, the screen area is divided equally between the number of roles currently active. These proportions can be easily adjusted – as one area expands, the others automatically shrink (they are not overwritten).

In general, however, it is easier to work in one role at a time, avoiding the problem of an over-cluttered screen. This is the method employed in the following screens. If only one role is active on the screen, to move from one role to another the user must return to the original log-on screen of Figure 4.2 by selecting *Quit Role*.

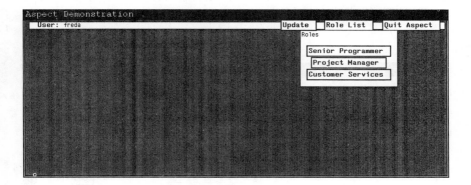

Fig. 4.2 Step 1: Logging on

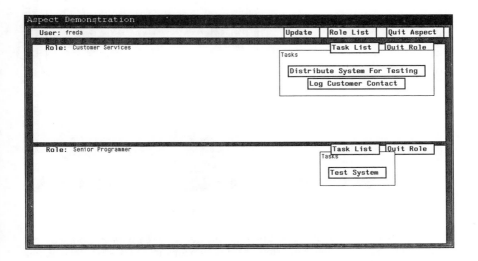

Fig. 4.3 Step 2: Selecting roles and task lists

Step 3: Logging the customer call

On initial customer contact, Customer Services selects *Log Customer Contact* task, logging the request, entering details in the IB and notifying the Project Manager responsible for the maintenance of the product in question.

This also automatically defines and forwards to the Project Manager a task to deal with the request, which then appears on the Project Manager's task list.

Every task has a task environment which is pre-defined in terms of the data and operations available in that task.

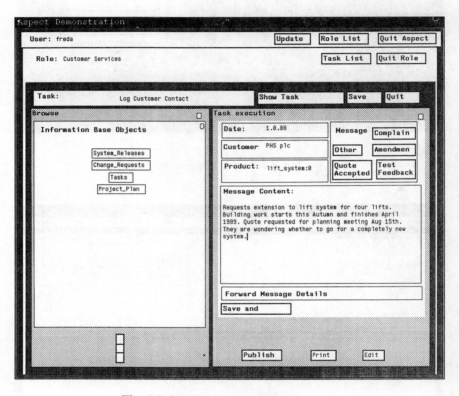

Fig. 4.4 Step 3: Logging the customer call

In Figure 4.4 we see the task environment for *Log Customer Contact*. All environments share the basic division of the screen area into two – the Browse area for access to a set of object types in the IB, and the Execution area with particular operations used in this task. At the base of the Browse panel is a menu of operations which "opens up" when an object is selected. The contents of the menu depend on the type of selected object.

Step 4: Producing the estimate

In the role of Project Manager, the user selects task *Respond to Customer Input* (Figure 4.5). This is the pre-defined task which was assigned to this role from the action of Customer Services on the previous screen.

A comparison between this task environment and that of Figure 4.4 shows the same overall design, although the Execution panel is quite different.

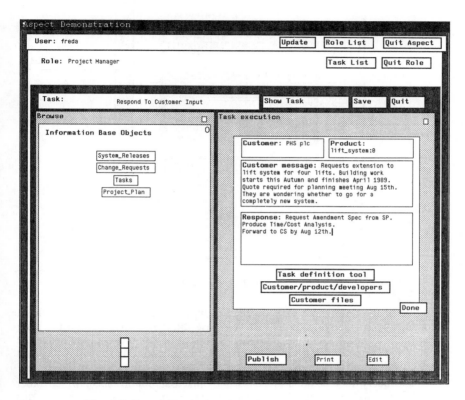

Fig. 4.5 Step 4: Producing the estimate – Project Manager

The *Task definition tool* allows the Project Manager to assign tasks to this or other roles using his judgement in response to the change request. In order to do this, the change request must first be read; it is therefore presented on the screen on entry to the task. The other tools available in the task definition panel are two task-specific query tools, the *Customer files* query and the *Customer/product/developers* query. Figure 4.6 shows this latter tool opened by selection.

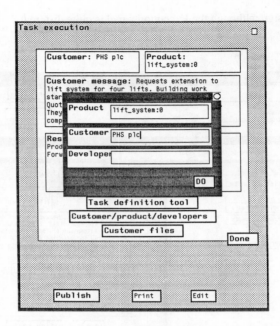

Fig. 4.6 Step 4: Customer/product/developers query tool

Any two of the three fields may be entered, with the third field being completed automatically by querying the IB. In this case the tool is used to find the team responsible for maintaining this customer's version of this product, and hence the product and customer fields have been entered. The answer (not shown) is the team headed by the Project Manager, which is, in fact, the only team set up in the IB.

The query tool could also be used to find out, for instance, which other products by this company are used by this customer. As with all tools in this demonstration, it can be closed by selection of the small circle in the top right-hand corner.

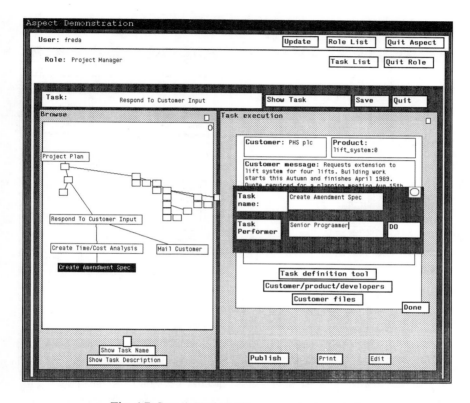

Fig. 4.7 Step 4: Project Manager assigning a task

In Figure 4.7, the Project Manager uses the *Task definition tool* to give the Senior Programmer the task of preparing an Amendment Specification, an initial investigation into the implications of the proposed modification, in order to cost it for the customer. This is a crude first attempt at such a tool, and simply records in the IB that the named task has been assigned to a particular role. Tasks valid for this purpose have been set up in the IB with pre-defined data, tools and a task environment, and the user only has to type in a recognised task.

A more sophisticated tool would allow the user to specify the availability of data and tools in the task, and the permission held by that task on those data objects. The user should also be able to build tasks from sub-tasks, specifying relationships between them of sequence, selection etc., in other words building up a project plan. As defining a task in this way could be time-consuming, such a tool would rely heavily on sets of defaults. These would be associated with generic tasks which could be selected from the Browse area (see Figure 4.7). In the demonstration, the pre-defined tasks can be considered as generic tasks whose default values need no customisation.

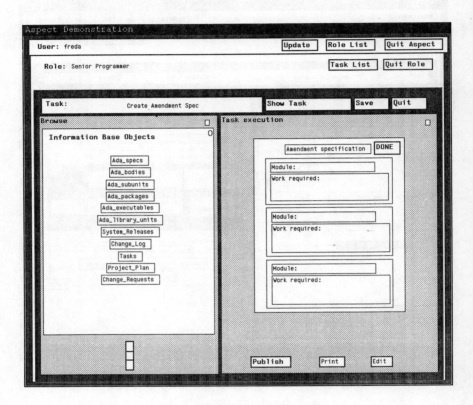

Fig. 4.8 Step 4: Senior Programmer's environment

Having quit the role of Project Manager, our user is now playing the role of Senior Programmer and has accessed the *Create Amendment Spec* task assigned by the Project Manager. Note that more and different types of objects are available in the Browse panel in this task environment (Figure 4.8), and also that the main tool to be used, the form-fill of an Amendment Specification, is open on entry to the task.

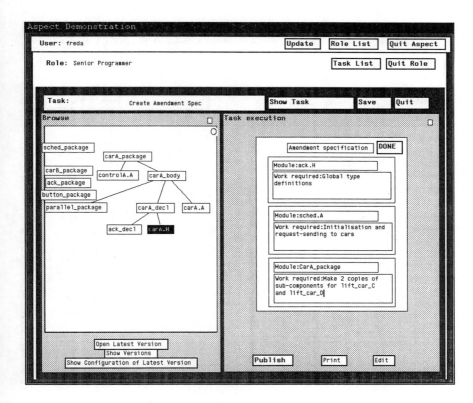

Fig. 4.9 Step 4: Amendment specification tool

The Senior Programmer examines the Ada modules in the lift-system configuration via the *Show Configuration* operation in the Browse panel. In Figure 4.9 we see the sub-components of the Ada package handling lift-car "A". The Ada code of the latest version may be browsed (but not edited) by selecting *Open Latest Version*, or of earlier versions through *Show Versions*. There are more examples of use of this tool later in this chapter, and the underlying representations in the IB are explained in Section 6.5.

The Senior Programmer decides which modules need updating to extend the system to control four lift-cars. The items of work are listed in the tool in the execution panel. Ideally, these would be linked in the IB to the subsequent assignment of tasks to individual programmers. In this demonstration, however, these tasks have already been defined.

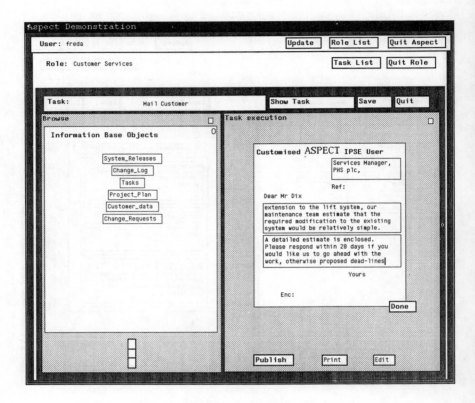

Fig. 4.10 Step 5: Mailing the customer

Step 5: Customer acceptance of the estimate

The Senior Programmer publishes the details in the Amendment Specification to the Project Manager who uses them to estimate the time and costs for the modification. This estimate is then published to Customer Services with a task to prepare it in suitable form for mailing to the customer.

Step 6: The production of the new variant

When the customer has accepted the estimate and the acceptance has been logged in the IB by Customer Services, the Project Manager assigns tasks to perform the updates necessary to create a new version of the lift system.

These tasks – *Update Globals, Update Scheduler* and *Create New Lift Shaft* – are the three items of work specified by the Senior Programmer in the Amendment

Specification (Figure 4.9). The following six screens illustrate the use of tools in the Update Scheduler task, which is assigned to the Senior Programmer, and also examine the Browse facilities in more detail. Figure 4.11 shows the objects and tools available in this task.

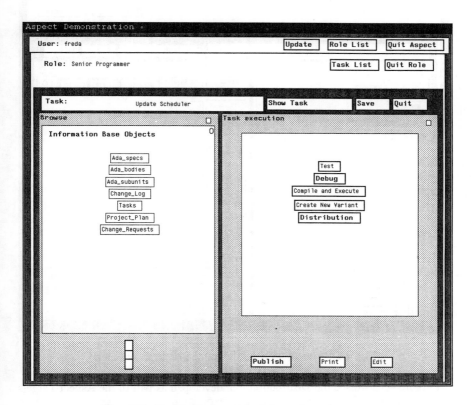

Fig. 4.11 Step 6: Update Scheduler task environment

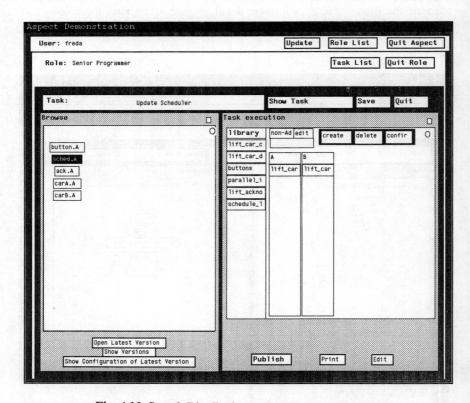

Fig. 4.12 Step 6: Distribution tool and component menu

In Figure 4.12 we see the Distribution tool developed as part of the Aspect Targets work (details in Chapter 10). It is used to experiment with different configurations of processes to processors in the distributed lifts system.

In the Browse panel, the programmer has selected *Ada_bodies* from the object list. Components of that type are displayed; these are the bodies of Ada packages displayed in the configuration of the whole lift-system (Figure 4.1). The programmer has selected *sched.A* (the scheduler package body), which is highlighted on selection. The menu of browse operations on components appears at the bottom of the Browse panel when a component is selected.

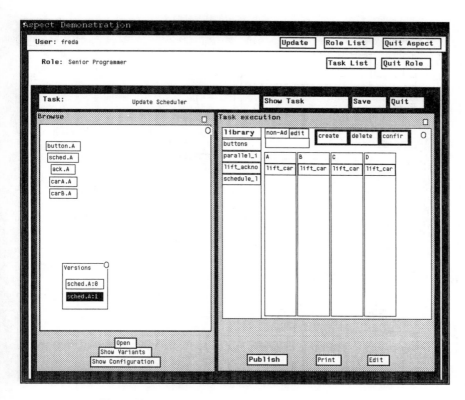

Fig. 4.13 Step 6: Distribution tool and version menu

Figure 4.13 shows the Distribution tool after the creation of new processors. Packages have been selected from the library and allocated to the new processors.

On the left, in the Browse panel, the operation *Show Versions* has been selected on the previously selected component, *sched.A*. This displays a list of versions – two in this case (*sched.A:0* and *sched.A:1*). These are the versions of its main line of development. When one of these is selected, a different menu of browse operations replaces those given for components.

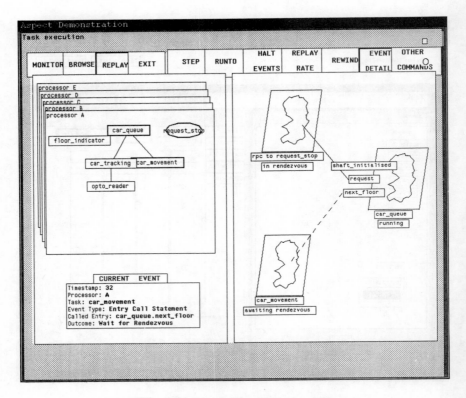

Fig. 4.14 Step 6: The debugging tool

Figure 4.14 shows the suggested graphical interface to the Debugging tool which exists at the moment in non-graphical form only. The tool is described in detail in the Targets work in Chapter 10.

The tool has been "blown up" to fill the whole screen by selection of the small square in the top right-hand corner. This is available on the Browse panel and the Execution panel, and operates as a toggle between original size and full screen.

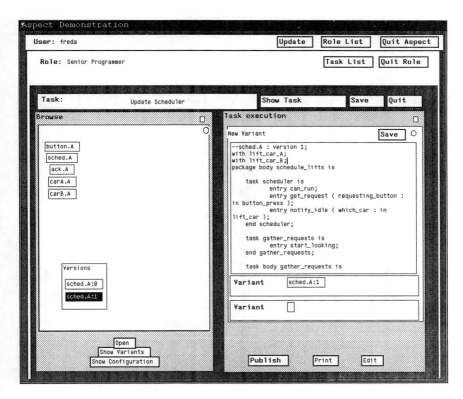

Fig. 4.15 Step 6: The variant tool

The variant tool in Figures 4.15 and 4.16 can be selected with a version or a component. If the latter, it operates on a default version. In Figure 4.15 the programmer is going to create a variant of the last version of *sched.A*. The tool reads in the file contents of that version, and allows the programmer to edit this and give the new variant a name. Selection of the *Save* button creates the variant.

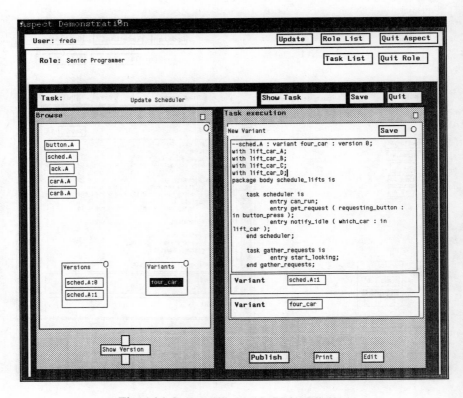

Fig. 4.16 Step 6: The version/variant display

In Figure 4.16 the source file displayed in the variant tool has been edited to create a variant as part of a four lift-car system. This has been saved. In the Browse panel, the source version (*sched.A:1*) has been selected with the operation *Show Variants*. This displays the list of variants for this version. In this case there is only the *four_car* variant which has just been created.

Selection of a variant causes another list of browse operations to appear. For variants, there is only one valid operation – *show versions*. Details of the version/variant IB structures are given in the Version Control section of Chapter 6.

4.4 Summary

We have tried in these few pages to give an impression of the flow of the mini-IPSE demonstration. It has not been possible to show every state of every task, but we have tried to choose screens to cover all the main principles of Aspect.

We hope that this broad, concrete introduction will provide readers with a context in which to place the detailed structures and arguments of the following chapters, and thus aid their understanding.

Chapter 5

The Information Base Engine

A.N. Earl and R.P. Whittington

5.1 Introduction

Updates to a design database, and, indeed, to a typical business database, tend to involve entity-sized granules: a new version of a source code module is added, a new tool is installed, a person is assigned to a project, a process is initiated, and so on. By contrast, retrievals tend to involve sets of entities: the set of modules that comprise a configuration unit, the tools that assist with a particular type of task, the people involved in a project, the current set of processes, and so on. This observation suggests that two kinds of interfaces are required to an information base: one that supports entity-oriented updates, and one that supports set-oriented retrieval. The former should enforce integrity whereas the latter should provide for the efficient formulation of arbitrarily complex enquiries, and thus provide an algebra for the expression of arbitrarily complex abstractions.

The ideal basis for an information base engine for a system development environment is a model that provides the above, based on a common underlying formalism. To a large extent, this requirement is met by Codd's extended relational model, RM/T [35]. This model – with a few modifications – provides for the two types of interface outlined above, and implements these in terms of an underlying relational formalism whose semantics are driven by the contents of a core of self-referential *catalog* relations. Consequently, the model allows for the definition of integrity at the entity level (via the catalog) and also for the manipulation of all data (including the catalog) in terms of an extended relational algebra.

In addition to satisfying this requirement, a modified RM/T is readily imple-mentable using a conventional relational database management system, and thus was selected as the basis of our engine. The model adopted is referred to as RM/T++ (from the C operator to increment).

The modifications made to Codd's original proposals are described later in this chapter; essentially they follow from the lack of a clear distinction in Codd's proposal between the entity interface and the extended relational interface. These changes have been discussed previously in [45] They were agreed by the project team following a formal specification exercise, using the language Z [97], which revealed the shortcomings of the original proposal and prompted further insight into the potential of the approach.

A prototype implementation of the engine is now complete. It is built as a set of modules developed using the C library offered by the relational database management system db++ [3]. These modules manipulate a relational database, and are available as a library for tool writers. Because an extended relational database is, at root, a collection of relations, the db++ query language has been available for prototype investigation in an end-user manner. More sophisticated, graphically-oriented enquiry facilities have also now been implemented, making use of Presenter.

Although, to the programmer, the Aspect information base engine can appear similar in concept to PCTE and CAIS, the existence of the additional, relational, facilities distinguish this system, and proved to be an invaluable mechanism during superstructure development.

This chapter presents RM/T++ in detail, and discusses the implementation (with extensions for distribution) that was carried out as part of the project.

5.1.1 Entity types and entities

The objects held in an RM/T++ database are called entities. The entities in a data-base represent, or model, either entities in the real world or other entities in the database.

In order to impose some regular structure upon the database, every entity is declared to be a member of at least one entity type; all entities of a particular type share the common properties of that entity type. Entities can belong to more than one entity type but all except one of these will be supertypes of its immediate type. The type hierarchy is described in the next section.

5.1.2 Type hierarchies

The subtyping relationships between entity types in RM/T++ constitute a type hierarchy. There is a single type hierarchy in RM/T++ because all entity types are descended from a single root type. In the type hierarchy, all subtypes inherit all the attributes of their supertypes. For instance, suppose PROGRAMS is an entity type with the attribute *creation-date*. Then subtypes of PROGRAMS might be C_PROGRAMS, PASCAL_PROGRAMS and ADA_PROGRAMS (see Figure 5.1). They too, all inherit *creation-date*.

RM/T++ also supports the concept of distinct categories of subtypes. In the above example the single category for PROGRAMS might have been called

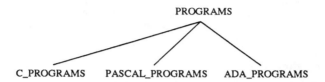

Fig. 5.1 Simple subtyping

language. But a further category for PROGRAMS could have been incorporated, called *application,* associated with further subtypes, SYSTEM and DATABASE (see Figure 5.2).

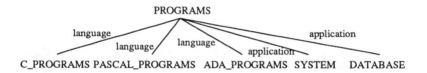

Fig. 5.2 Subtyping per categories

In addition, RM/T++ incorporates multiple supertypes. This is where a given subtype may simultaneously be an instance of more than one supertype. In this example PROGRAMS could be a subtype of both the IMPLEMENTATIONS and TOOLS types (see Figure 5.3).

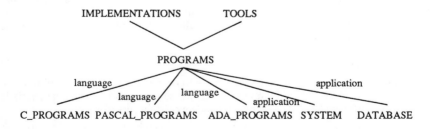

Fig. 5.3 Multiple inheritance

One of the most important reasons for having a subtype hierarchy is that it enables the use of null values meaning "value inapplicable" to be avoided. For example, suppose one of the attributes of an Ada program was the Ada library it belonged to. Without attribute inheritance, all programs would have to have that attribute. In the case of Pascal or C programs the value of that attribute would always be null.

5.1.3 Entity attributes

Attributes are the means by which immediate single-valued pieces of information about an entity can be held. *Immediate* here means that it is not an attribute of some related entity but really an attribute of the entity itself.

5.1.4 Values and value types

Attribute values are restricted to a defined *value type*. Furthermore, a value type itself is defined over a *domain* of values. The initial set of value types, each with a corresponding domain, are integers, reals, strings, dates, durations, identifiers, a surrogate type, a file type, and a relational expression type.

RM/T++ also supports value subtyping. A value type can be a subtype of another if its domain is a subset of the latter's.

5.1.5 Attributes and values

All attributes in the database are associated with a value type. This is so that it can be ensured that all the values of all attributes come from the correct domain.

5.1.6 Surrogates

Surrogates are system generated entity identifiers. Every entity is permanently associated with its unique surrogate. Surrogates are never reused so that problems are not encountered when reinstating information from archives. RM/T++ itself does not deal with naming at all, but see a later section in this chapter for an integrated treatment of names.

5.1.7 The classification of entity types

All entity types are classified to be either kernel, characteristic or associative. They may also be designative in addition. In the following subsections these classes are described in more detail. The main reason for this classification is to provide the system with sufficient information to enforce the integrity rules associated with the various classes of entity types.

Characteristic entity types

The function of a characteristic entity type is to describe some other entity in more detail. The other entity is often referred to as the superior entity. The characteristic entity is subordinate to, and existence-dependent on, that superior entity.

For example, the individual COMMANDS which have to be executed to keep a target up-to-date in a Makefile, could be considered characteristic of the RULES they appear in. The attributes of the individual COMMANDS can then be regarded as non-immediate attributes of the RULES.

The way in which a characteristic entity references its superior entity is that it has an attribute, the value of which is the surrogate of the superior entity.

Characteristic integrity says that a characteristic entity can only exist if what it describes exists.

Designative entity types

A designation is defined as a many-to-one relationship involving two otherwise independent entities. For example, a PROGRAMMER may only be allowed to belong to one DEPARTMENT and assigned to one PROJECT. It would be said that a PROGRAMMER designates a DEPARTMENT and a PROJECT.

The way in which the designation is achieved is that the designating entity type has an attribute for each entity type designated. Each of these attributes takes the values of the surrogates of the entities designated. One entity type designates another *via* an attribute.

Designative integrity says that a designative entity can only exist if all the entities it designates also exist.

Associative entity types

An association is defined as a many-to-many(-to many etc.) relationship involving two or more otherwise independent entities. For example, a COMPILER associates a PROGRAMMING_LANGUAGE with a MACHINE_KIND.

The concept of designation is actually a more primitive notion than that of association. The means of achieving associations are also very similar. It is important to note that there must be at least two participants, not necessarily of distinct types, in an association.

Associative integrity says that an associative entity can only exist if all the participants in the association also exist.

Kernel entity types

A kernel entity type is one which is neither characteristic nor associative.

5.1.8 The RM/T++ diagrammatic notation

Figure 5.4 illustrates the notation developed for documenting diagrammatically RM/T++ formulations. In fact it illustrates an application of RM/T++ to the capture of the information objects used by the Unix tool Make [49], This example is described more fully in [44].

An entity type (for example, Makefiles, Files, Rules, and so on) is represented by a box containing its name, and its class. The latter is indicated by capital letters for Kernel, Associative, Characteristic or Designative, written in the top left-hand corner.

Subtypes with a single supertype − Makefiles as subtypes of Files, in the above example − are represented as boxes within boxes; more complex subtype relationships, however, can be detailed on a separate subtype hierarchy diagram.

The associations captured by Associative entity types − Dependents associating Rules with their dependent Files, and Targets, associating Rules with their target

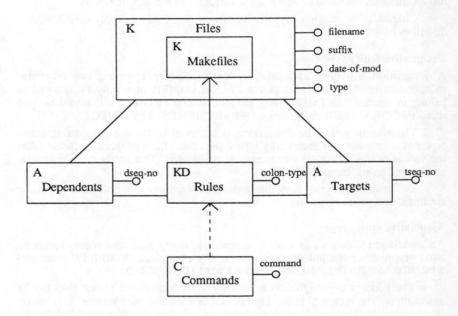

Fig. 5.4 RM/T++ notation illustrated through the
formulation of Make information

files, in the above example – are indicated by lines connecting the entity types
involved.

Designative relationships between entity types – for example, the designation
within Rules of the Makefile to which they relate, in the above – are again
represented by lines, except that these have arrows to indicate the direction of the
designation. Where multiple designations ensue from an entity types, these must be
labelled with the name of the designative attribute for clarity.

Characteristic relationships – in the above example, the collection of Commands within Rules – are represented by dashed lines, again, with directional
arrows (although these are not strictly necessary).

Simple attributes – for example, *filename, suffix* and *type* are attributes, or
properties of Files – are represented as small circles attached by a line to the
appropriate entity type.

5.1.9 Relations

The description of the database has so far centered around entities and entity types. But the way in which information is manipulated is via relational operators. This section describes how entities and entity types are represented as relations in the database.

The relations dealt with are those described in the relational model [34]. That is, they can be thought of as tabular structures whose headings are called attributes and whose rows are called tuples. A relation has a set of attributes and a set of tuples.

Every entity type in the database has an e-relation: a unary relation holding the surrogates of all the entities of that type.

Every entity type in the database has a set of p-relations recording the values of the attributes of entities of that type.

5.1.10 Self-referential aspects of RM/T++

One of the most important features of an RM/T++ database is that *all* information in the universe of discourse is represented as entities within the database. This information includes information concerning the structure of the database itself.

A section later in this chapter discusses in more detail exactly what information is held concerning the database structure, but two points are made here. Firstly, there are entities which represent all entity types, attributes, and so on. And secondly, there are no special distinctions between these entities and any others, and so the information concerning the database structure is held in entity types exactly as any other information would be. A consistent interface is thus provided to the user who does not need any special operations to query about the structure of the database. The set of entity types holding such information is referred to as the Catalog.

5.1.11 The conventional relational operators

The basic relational model includes a set of operators. RM/T++ includes all of these operators. These operators have been presented in several ways. The presentation chosen here follows closely that of the Peterlee Relational Test Vehicle (PRTV) [56]. The set consists of generalised intersection (specialised cases of which include restriction, join and intersection), union, difference and project.

These operations are so well known that a description of them is not presented here. However, it should be noted that the operators do not introduce null values. The generalised union operator is restricted to the special case of union compatible relations.

5.1.12 The extended relational operators

The operators in this category consist of a set of the new relational operators designed to provide better support within the context of RM/T++ for dealing with sets of relations and relations representing hierarchies. The operators are divided into the set operators and the graph operators.

The set operators

There are six so-called set operators in RM/T++ (taken from Codd): COMPRESS; APPLY; Partition by Attribute (PATT); Partition by **Tuple** (PTUPLE); and Partition by **Relation** (PREL). Their definitions are presented here.

Let f be an associative and commutative operator that maps a pair of relations into a relation. Let Z be a set of relations such that f can be validly applied to every pair of relations in Z. Then COMPRESS(f,Z) is the relation obtained by repeated pairwise application of f to the relations in Z.

If f is a unary operator that maps relations into relations, then APPLY(f,Z), where Z is a set of relations, is the set of relations $f(z)$, where z is a member of Z.

Let r be a relation with attributes a (possibly compound). r may have attributes other than a. Then PATT(r,a) is the set of relations obtained by partitioning r per all the distinct values of a.

Informally, PTUPLE(r) promotes each tuple of a relation into an individual relation.

If r is a relation, then PREL(r) is the set containing just r.

The graph operators

The graph operators are provided for manipulation of special kinds of relations, directed graph relations. The only graph operator in RM/T++ is CLOSE, returning the transitive closure of a relation. In order that this operation does not generate null values its application is limited to graph relations with just three attributes to hold the values of two nodes and the relationship which exists between them.

5.1.13 Database manipulation operations

This section covers those extended relational operators which cannot be specified without reference to an encompassing database, plus manipulative database operations such as create/destroy relation, create value type and create value subtype.

The name operators

The so-called name operators comprise DENOTE, TAG and SETREL, and deal with associating an identifier with a relation.

DENOTE comes in two forms. It can be applied to a relation surrogate or to a unary relation which contains only relation surrogates. DENOTE (surrogate) simply takes a surrogate of a relation and returns that relation whereas DENOTE(r) (where r is a unary relation which contains only surrogates of relations) is the set of all those relations whose surrogate is in r.

The result of TAG(r,x) is a relation formed from the cartesian product of r and a unary relation with attribute, x, containing only the surrogate of r.

SETREL returns a set of relations from a set of relation surrogates.

The manipulative operators

These operations deal with changing the contents of the database. They can be partitioned into two sets. The first, and most important, includes the set of logical-level operations to create entity types, value types, value subtypes, categories and attributes. It also includes the operations to create, update and delete entities.

The second set supports the provision of a conventional relational database management system (RDBMS) within an RM/T++ database system but without the integrity checking which goes with e-relations and p-relations. The operations to create, update, and delete *user*-relations (i.e. those not created through the entity interface) are not a very important part of the RM/T++ model.

5.2 Differences between RM/T and RM/T++

The work done on the original descriptions of RM/T is brought together here by stating the changes made by RM/T++ followed by those ideas omitted and those which are extensions to RM/T.

5.2.1 Changes

Some changes are simply use of terminology. For instance, influenced by Z, RM/T++ does not use the term *property* since *attribute* seems more appropriate at both the logical and relational levels. Both Codd and Date, in his tutorial exposition of Codd's RM/T [40], call *any* attribute holding surrogates an E-attribute. In RM/T++ the term is restricted to the attribute of an E-relation.

The changes made to the naming and structure of the Catalog and the reasons for them are described in a later section. Although only Date introduces designative entity types, they *are* included in RM/T++. The differences resulting from the RM/T++ approach to defining manipulation operators at the entity (type) level rather than at the relational level are discussed in more detail under *Extensions* but are clearly a change from RM/T. However, this does not affect the approach of the model with regard to actions taken should an integrity rule be broken. Just as Codd considers a cascading delete* constraint as part of the *application* of RM/T, so RM/T++ does not directly support any cascading operations. Clearly, the availability of Catalog information allows higher-level tools to provide this type of functionality where appropriate to certain applications.

One of the most far-reaching changes concerns the naming issue. Codd and Date present the advantages of surrogates, yet then go on to propose rules about the naming of relations. From a pedagogical point of view this perhaps offers simplicity. Yet their definition of RM/T is further complicated by naming and its strengths and self-referential properties are devalued.

A discussion of how this situation is rectified within RM/T++ by omitting naming from the model but using the model to support a naming system is described later in this chapter. The operators changed to use only surrogates rather than names are DENOTE, TAG (to which an attribute parameter is added to Codd's

---

* A cascading delete operation is a delete operation which not only deletes the requested entity but also any entities which are recursively dependent on the requested entity.

definition) and SETREL.

Both Codd and Date state that the subtypes of a kernel entity type are always kernel. No justification is presented in their papers and research by this author has concluded that the restriction is too strong. It disallows, for example, the use of a single root type to enforce that every entity should have an owner. The constraint does *not* appear in RM/T++, although the similar constraint that subtypes of associative, characteristic and designative types should be associative, characteristic and designative, respectively, *does* apply.

5.2.2 Omissions

The operation NOTE, defined by Codd to return the name of a relation, is not included in RM/T++ (see the section later on naming issues). *Non-entity associations*, which are only included in RM/T for expository reasons, are not defined in RM/T++. *Event precedence*, defined to provide some dynamic semantics is not defined in RM/T++ since a more comprehensive approach is defined in the Aspect activity model.

Codd's RM/T paper presents a treatment of null values within the relational model. The null value can have the meaning *value unknown* or *value inapplicable*. The latter can be avoided by entity subtyping. Date presents a convincing argument against the inclusion of null values, preferring more application-specific default values without problems of semantics. The specification of RM/T++ does *not* allow null values to be entered into the database nor be generated by any of the operators. There is no reason why the specification could not be extended to include null values, but, as concluded by the investigators of Taxis [79], the increased complexity of the specification would be considerable.

In another area of complexity, *Alternative generalisation*,† RM/T++ follows the advice of Date that considerable study is required to overcome the complexity without guarantee of a worthwhile increase in functionality, and so RM/T++ includes only *unconditional generalisation*. Codd's *Cover Aggregation*, where a set of instances of unrelated types are considered as a whole (e.g. a **convoy** of ships, planes and submarines, or a **library** of records, tapes, books and magazines), has, as in Date, been omitted from RM/T++. Its addition to RM/T++ would be straightforward and not introduce great complexity to the data structures but would require the invention of a set of suitable operators. The requirement for *complete* mappings, documentation and implementation of any feature within Aspect has encouraged such additions only where a definite requirement or advantage can be seen. It is for similar reasons that, of the graph operators, OPEN, CLOSE, and STEP in RM/T, only CLOSE is incorporated in RM/T++.

---

† Y may be a *conditional* subtype of a set of $X_1...X_n$, in the sense that every instance of Y is also an instance of exactly one of the X_i (i=1..n), but not every instance of the X_i is an instance of Y.

5.2.3 Extensions

Neither Codd nor Date present any details of the set of base value types supported by the model nor how new types should be defined. RM/T++ allows the creation of new value types strictly as subsets of existing ones, and supports, initially, ordinary types (string, integer, and real), some well-known extensions of these (date, duration, and identifier), plus the following types specifically important for the model and its application within an IPSE.

There is, of course, a value type specifically for surrogates (e_type). There is a type (x_type) to record relational expressions in the database. This helps maintain integrity for the support of rules especially. And a *file* value type provides support for unstructured data to be held, or presented as held, in files of the underlying operating system.

The major extensions to RM/T are a result of having an explicit semantic level at which a set of operations is defined. All of these operations, dealing with entity types, entities, attributes etc., and their creation, update, and deletion are not discussed in RM/T. RM/T++, in its specification at least, allows the system to support an ordinary relational database. The envisaged purpose of this is to support management of temporary results or experimental queries from the semantically controlled information. It would be a way of gradually introducing RM/T++ to existing RDBMS users.

5.3 Implementation of RM/T++

5.3.1 Designing a catalog structure

The Catalog structure proposed by Codd for RM/T is shown in Figure 5.5. It suffers from the following problems:

(a)   Mixing levels – associations are with relations, not entity types;

(b)   An attribute can exist without an associated domain;

(c)   The association and characteristic graphs do not indicate the attributes involved;

(d)   Information is collected in a string of characters in the single **reltype** attribute of **relation** (e.g. 'A' for associative and 'P' for property relation) which seems not to be a *single-valued piece of information*;

(e)   Names are attributes of some, but not all, of the entity types.

Date's RM/T Catalog proposal is shown in Figure 5.6. It is inadequate for reasons (a), (d) and (e) stated above as well as the following reasons:

(f)   The characteristic graph does not indicate which attribute holds the characteristic reference;

(g)   **Attribute** associates relations and domains implying that an attribute cannot exist alone, but also implying that each attribute appears in only one relation. This cannot be true since every set of P-relations has a common E-attribute.

The Catalog specified for RM/T++ is shown in Figure 5.7. Note the following points:

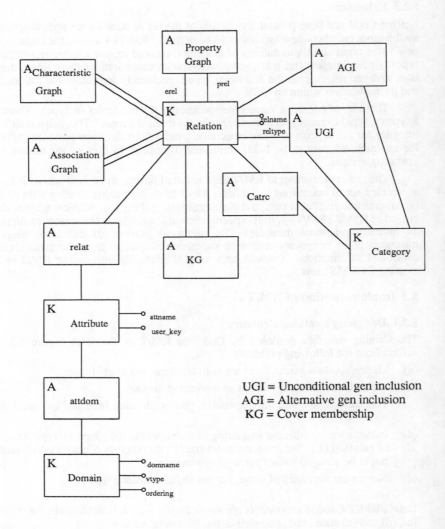

Fig. 5.5 Codd's Catalog structure

- There are kernel entity types representing attributes, entity types and relations. They are associated separately via **etat** and **relat**;
- All the graph relations include the attributes involved;
- An instance of **Entity_Type_Reps** designates its e-relation, providing the key link between the abstract and relational levels;

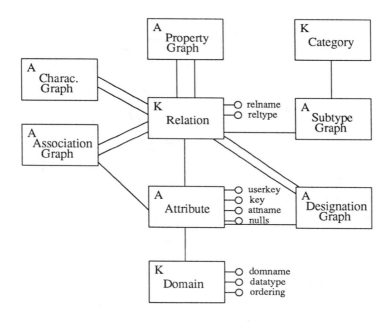

Fig. 5.6 Date's Catalog structure

- Naming is not involved in the Catalog information (see next section);
- No entity types in the Catalog have attributes except to hold entity references.

This Catalog structure is, however, deficient in that it lacks an association between **Value_Type_Reps** to record the value-type hierarchy. The correction has in fact been implemented, but is not made here so as to maintain consistency with the currently published specification of RM/T++.

Apart from supporting integrated functionality required by an IPSE, the ease with which graphical presentation of models can be prepared is noted. This IPSE is certainly self-referential since it is used to control its own development.

5.3.2 Naming and surrogates

The problem of how to identify objects is a fundamental one to which a generic solution is required. The term *surrogate*, introduced in [57], captures the idea that every entity of the outside world is associated with a surrogate which stands for that object in the model. In other words, a surrogate is a unique, system-generated identifier which is never re-used.

The problems of using user-controlled keys as surrogates are threefold:

(1)   The actual values are user-controlled and thus users are responsible for keep-ing them consistent. Each user would be impacted by an event such as a

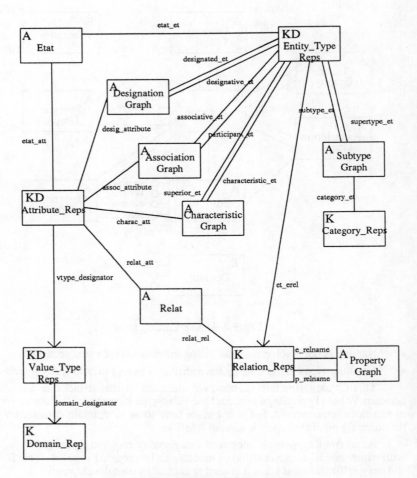

Fig. 5.7 The RM/T++ Catalog structure

company merger which changed all serial numbers;

(2) Different user-controlled keys may be denoting the same entity, but this cannot be recognised if those keys are on different domains. For example, part of the database may be identifying people by their full names and addresses, while another uses a health service number;

(3) The value used as the key may not be known at the time the entity is introduced into the system. For instance, if a job applicant needs to be recorded as a person using a health service number then their key is unknown until that information is obtained.

Surrogates overcome these difficulties by allowing the system itself to have control of surrogate values, which are defined over a single domain, and by allocating surrogates when the entity is introduced to the system. It is therefore always true that two entities are the same if, and only if, their surrogate values are identical. Surrogates are never re-used to ensure that events such as restoring entities from a backup storage system cause no conflicts.

Some observations on the fundamental differences that exist between surrogates and identifiers are given in [73]:

- A surrogate might not be exposed to users;

- Users do not specify the format, syntax, structure, uniqueness rules, etc. for surrogates;

- Surrogates are globally unique, and have the same format for all entities;

- The system does not have to know the entity type (or the identifier type) before knowing which entity is being referenced, or before knowing what the surrogate format will be;

- Surrogates are purely information free. They do not imply anything about any related entities, nor any kind of meaningful ordering.

The surrogate concept does not necessarily imply that surrogates should be either totally visible nor totally invisible to the external user. There can usefully be degrees of surrogate visibility:

(i)   User-keys are still used extensively, and surrogates, hidden completely, simply help maintain the integrity of the system;

(ii)   Users are aware of an attribute recording surrogate values which can be taken advantage of in queries, but actual values are always hidden;

(iii) All entities are named, and whenever a user would see a surrogate value, a name is presented instead;

(iv)   Surrogates are completely visible to the user, but they cannot, by definition, update, or in any way control, the values presented.

Within an IPSE context, option (iii) is generally the most useful. However (iv) can be useful to the IPSE developers or toolwriters while new elements are being developed or debugged. And (ii) is appropriate more especially for tools which do not want to have to generate names where it would be more appropriate to identify an entity by its properties. An example might be the symbol table generated in a compilation. The use of surrogates for engineering databases in general is investigated in [77].

Any surrogate can be associated with a name which is unique within the context of a namespace. Since names and namespaces are entities themselves, a very flexible approach to naming is supported. For example, the naming mechanisms of PCTE or Unix are easily modelled, and the Aspect approach clearly distinguishes the name of an object from the means of accessing it. Data independence is thus not compromised and it is clear whether or not two different names refer to the same entity.

It is interesting to note that, in the description of SHM [91], it is recommended that *names should be meaningful nouns*, implying that naming is intrinsically concerned with semantics. Despite describing the advantages of surrogates over names, both Codd and Date use rules about names to describe RM/T. Strictly, naming is not dealt with by the RM/T++ model, but it does provide support for naming mechanisms as demonstrated within Aspect.

With the Aspect approach to naming, a bootstrapping problem arises if an initial namespace does not exist. At first glance it appears that since users are free to create namespaces and assign names to them, then an initial namespace is not essential. Indeed, there is no problem within the process which creates a namespace to work in. However, if a process starts and is required to use a named namespace then the surrogate of that namespace can only be recovered by giving its name *and* the namespace in which it is named. Only the existence of an initial namespace, the surrogate of which is available to all processes after Aspect initialisation, overcomes this problem.

5.4 Building a Prototype Implementation

Earlier parts of this chapter have described how RM/T++ was investigated in isolation by means of a specification far removed from any machine language. In order to carry out further investigation and experimentation to validate the claim that RM/T++ was a suitable candidate for the core of an IPSE information base it was necessary to implement the specification on some machine.

This section reports on the requirements of such an implementation and the background to some of the decisions made. It describes how the transition from a high-level specification language, to a reasonably high-level programming language was carried out. Finally, some of the more interesting points about the implementation are discussed together with its limitations.

5.4.1 Properties required of the prototype

The Aspect project itself was distributed over more than three sites and went through a number of political changes impinging on the hardware used. Although the decision to build on top of Unix was stable, it was essential that the software produced was portable across different hardware configurations. The information base was to be used by all parts of the project and thus had to work on the hardware used at any of the sites as well as other demonstration sites. A project decision, closely linked with the Unix dependency, was that the implementation language would be C.

The implementation of the information base engine was to be started at the same time as that of the information base superstructure. The IB implementation was thus on a critical path and had to be implemented speedily to provide the capabilities for other areas to be tested. Linked with this was the constraint that the implementation should proceed in stages, providing the most-needed facilities initially before supporting the least-used operations.

Although the implementation had to be available quickly, there were no stringent requirements on its performance. So long as the resources it consumed were available, and it performed with a speed sufficient for demonstration purposes it would be considered an adequate prototype.

The properties considered more important than performance were, firstly, that it should perform functionally as specified. Secondly, it should be simply built and well-structured so that it could be easily understood and easily modifiable. In other words, maintainable.

The Z specification documented *what* the operations would do, it did not explain *how* these facilities were to be made available through a programming interface. There was thus a requirement to provide good, clear, up-to-date documentation of both installation and use of the RM/T++ library. Since all work was being carried out upon Unix, the RM/T++ documentation led the way in using Unix-style manual pages as the major documentation device.

5.4.2 Choosing a database management system

This section firstly describes the reasons for building the prototype implementation of RM/T++ on top of an existing RDBMS, and secondly describes the reasons behind the choice of db++ [3] as that vehicle.

The choice to make use of a commercially available RDBMS was based on three major points:

(1)   RM/T++ maps the logical view of a model onto a relational view;

(2)   The main aim of the prototype was *not* to investigate optimal methods for implementing RM/T++, but to produce a usable, demonstrable system quickly;

(3)   Ports to different relational systems or even database machines would thereby be possible.

The reduction of effort in not having to write code to manage data in a relational manner was certain to be great. Both maintenance and overall complexity of the system would be reduced. The use of a relational DBMS would, by definition, implement a subset of the RM/T++ query facilities immediately. The extent of the reduction in work would depend on how closely the query facilities of the chosen system matched those specified. Such facilities would also provide an easy method of directly querying relations for debugging purposes. Other database facilities such as locking and access control found in a DBMS might also be taken advantage of.

If the RM/T++ implementation made little or no use of facilities specific to the chosen DBMS, then it should be the case that the RM/T++ implementation would be portable over relational different DBMSs rather than just operating systems.

The main point against using an underlying relational DBMS is that its generality sacrifices to some extent the performance of systems built using it. This is particularly relevant with respect to RM/T++'s integrity checking where one could imagine some hierarchical or network system performing substantially better. But, as stated above, in the implementation of this prototype, performance was definitely of secondary importance.

The choice available, when a study was carried out of candidates to build upon, was drastically limited by a pragmatic requirement that the DBMS should run on a GEC-63 machine. Only three vendors said they could supply such a system.

A study of those systems resulted in a system called db++ [3], from Concept Asa in West Germany, being selected. The main advantages and drawbacks of the use of db++ for this application can be summarised as follows:

+   It is based upon the relational algebra. This is a closed algebra and is easier to translate into from higher level statements than the only option, relational calculus;

+   There is very close integration with Unix, both through shell scripts which would allow fast and easy prototyping, and through the C-interface routines. This fits the Aspect approach well;

+   It is available on a wide range of machines running Unix;

+   Results can be piped for further relational processing or to standard Unix tools;

-    Lack of support for null values;

-    Little on-line documentation;

-    Locking of entire relations may be restrictive;

-    The data-dictionary facility does not keep the relational form up-to-date.

5.4.3 Functional structure of the implementation

It was not simply a matter of good design that the RM/T++ software should be layered into distinct functional areas. Apart from the fact that distributed and non-distributed aspects of the implementation had to be identified to allow a distribution layer, there was a need to separate out both query facilities and primitive RDBMS facilities (such as open relation, or delete tuple). This section describes the layers developed and their functionality.

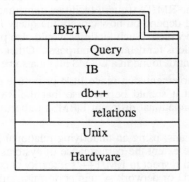

Fig. 5.8 Functional layering of the implementation

Figure 5.8 shows that immediately beneath the Public Tool Interface (PTI) is the Information Base Translation and Validation (IBETV) layer. In general, a PTI operation or function (where the distinction is that only the former changes the state of the IB) will make queries on the IB layer to verify that it can be carried out with the given parameters. These queries are made in terms of those relational algebra facilities provided at the PTI by the query layer. Any recursion is terminated within the query layer by recognising a Catalog relation being the target of a query.

The translation functionality of the IBETV comes from observing that in the Z specification many PTI operations and functions are expressed in terms of more primitive operations and functions. It is most clear with operations which act upon the *abstract database* (e.g. create entity type, or delete entity) because their specification describes the operations to be carried out on the underlying *Physical Database*.

In fact, the IB layer, which provides those primitive operations, supports only the following:

- create relation();
- add tuple();
- delete tuple ();
- update tuple();
- denote surrogate();
- generate surrogate().

This set of functions is readily supported by db++, which in turn resides on Unix-running hardware.

This layering would both ease the introduction of a different RDBMS or even a relational database machine to improve performance, and would allow the query layer to incorporate optimisation techniques without affecting the other layers. The latter was carried out for the Catalog queries within PTI operations and proved extremely effective in improving performance.

5.4.4 Limitations on the implementation

A complete implementation of the entire specification was beyond the resources available to Aspect. Fortunately, not all RM/T++ operators are born equal. For example, of the extended relational query operators, only **close** has come close to finding an effective use. Simplifications of the structures as specified can also be made.

Although these compromises are currently being made out of necessity, their practicality has been established during demonstrations. It is the purpose of this section to make clear the simplifications that have been made. Some justification for making each simplification will be given.

Value types

The problems of domain checking of values are well understood in both database systems and programming languages. The implementation of such would take significant coding without demonstrating anything new. Also the Catalog structure would have to be added to in order to support such checking. For these reasons the operators **create_VALUE_TYPE** and **create_VALUE_SUBTYPE** are *not* implemented.

User relations

The specification of an RM/T++ database allows the database to contain relations which are neither e-relations nor p-relations. Such relations have been termed *user relations* or *U-relations*. A traditional database management system would contain only U-relations. It is imagined that the only effective use of U-relations within an RM/T++ database would be as temporary snapshots made by one-off queries, since no integrity checking (except for value types) would be imposed. Clearly the provision to create and manipulate results in the canonical form of relations would be useful in a real system, but again would not demonstrate anything new.

A further problem with U-relations is that they are not immediately amenable to the method of distribution. This is because Aspect distribution is based on ownership and there is no reason to assume that a U-relation will have the ownership attribute.

For these reasons, the following operators are *not* implemented: **create_REL, overwrite_REL, delete_REL** and **delete_TUPLE**.

Subtype graph

Purely to simplify the implementation, it is assumed that the subtype hierarchy is a tree. This disallows multiple inheritance. Allowance is made in the implementation for adding the full graph structure.*

The root type

For the purposes of implementing distribution and publication, an attribute designating an owner has been added to the root entity type implementation. Since this is a specific instantiation of RM/T++ for Aspect, it does not appear in the specification. The ownership attribute of the root type should not be given explicitly as would be required by the specification. The integration of domains as owners (described in the following chapter) in the implementation means that the value of the ownership attribute is found in a Unix environment variable.

Naming

The entity-type structure set up in the specification for naming makes named_type a subtype of the root type. Since, for demonstration purposes, all entity-types are nameable, space and time can be saved by making named_type exactly equivalent to the root entity type. So, in the implementation, named_type does not explicitly exist, and all its connections are redirected to root.

The specified structure is shown in Figure 5.9 and the structure as actually implemented in Figure 5.10.

---

* In fact the current implementation supports the construction of types with multiple inheritance, but does not yet cope with instances of them.

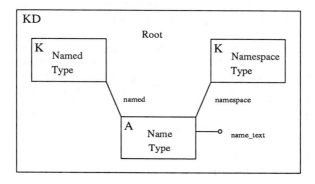

Fig. 5.9 Specified naming structures

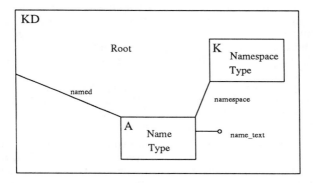

Fig. 5.10 Implemented naming structures

Extended relational operators

There was simply no great need for any of the extended relational operators, except DENOTE_SUR, to be implemented although an optimised transitive closure operation was often identified as being desirable.

5.5 Distribution

There are a number of advantages to be gained through using a distributed rather than a non-distributed IPSE. All of these are comparable to the reasons why other systems are distributed but some gain particular significance within an IPSE context.

A good overview of the concepts, problems and ideas associated with distributed information systems is given in [31]. The purpose of the first subsection here is not to re-address those ideas, but to look in particular at how they relate to the development and use of an IPSE. This is followed by a look at what information concerning distribution issues is captured by an Aspect IPSE and how it is modelled in the information base. The final subsection describes a method of distributing RM/T++ to support this distribution model.

5.5.1 IPSEs and distribution

There is little doubt both that any IPSE will consume a large amount of computing resources and will provide the greatest benefits when used to support a project consuming large amounts of human resources. The advantages of a distributed IPSE become more easily apparent if these two facts are borne in mind. The advantages become even more attractive when it is noted that not all the traditional problems associated with distribution have to apply to IPSEs.

No system can be expected to be completely available at all times. Despite the IPSE attack on reducing faults in the developed systems and hence reducing future maintenance, IPSEs themselves are no less susceptible to these problems. The cost of depriving a whole project of its entire support environment, let alone the cost of restoring the whole system to some consistent state, will be great. Despite the added complexity of distributing a system, it can become more resilient since any problem is likely to affect only a subsystem leaving the rest of the system able to operate with a potentially reduced functionality. For example, the technical architect of a system may be preparing a status report on development when the machine being used is accidentally switched off. This should not affect those using formal specification tools to develop subsystems on separate hosts, except that they receive no confirmation of their report to the architect.

Security is an issue in IPSEs for at least two major reasons. The first is that resources in terms of hardware, software, or even personnel, used to develop a product may be sensitive. Distributing an IPSE forces channels of communication to be more formal and allows sensitive work to be carried out in secure isolation. Monitoring of security can then be focussed on instances of communication. The second security issue is the product itself. Again, sensitive parts of the product can be isolated on more secure parts of the system. It may be the case that the product as a whole can be kept secure simply by ensuring that it is not available as a whole on a single node.

The cost and effort involved in moving personnel to the site where their expertise is required can be substantial. A better, and more economic, solution may be to bring a node of the IPSE to the current site of the personnel. This approach is only feasible with a distributed IPSE and is most effective at any stage of the development where particular expertise, or a special skill is required. A similar situation arises when a member of the team finds it more effective to work at home for example.

Non-distributed IPSEs are currently used to develop distributed target systems (e.g. Perspective). A distributed IPSE could integrate the information about its own distribution with the information about its distributed targets. The resultant benefits are the possible reuse of tools and techniques applicable to distribution information.

A further economic consideration provides the final advantage of distributing an IPSE. It concerns the cost of computer power. If communication overheads can be kept reasonable, as is possible in good IPSE designs, it makes economic sense to compute on many smaller machines rather than a single large one.

5.5.2 Aspect and distribution

The purpose of an investigation into the strategies for IPSE distribution within Aspect was to develop a logical model of distribution providing a set of facilities useful within a distributed IPSE. The concepts of distribution present within a system depend on the viewpoint taken to look at the system. Within an IPSE that viewpoint may vary from a user who is completely unaware that the facilities being used are not entirely local, to a sophisticated optimisation tool attempting to find the most powerful processing power currently available to it.

The Aspect distribution model must support several functions. It must enable distribution information to be available. It must manage that information and provide an interface to update what cannot be updated automatically, such as the introduction of a new processor to the system. And it must support transparency, particularly in the case of the publication mechanism where the invoker of the publish operation is unlikely to be aware of the exact location of the domains published to. It is the intimate relationship of the distribution model with the publication model which enables Aspect distribution to cause fewer problems than in conventional distributed systems.

In order to support the logical model of distribution, a physical model was also developed, mirroring more closely the hardware configuration upon which the IPSE exists. Within this layer, planned partitions are handled, recovery from unplanned partitions is managed, other distribution information is managed, and the higher level PTI calls are translated into non-distributed lower level calls. Further problems associated with identification arise in conjunction with distributed systems and their implementation, but we do not address these here.

There are two kinds of entities within an Aspect system: published and non-published (or private) entities. A domain can access and update its own private objects. A published entity cannot be updated, and can be accessed by the owning domain plus all the domains that have acquired it. In a non-distributed system multiple copies (or replicates) of such shared entities do not have to be made, since an extra link is sufficient. A similar mechanism would have been possible within Aspect (through the Newcastle Connection) but access across potentially slow, unreliable networks is inconvenient, and impossible if the network or the node upon which the single copy exists fails.

The need to make published entities more available by replication does not cause multiple-update problems since published entities are not updatable.

However, a decision has to be made as to *when* the replication takes place. There are three options:

    (a)   Replicate upon publication;

    (b)   Replicate upon acquisition; or

    (c)   Replicate upon first access after acquisition.

The advantage of (a) is that if a domain is aware of an entity published to it, then that entity is accessible. The disadvantage is the potential for replicates made for domains which never acquire them. This problem is solved by (b) and (c) but they suffer from a domain being aware of an entity which is not acquirable (in (b)) or not accessible (in (c)) should the system be partitioned. Only in (c) is it guaranteed that a replicate will be used.

The implemented choice was (a), since it was felt that, in practice, few replicates would be unused, and the inaccessibility of a visible entity was unacceptable, particularly in the case where a user may take home a workstation and find that all acquired entities are inaccessible.

The immediate availability of a published entity is not guaranteed in a distributed system as it is in the centralised case. Different domains are likely to receive notification at various times later, but so long as each domain does eventually receive notice then the asynchronous delays are acceptable in an IPSE.

A further interesting difference in the publication idea on a distributed system is that the information published may be completely useless on the remote node. Examples of such information could be Ada binary code, or troff input sent to nodes unable to execute Ada or interpret troff. Of course, Ada code *may* be useful information if the node can process it in some other way rather than executing it. It becomes a question of semantics (with which the Aspect IPSE has been designed to cope). A similar problem can occur in non-distributed systems where resources are not globally available.

Distribution and self-reference

As has been described previously, an Aspect philosophy is to maintain all information about the IPSE itself within the information base. The advantages and problems of such a policy with regard to distribution information are described here. If the information concerning the distribution of the IPSE and its elements were held in some other form, it would be necessary to develop not only a separate model to maintain that data, but also develop a different way to present that data to the user. By means of Aspect's self-referential model, the need to develop a different type of model is eliminated and integration is aided through a consistent interface.

One problem of such an approach to maintaining distribution information is that of performance. Supporting a good, clear, logical model through the information base primitives gives little consideration to performance, especially in the prototype implementation. The additional software layers responsible for poorer performance are described later.

In any self-referential system there is a need to identify a condition to end the recursion. In Aspect's case the recursion was always ended at the second level where a query on a distributed relation would result in a query on a relation containing information concerning how the original relation was distributed. For this reason a small number of relations representing distribution entity types have to be treated specially by the distribution software layers.

Transferring distribution information is achieved in almost exactly the same way as any other information is transferred throughout Aspect: via the publication mechanism. Information is published from one domain to another and once the second domain has acquired it, it becomes accessible within that domain. Distribution information has to be kept as up-to-date as possible, and so the important difference is that all published distribution information has to be acquired as soon as possible. The implication is that before any operation using distribution information is carried out, a check should be made that no distribution information is available to be acquired.

5.5.3 The distribution model

Taking a look firstly at the physical aspects of distribution within the model, it is a relatively straightforward set of associations between types and their specialisations (see Figure 5.11).

A **device** represents pure processing power without permanent memory. A **computer** is a device upon which Aspect primitives and tools can be executed. An **interface_unit** is a device serving as either an interface between peripherals and channels, or an interconnection between channels. A **channel** models the communication medium enabling properties such as protocol, signal speed, baud, and cost to be recorded. The **peripherals** are divided into either **I/O_units** such as terminals and printers, or **drives** which control disks and tapes. The latter are special cases of **volumes** which represent the pure storage capacity for holding Aspect objects.

To relate these physical elements at a more logical level, the concept of a **node** is introduced. A node consists of one computer with at least one drive and one terminal available either directly or over a network via interface units. A publication **domain** is said to reside on a node which provides a distinguished workspace for each resident domain.

The idea within the distribution model which relates both RM/T++ and the publication model is based on combining one basic concept from each to form the unit of central importance within Aspect distribution. The publication model is based upon ownership and this is provided for in Aspect's use of RM/T++ by the root entity type having an ownership attribute. The representation of entity types is achieved by relations. A **chunk** is a horizontal partition of a relation based on ownership. Thus a chunk is a relation itself, and the term used for a tuple within a chunk is an **object**. The replication policy within Aspect distribution is with regard to objects.

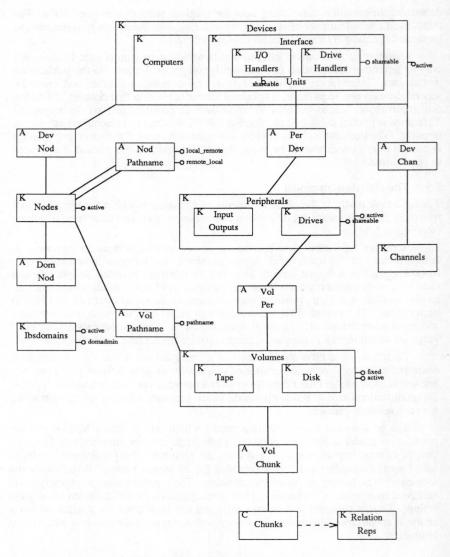

Fig. 5.11 Entity types for distribution

An example will help to illustrate how all these concepts relate. Suppose a manager is responsible for assigning change requests to programmers. The manager, called *manager1*, will see an entity type called *Change Request* with properties such as *difficulty* and *deadline*. The manager will also have a view of the representation of that entity type and its instances, as a relation with an e-attribute and attributes difficulty and deadline. So far, this is exactly what RM/T++ provides. The non-distributed form of RM/T++ simply implements that relation by means of a relational DBMS.

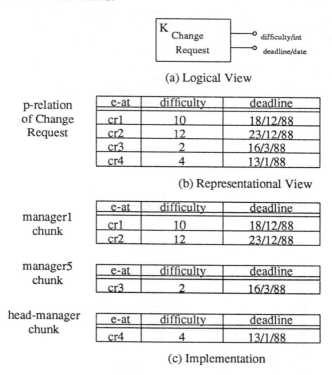

(a) Logical View

(b) Representational View

(c) Implementation

Fig. 5.12 The chunks of an entity type in a domain

In the distributed case, the relational implementation, hidden from the manager, is as follows (illustrated in Figure 5.12). All the change requests which manager1 owns are held in one chunk. But all the ones he has acquired from, say, manager5 and his head-manager are held in separate chunks. In general there will be **n+1** chunks for each p-relation where **n** is the number of domains which have published change requests to the domain in question. Note that all the chunks are union-compatible, thus making the task of presenting the whole p-relation straightforward.

The disadvantages of having such a large number of chunks, each implemented as a relation by the RDBMS, are offset, at least in the prototype implementation, by the simplicity of the distribution and publication routines which access and manipulate the chunks. Note that any operation by manager1 can write to manager1-chunk, but only read any of the other chunks. Conversely, the publication operations, supported by distribution routines, will only update the chunks which hold published objects.

5.5.4 Implementing the distributed IPSE

Figure 5.13 shows how the structure of the implementation is altered in the distributed case. The PTI is extended (by Con_dist) to include operations on the conceptual model of distribution such as add_volume or attach_node (to a location). The IBETV and query layers are unaffected, but are now supported by a distribution layer. This layer provides almost the same interface as previously provided by the IB layer, but accounts for distributed information. Access to remote machines is provided by the Newcastle Connection [25] layer which supports a logical view of a single Unix system over a set of distributed Unix systems.

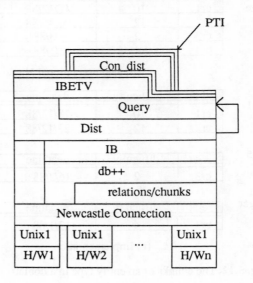

Fig. 5.13 Functional layering of the distributed implementation

It is useful to look at an example to see what type of functions are carried out within each layer. Suppose a new node is to be added to an Aspect IPSE. The invocation of **add_node** at the PTI would cause some queries to check preconditions on the operation (e.g. to check that the node is not already in the system). It would also invoke some RM/T++ operations such as **create_entity** to record the new node's addition. The IBETV layer invokes queries to ensure the integrity of the information base. The IBETV layer also uses functions supported by the Dist layer (e.g. to add a tuple to the NODE p-relation).

The Dist layer will itself make queries (e.g. to find the appropriate chunks representing the NODE P-relation) but these will be on its own distribution catalog thus terminating the recursion. The IB layer supports the Dist layer by calling db++

to add tuples to the chunks involved for example.

The Dist layer will need to add tuples to relations on remote machines in supporting publication routines (e.g. to let other nodes know of the new addition). For this reason db++ uses the Newcastle Connection interface rather than Unix directly.

The working system was demonstrated on two Sun workstations running the Newcastle Connection and connected by Ethernet.

Chapter 6

The Information Base Superstructure

A.W. Brown, A. Pearcy, A. Petrie,
R.J. Stroud and R.A. Weedon

6.1 Introduction

In this chapter we enlarge upon the Aspect process model described in Chapter 3 and show how it may be implemented using the RM/T Information Base Engine (IBE) described in Chapter 5. The facilities built on top of the IBE to support the Aspect process model are collectively known as the Information Base Superstructure (IBS). Individually, they are realised as a number of entity types supported by operations which implement the various abstractions needed to model the software development process as represented by the Aspect process model. These facilities may be thought of as a generic IPSE kit that can be customised to suit the project management needs of a particular project or organisation. One example of such a customisation is the demonstration IPSE presented in Chapter 4. This is used to illustrate the discussion of the implementation of the IBS in this chapter wherever possible.

Although not all the components of the IBS described in this chapter were used in the demonstration IPSE, most of the ideas discussed in this chapter have been implemented in one form or another. Where this is not the case, the tentative nature of the proposals has been stated explicitly. Because the design of the demonstration IPSE was a learning experience, possible improvements to the design are identified where appropriate. In particular, there are several discussions of ways in which the various elements could be integrated more fully to provide a complete implementation of the Aspect IBS.

Section 6.2 describes the basic components of the IBS and explains how they were intended to fit together. The next four sections describe the implementation of the Aspect process model for the demonstration IPSE presented in Chapter 4. The project plan was realised in the IBS by a model of tasks and bindings described in Section 6.3. The project organisation was realised by a model of people and roles described in Section 6.4. The product was realised by the versions and configurations described in Section 6.5 and the domain based concurrency control mechanisms discussed in Section 6.6. Two other components of the IBS which were not integrated with the demonstration IPSE are described in the next two sections, namely rules (Section 6.7) and views (Section 6.8). Finally, Section 6.9 summarises the facilities provided by the Aspect IBS.

6.2 An Overview of the IBS

6.2.1 Introduction

The Aspect Information Base Superstructure (IBS) provides a framework within which all interactions with an Aspect IPSE take place. It is therefore an integrating mechanism, effectively implementing the Aspect process model by managing the relationships between people, information and activities.

The development of the IBS within the Aspect project has a complex history. During the first three years of the project, the components of the IBS were identified, formally specified in Z as part of the Aspect PTI, implemented in C and incorporated into various prototype IPSEs. Although the formal specification of these components was itself a major achievement, the essentially bottom-up nature of this process meant that difficulties were experienced in integrating the various components of the IBS with the result that some problems were left unsolved. In particular, the facilities for version control and configuration management were not integrated with the rest of the IBS and there were some outstanding problems with the concurrency control mechanisms.

During the fourth year of the project, an alternative approach was taken. The IBS was reconsidered from a top-down viewpoint in order to come up with a more integrated architecture. This resulted in the process model presented in Chapter 3 from which a rather more abstract and therefore simplified model of the IBS was derived. However, it was intended that this architecture could be refined into and built from the original components of the IBS developed bottom up.

Unfortunately, lack of time and resources meant that it was not possible to complete this mapping process and achieve complete integration between the various components of the IBS. Indeed, the integration of the various facilities provided by such an IBS proved to be a very difficult problem. Nevertheless, the exercise was a valuable experience and much was learned from the successful development of a demonstration IPSE based on the Aspect process model and those parts of the IBS which were integrated.

Because of this history, the structure and contents of this chapter are perhaps rather confusing because they attempt to present the achievements of both the first three years and the fourth year of the Aspect project which are not entirely compatible. The bulk of the chapter describes the implementation of the process model and demonstration IPSE developed in the fourth year but the chapter also includes two sections that describe important work from the first three years of the project which was not integrated in the final demonstration (although these ideas were implemented and used in an earlier prototype IPSE). The purpose of this overview is therefore to put the work on the IBS described in this chapter into context by first reviewing the original IBS and then describing the simplified IBS adopted for the demonstration IPSE built during the fourth year of the project. Given an appreciation of the overall structure of the IBS and the way in which the various components are intended to fit together, it should be easier to understand the details of any particular component.

6.2.2 The original IBS

The original IBS for Aspect was built from the following components: configuration management and version control, activities, rules, views, domains, publication. The work on configuration management was rather abstract and self-contained; it was not integrated with the rest of the IBS and was completely replaced in the fourth year so it is not discussed further here.

Activities were the central part of the original IBS. They served both as descriptions of what needed to be done (i.e. plans) and of what had been done (i.e. histories). Every action that took place in the IPSE occurred as part of some activity. Activities could be built up from other activities and were constrained by rules. Rules were used as pre- and post-conditions for activities and were also used to enforce constraints during the execution of an activity. Certain rules were inviolate but others could be relaxed during sub-activities. Rules were simply database queries and could therefore express any condition that was modelled in the IB. The intention was that a generic Aspect IPSE would come with a minimum set of activities and rules to ensure the integrity of the IPSE itself and that customisation would occur by defining additional activities and rules in support of a particular project methodology.

Activities were executed in a context provided by a combination of a domain and a view. Domains were a concurrency control mechanism whilst views were an abstraction mechanism. The objects and operations in the IB available to an activity would be defined by its view but their availability would be subject to them having been published to the domain associated with the activity. Thus, although the view was a view of the whole IB, in fact the activity was always constrained to be only able to see the things in its domain. Views were built on top of other views recursively but provided a more general mechanism than just a simple restriction to a subset of the objects available. They could be used to redefine the structure of the database by defining a mapping from the old structure to the new and specifying new operations in terms of old operations.

Domains were the basis for concurrency control. There was a notion of publishing objects to domains involving a two-way handshake to ensure that the contents of a domain did not change without the activity associated with it doing something explicit. Publication effectively granted read permission to the object published and there was a similar notion of allocation that granted development permission. In fact, both of these concepts were imported from the Systems Designers' product, Perspective. However, Perspective uses allocate to publish tasks to roles meaning "here's some work, get on with it". In Aspect we were concerned with a greater understanding of the relationship between domains, roles, activities and publication. As a result of our work we had a better understanding of the problems involved in this complex relationship.

6.2.3 The revised IBS

In an attempt to address the problems with the original IBS and as an aid to describing Aspect, during the fourth and final year of the project a simple top-down view of an Aspect IPSE was developed that became known as the Aspect process model. This model had three components representing people, tasks and information that were referred to as the project organisation, the project plan, and the product.

The intention of the model was to provide a framework in which actions took place. Every action was the result of somebody assuming a role to perform a task that accessed or modified some information in the IB. Despite its simplicity, the model proved to be adequate for this purpose and provided a useful focus for the development of the demonstration IPSE.

The project organisation part of the model recognised a three part relationship between people, roles and tasks. There was a lot of discussion about the granularity of the role concept and in particular whether the relationship between roles and people was 1-1 or 1-many but in the end it was decided that tasks required the skills associated with a role, people were capable of performing roles and tasks were assigned to people. These relationships are quite different in kind and would normally be the responsibility of different roles: assigning tasks to people is a managerial problem, assigning people to roles is a personnel decision, and assigning tasks to roles is a technical decision. The important thing that the IPSE must ensure is that the three part relationship is always consistent; in other words, that nobody is assigned a task that they are not deemed to be capable of performing.

The product part of the model was based on the notion of components. Components were typed and could exist in many versions. The versions of a component formed a graph structure sub-divided into variants which were sequences of versions. Versions could be revised to create the next version in the sequence or used to start a new variant. There was also the idea of a configuration. The original work on configuration management was thought to have adopted an overly complex scheme for representing versions of configurations and the model that was finally agreed upon was felt to be an elegant simplification. It had the notion of a logical design expressed in terms of components (not versions) that was itself a component and therefore potentially existed in many versions. Actual versions of a component were built according to a version of a design and were therefore constructed from versions of the components of that design. In this way it was possible to re-use a logical structure by binding its components to different versions and thus create different versions of the component for which the structure was a design. The model was recursive in the sense that designs could themselves have designs; primitive components (i.e. those not built from sub-components) were deemed to have specifications rather than designs, the word design being rather misleading in this context. In the event, a simpler model of configurations as graphs of physical versions was implemented for the demonstration and designs were not factored out in this way. The problems with the concurrency control mechanisms provided by the original IBS were addressed by attempting to generalise the notion of publication to allow objects to be published with a range of different permissions. In particular, versions could be published with read permission whilst variants could be published with development permission.

The project plan part of the model described a simplification of the original activity concept called a task. The idea was that a task description would specify exactly which items of information the task required for its execution, thereby achieving the previously missing link between configuration management and activities. In effect, these information items would parameterise the task description. There was a notion of re-using task descriptions by binding these parameters to varying degrees – type, component, variant and version being an obvious hierarchy. During the execution of the task, the only part of the IB visible would be the information items represented by these bindings. These would therefore have to include not only the inputs and outputs of the task but also the tools needed by the task to perform its function. Tasks could be built out of sub-tasks and joined together in a plan using a notation based on JSD (choice, sequence, iteration, etc.). Of course this plan was not fixed but could be developed as the project proceeded. Indeed, the initial plan in an Aspect IPSE might be a task description "write a better plan" parameterised with task writing tools. The IPSE could be customised by supplying generic task templates and fragments of plan representing particular steps in a method. By restricting the ability to create arbitrary task descriptions and plans, it would be possible to constrain the project to proceed along a certain path. Tasks required a workspace and this is where concurrency control came in. Each parameter to the task represented an object that needed to be made available in the workspace with appropriate permissions, according to whether the parameter represented an input, an output or a tool. Development permission went with variants rather than versions.

6.2.4 The implementation of the IBS for the demonstration IPSE

The implementation of the demonstration IPSE provided an opportunity to see how well the various components of the revised IBS fitted together. However, in the time available, it was not possible to include everything in the demonstration IPSE and not everything that was included was completely integrated. Thus, the demonstration shows the grouping of tasks to form a project plan, the assignment of tasks to roles and the building of components out of versions and configurations. However, although a task parameterisation mechanism was implemented, the tasks used in the demonstration were not parameterised and it was not possible to illustrate the intended integration of tasks, versions and configurations. This in turn meant that it was not possible to demonstrate the implementation of domains and publication although the demonstration does illustrate the concept of different tasks having different views of the IB and shows a change request being published from one role to another. If it had been possible to continue work on the demonstration IPSE beyond the end of the project, then a more impressive and more fully integrated demonstration could have been built. Achieving a fully integrated IBS might require some slight changes to the implementation of the various components of the IBS described here, but we believe that our basic mechanisms and concepts are sound enough.

6.2.5 Summary

The original IBS identified activities as a fundamental concept around which domains, rules and views were integrated. Configuration management and version control was unfortunately left out of this integration. The revised IBS adopted a simplification of an activity called a task which was used to unify a model of software components (versions and configurations) with a model of people and roles.

6.3 Tasks and Bindings

This section describes the realisation of the project plan part of the Aspect process model in the IBS. The project plan was implemented using task objects that could be grouped together to form plans. Separate binding objects were used to implement parameterised tasks.

6.3.1 Tasks vs Activities

The activity mechanism proposed for the IBS during the first three years of the Aspect project was very elaborate, providing several mechanisms for describing activities and constraining their execution. However, the time and resources available for implementing the demonstration were limited and it was therefore felt to be too ambitious to attempt to implement the full functionality of activities and integrate the different elements of the IBS. Instead, the demonstration concentrated on integrating a subset of the IBS, bringing together users, roles, domains, version control and configuration management in a simplification of an activity called a task. In effect, this was a customisation of the IPSE kit provided by the IBS with tasks providing a more user-oriented view of the Aspect process model than activities. Tasks can therefore be thought of as an abstraction of the more detailed but lower-level notion of an activity.

Although no attempt was made to integrate tasks with views and rules, the model chosen for tasks embodied some of the features which could have been implemented using these components of the IBS. Tasks were parameterised and could be bound to particular objects. Similarly, tasks could be decomposed into sub-tasks according to a plan. Had the task model been refined to a lower level of abstraction (something closer to the original design for activities), then views could have been used to implement bindings and rules could have been used to control the way in which tasks were decomposed into sub-tasks. However, integrating tasks with views and rules would have presented some serious implementation difficulties because of limitations of the RM/T data model underpinning the Aspect IB and in particular the inability of this model to handle abstraction and capture the operational semantics of the objects it models. For this purpose, an object-oriented data model would have been more suitable.

6.3.2 Implementation philosophy

The approach taken in the implementation of the demonstration was to model each element of the task model as a separate RM/T kernel entity and then to integrate the elements together with a series of associative entities. Using associations rather than designations or characterisations to link entities together was a way of delaying decisions about integration, intended to make the IPSE kit more flexible and easier to reconfigure.

An example will illustrate this philosophy. It proved difficult to decide whether domains should be associated with users, roles or tasks. The trade-offs between these choices are explained in more detail in Section 6.6 on Concurrency Control. However, by using indirection to delay the decision, it was possible to associate domains with all three if appropriate. The actual implementation decision taken could be hidden by an operation which returned the objects available to a task, perhaps by querying the domain associated with that task, perhaps by querying the role to which the task has been assigned, or perhaps by querying both and returning a union. The use of an association rather than a designation also makes it possible for more than one domain to be directly associated with a task should that be considered appropriate.

This use of indirection by association also makes the IBS more flexible. Role or user specific domains can be shared between tasks assigned to the same role or user without losing the ability for tasks to have their own private domains as a workspace. In the same way, by modelling bindings as separate entities, it is possible either for tasks and sub-tasks to share the same bindings or else for sub-tasks to inherit by indirection the bindings associated with their parent tasks.

6.3.3 Modelling Tasks and Plans

A task describes a piece of work that has to be done and it was therefore natural to model tasks in this way. Thus, the *task* entity type used to model tasks in the IB has a single string attribute *task_description* which describes the purpose of the task.

Task	
task_eatt	task_description

For the purposes of the demonstration, this string only needed to be a simple title such as "Produce Time/Cost Analysis" or "Build System" rather than a more elaborate description. For a more realistic system, a task might be modelled as a short description like this together with the name of a file giving full instructions. Parameters to tasks were modelled separately in keeping with the philosophy of indirection described above.

In order to allow tasks to be decomposed into sub-tasks according to a plan, it was necessary to provide a way of modelling the task hierarchy in the IB. The intention was that the various tasks in the IB should form part of a tree representing the overall project plan. The root of this tree would be a task describing the execution of the project plan in terms of performing various sub-tasks in a particular order. Each of these sub-tasks would have their own sub-tasks arranged according to a sub-plan and so on.

The task hierarchy was modelled in the IB using the *plan* entity type, a simple parent/child association between tasks.

Plan		
plan_eatt	plan_parent	plan_child

However, this model was not sufficient because the intention was to allow tasks to be composed of sub-tasks in various ways: the plan for a particular task could consist of a choice between sub-tasks, an iteration over a particular sub-task, or the execution of a series of sub-tasks in sequence or in parallel. It was therefore necessary to capture the information about the type of plan associated with each task somewhere in the IB.

Modelling the project plan to this level of detail requires capturing two things in the IB:

1.   An optional association of a set of sub-tasks with each task to form the plan for that task.

2.   A property of that association (if it exists), namely whether the plan is a sequence, choice or iteration.

The problem with achieving this is that the RM/T relational data model does not allow these two things to be expressed directly because it provides no direct support for sets of objects or optional properties. The *plan* entity type described above models the parent/child association between tasks and sub-tasks; the type of plan (i.e. whether the grouping of sub-tasks is interpreted as a choice, iteration, sequence or whatever) must be modelled as an attribute of either this association or else the parent task of each plan.

Although it might seem natural to hold the type of plan as an attribute of the *plan* associative entity, this could lead to an inconsistent state of the IB. The division of a given task into sub-tasks is represented by several instances of the *plan* entity type, one for each sub-task. However, the attribute representing the type of plan would have to be the same for each of these instances. It would need to be duplicated for each sub-task in the plan because each sub-task associated with a given task is part of the same plan. This would mean that the relation representing the *plan* entity type in the database was not in normal form and it would be possible for an inconsistent state to arise. For example, if task A was comprised of sub-tasks B and C, it would be possible for B to be associated with A in an iterative plan but for C to be associated with A in a sequential plan which is clearly not a valid state. However, if the type of plan is modelled as a property of the parent task rather than a property of each task/sub-task association, then this inconsistent state cannot arise. The plan for task A could either be an iteration or a sequence of tasks B and C but not both simultaneously.

For this reason, in order to model the decomposition of tasks into sub-tasks according to a plan, it is necessary to model the type of plan as an attribute of the *task* entity type. However, this poses another problem. Tasks which are leaf nodes in the overall task tree representing the project plan have no sub-tasks and hence no plan associated with them. The attribute representing a task's type of plan is only meaningful if that task has a plan associated with it. Since RM/T does not allow optional or null valued attributes, it is necessary to introduce a special value for this attribute to represent leaf nodes or primitive tasks which have no plan. These primitive tasks represent real pieces of work which must be carried out and are therefore the building blocks from which the project plan is constructed.

The revised data model for tasks therefore looks like this:

Task		
task_eatt	task_description	task_type

For example, if task A were to consist of a choice between sub-tasks B and C, this would be modelled by setting the value of the *task_type* attribute to CHOICE for task A and PRIMITIVE for sub-tasks B and C.

Despite this enhancement to the basic representation of a task in the IB, even this model cannot capture the fact that a primitive task should not be allowed to have a plan (i.e. the surrogate of a primitive task should not appear as the *plan_parent* attribute of some instance of a *plan*). This could be modelled by introducing a sub-type of *task* thus:

Generic Task	
task_eatt	task_description

Non-Primitive Task (sub-type of Generic Task)		
task_eatt	task_description	task_type

and requiring the *plan* entity type to be an association between a *non-primitive task* (as parent) and a *generic task* (as child). Alternatively, this kind of semantic check could be expressed using the Aspect rules mechanism described in Section 6.7.

A further complication would be the modelling of the logical expressions used to choose between alternatives in a plan or to describe the terminating condition of an iterative plan. This was omitted for the purposes of the demonstration. However, the rules mechanism described later in this chapter could be used to model such expressions. Rules would be associated with plans in some way but again difficulties would arise because not all plans have rules associated with them (for example, sequential and parallel plans).

For a plan expressing a choice between several sub-tasks, it would not be appropriate to associate the rules governing the choice with the parent task of the plan (of type CHOICE) because the rules for each sub-task would be different. However, for a plan expressing an iteration over a sub-task it would be appropriate to associate the rule expressing the terminating condition with the parent task (although it might just as well be associated with the sub-task because it only makes sense to iterate over one task at a time since any iteration over a group of sub-tasks may just as well be expressed as an iteration over a single task made up of those sub-tasks). Therefore, unlike the attribute describing the type of plan, the rules associated with a plan should be a property of the *plan* entity type rather than the *task* entity type.

It is not necessary to use a further association between plans and rules because each sub-task involved in a choice or iteration is controlled by exactly one rule. However, not all instances of the *plan* entity type (associations between parent and sub-tasks) will have rules associated with them – it will depend on whether the parent/child task association forms part of an iterative or choice plan or a sequence or parallel plan. Since RM/T does not allow null values to be expressed, this must either be modelled as a sub-type of the basic *plan* entity type (like the *non-primitive task* sub-type of the *task* entity type suggested above), or else an additional entity type must be introduced to associate plans (i.e. parent/child task associations) with rules. Again, it would be difficult to capture the fact that only tasks whose plan type was CHOICE or ITERATION could be the parent task in plans associated with rules, although this could be achieved with an even more extensive use of sub-typing for tasks, perhaps ultimately using a different sub-type of the basic *task* entity type for each sort of plan, making it no longer necessary to represent the plan type as an attribute of the task.

Clearly, there is a trade-off between the complexity of the data model (and hence the amount of semantic checking that can be done by the database itself), and the amount of semantic checking that must be embedded in the programs outside the database that implement operations such as "create task T with plan P". It is always possible to overcome the limitations of the data model in a program but ideally the data modelling language recognised by the database should be powerful enough to capture the semantics of the system being modelled in a natural way. Object-oriented data models are better than relational data models in this respect because they can capture more semantics. However, the rules mechanism provided by the Aspect IBS goes some way towards addressing this problem.

6.3.4 Demonstrating the task model

For the purposes of the demonstration, a number of tasks were pre-defined and arranged in a tree to represent the project plan. This was possible because the demonstration had a fixed scenario which was known in advance. For a real IPSE of course, the project plan would not be known in any great detail before the project began but would rather evolve over time as the need for new tasks became apparent. However, for the demonstration, the project plan was mapped out in advance and fixed.

The project plan can be accessed from certain tasks in the demonstration via the *Project_Plan* box in the Browse panel. If this box is selected, the *Open* operation causes the *plan* and *task* entity types to be queried in the IB and the resulting structure to be displayed as a hierarchy. If a node in this hierarchy is selected, then the *Show Task Description* operation displays the *task_description* attribute of the *task* entity corresponding to that node as if opening the selected node. JSD notation [98] is used to represent the *task_type* attribute as iteration (*), selection (°) or sequence (no symbol).

Figure 6.1 shows part of the project plan displayed in this way. From this, it can be seen that for the purposes of the demonstration, the project plan is to repeatedly satisfy the customer. Satisfying the customer involves successfully dealing with either a customer enquiry or a customer request. A customer enquiry involves producing a quotation for a particular modification to the customer's system and a customer request involves carrying out that modification and producing a new version of the system. Each of these stages is refined to several further levels of detail.

Although the project plan used for the demonstration is static in the sense that it is mapped out in advance, what does change over time as the scenario unfolds is the list of tasks assigned to each role. This is represented in the IB as an associative entity between *tasks* and *roles* which can be queried by selecting the *Task List* menu in the demonstration IPSE (Figure 6.2). The implementation of this part of the

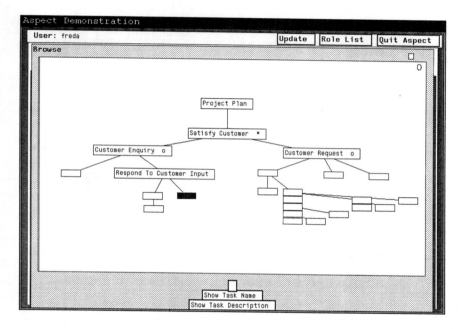

Fig. 6.1 The project plan

demonstration is discussed in Section 6.4 of this chapter which describes the way in which the project organisation was modelled in the IB.

At various points in the demonstration, tasks are assigned to roles either explicitly as a result of using the *Task Definition* tool or implicitly as a side-effect of executing some task whose post-condition requires the assignment of certain tasks to certain roles.

For example, the *Log Customer Contact* task from Step 2 of the demonstration which is illustrated in Figure 6.3 has the side effect of assigning a *Respond To Customer Input* task to the Project Manager when the customer's change request is logged in the database. In contrast, the *Respond To Customer Input* task provides the Project Manager with a *Task Definition* tool which is used explicitly in Step 4 of the demonstration to assign a particular task to a particular role (in this case, to assign the *Create Amendment Spec* task to the Senior Programmer).

Although a task may have been assigned to a role, it does not follow that the task is ready to execute. As a pre-condition, it may be necessary for another task to complete its execution (perhaps the previous task in a sequence) or for objects required by the task to become available and be published to a domain associated with the task's execution. Therefore, even when a task has been assigned to a role, it is not possible for the role to perform that task until all the pre-conditions for the

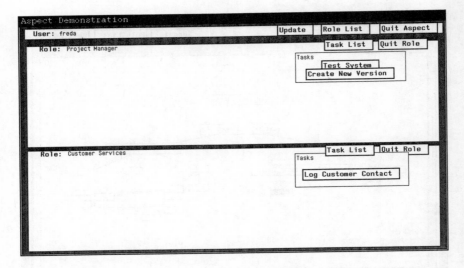

Fig. 6.2 Task lists for Customer Services and Project Manager roles

task's execution have been satisfied. Only then does the task appear in the task menu associated with each role, allowing a user logged into that role to execute the task. (Because rules were not used in the demonstration IPSE, the pre-conditions for each task were empty and therefore trivially satisfied, making this aspect of the demonstration easy to implement! However, this is how it would have worked in theory if not in practice.)

In summary, the demonstration IPSE illustrates the basic relationships between tasks and the assignment of tasks to roles. It was not possible to demonstrate the use of bindings to parameterise tasks because of lack of time for integration (and the additional complexity this would have introduced). However, this part of the code was certainly designed and implemented as we will now describe.

6.3.5 Modelling Bindings

The other important feature of the project plan from the Aspect process model implemented for the demonstration was the idea of parameterising task descriptions so that they could be re-used. In particular, the idea of a task having parameters which could be constrained to only assume certain values was modelled with the notion of a binding. This part of the IBS was designed and implemented but was not integrated with the rest of the demonstration because of lack of time. Consequently, the tasks used for the demonstration are not parameterised or bound to objects in the IB in the way described here. However, all the facilities were available for this next step in the development of the demonstration IPSE.

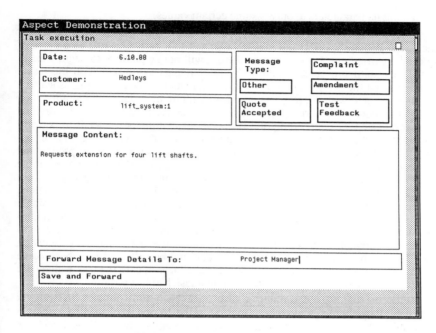

Fig. 6.3 Indirect assignment of a task

An overview of the binding mechanism

Before we describe the implementation of the binding mechanism in detail, it is useful to give an overview of how bindings may be used to implement generic tasks and how such tasks would be instantiated and executed. Thus, we describe the relationships between tasks, bindings, domains, views and rules. In practice, the only part of the mechanism outlined here that was implemented was the definition and refinement of binding objects themselves. Associating bindings with tasks would have been straightforward because of the philosophy of indirection by association outlined in Section 6.3.2. Implementing the rest of the mechanism would have required more work on the integration of tasks and domains in particular but the scheme we outline here would have formed the basis of such an integration.

Bindings are essentially name/value pairs which express constraints on the values that the formal parameters to a task may take. These constraints may be strengthened by refining the binding and in this way generic task descriptions may be specialised for particular tasks. Thus, generic tasks are modelled in the Aspect IB as an association between a parameterised task description and a set of generic bindings, with the bindings expressing constraints on the actual values that the formal parameters of the task may assume when the task is executed. By supplying different values for these parameters, the task may be instantiated and executed over and over again. Similarly, by refining the bindings associated with the task description, the task may be customised to fit a particular application by further constraining its parameters to only assume certain values.

Once the bindings to a generic task have been refined, the task is no longer generic but is quite specific and may be assigned to a particular role as a piece of work to be carried out. However, even then, it will not be possible to begin executing the task until the objects defined by the bindings associated with the task's definition to be the actual values of the task's parameters have been published to a domain associated with the task. This is dealt with in more detail in Section 6.6 on concurrency control but briefly, parameters (and hence bindings) may be divided into several categories depending on the operations that the task intends to perform on the actual object denoted by the parameter. These different categories (effectively levels of permission) may be chosen as part of the customisation process but are modelled as properties of the task/binding association. For example, a simple choice of categories would be input and output parameters requiring respectively read and write permission on the actual objects in the IB bound to the parameters, and the concurrency control system might allow multiple readers but only single writers for each object. The task would therefore be unable to begin execution until actual objects corresponding to each of its formal parameters had been published to its execution domain with appropriate permissions. To avoid deadlock, publication would have to be an atomic operation – it would not be sufficient to publish some objects and then wait for the others to become available in case the task which held those objects was waiting for the objects the first task had just acquired.

Once the bindings describing a task have been fully refined, the objects denoted by those bindings have been located in the IB and published to a domain associated with the task, and the task has begun execution, the bindings associated with the task are fixed and cannot be refined any further. However, since they describe an association between names and values, they may be used to construct a view and hence an abstract context in which the task executes. Rules which govern the execution of the task (in particular the logical expressions governing choice or iteration in a plan for the task) may be written in terms of the names of formal parameters to the task (i.e. the names in the bindings associated with the task) and can therefore be expressed as queries against this view of the IB. In this way the name part of the binding may be used to integrate tasks with views and rules and hence provide the full functionality of the IBS.

The representation of bindings in the IB

The *binding* entity type is used to model task parameters in the IB. Bindings are defined, refined and used to provide a generic task facility in the IBS. Effectively, a copy is made of the bindings associated with a generic task and these copies are then refined until they denote particular objects (or versions of objects) in the IB. Once this refinement has been made, the task may be assigned to a particular role or user as a piece of work to be carried out.

Bindings may be modelled as simple associations between names and values.

Binding		
binding_eatt	binding_name	binding_value

It is intended that there should be a separate associative entity type linking tasks and bindings, making it possible for several tasks to share the same bindings. This is another example of indirection being used to make the model flexible and easy to configure. For example, using this technique it would be straightforward to arrange that each sub-task inherits some or all of the bindings associated with its parent task, and to allow the parent task to select which of its bindings are made visible to each of its sub-tasks. The use of different associations between bindings and tasks would also make it possible to model the *uses*, *produces* and *requires* relationships described in Section 3.7.2.

The *binding_name* attribute of the *binding* entity type has no particular significance in the database as a whole, but simply serves to identify the formal parameter represented by the binding. In particular, the name does not denote some object in the database – the actual object in the database which the binding refers to (the value part of the name/value association) is represented by the *binding_value* attribute which is a surrogate. The name in the binding was simply intended to be a convenient handle or label by which a description of a task to be carried out in the context of that binding could refer to the parameter which the binding represented. Such parameter names could be used in written instructions accompanying the task. For example, if a task was to be associated with a binding of a name A to a particular object of type program in the IB, then the instructions for the task might refer to "program A". Similarly, someone performing that task at a terminal might see on the screen a box labelled A representing the actual parameter on which could be performed operations appropriate to the type of object represented by the binding (in this case a program).

Used purely as a label, the name part of a binding is only of human significance and has no particular meaning to the IBS. Ideally, there should be a check that the bindings associated with a particular task at any one time have different names to prevent ambiguity, but this requirement would be difficult to model in RM/T and would therefore need to be enforced by programs implementing operations on the task/binding association such as "add binding B to task T", perhaps by using the Aspect rules mechanism. Alternatively, an automatic renaming function could be provided since names only have significance as labels. Even if unique naming was not enforced, it would still be possible to distinguish individual bindings by their surrogate; names were added to bindings as a human convenience, not a machine convenience. However, the possible integration of tasks with views and rules described above would give the names in bindings more significance.

Refinement of bindings

Bindings may be refined to further constrain the values of the formal parameters they represent. This is the way in which bindings are used to provide a generic task capability and there would be no point in modelling bindings as separate entities if it were not possible to refine them in this way. Because bindings can be refined, it is necessary to think of the value part of the binding as denoting not a single object in the database but a set of objects. The constraint expressed by the binding is therefore that the object eventually supplied as the actual value of the formal parameter represented by the binding must be a member of this set. By restricting the set to be some subset of itself, the binding may be refined and the constraint narrowed until eventually the set is a singleton and the actual parameter has only one possible value. In this way a binding may be refined through a chain of sub-bindings, each expressing a constraint which is a subset of the constraint represented by their parent binding.

This subset relationship between the constraints at each stage of the chain guarantees that every binding in the refinement is compatible with all previous bindings. Otherwise, it would be possible for a binding to permit an actual value that was not allowed by its parent binding which would be contrary to the whole notion of progressively refining a constraint.

The mechanism for recording the refinement of a binding could literally be to construct a chain of sub-bindings by maintaining a relationship *is-a-refinement-of* between bindings as a further associative entity type. However, this is only necessary if for some reason it is felt important to model the various intermediate stages in the refinement of a binding. Although it would be possible for the IBS to implement this, in practice it is probably sufficient to just keep track of the end-result of the refinement and the original generic binding from which it was derived. This can be achieved by making a copy of each generic binding that is to be refined, maintaining the *is-a-refinement-of* relation between the copy and the original, and updating the copy in place. Although intermediate stages in the refinement will be overwritten when the binding is updated in place, the basic relationship between the original binding and the end-product of its refinement will always be maintained.

It is worth noting that this design is flexible enough to allow bindings to be refined in place to any desired extent and then frozen, copied and used as the basis of further refinements themselves. Thus, a generic set of bindings may be customised at several different levels to reflect the needs of a particular methodology or project.

The association of tasks and bindings provides a parameterised task facility in the IBS. Bindings are used to model task parameters and express constraints about the actual values that these parameters may assume when the task is instantiated. The only part of this mechanism which has not been explained is the way in which a binding represented as a single name/value association can express the constraint that a named parameter may only assume a value from a particular set of values. How is it possible for the *binding_value* attribute of a *binding* entity (a single surrogate) to represent a set of values?

RM/T does not provide any direct method of representing sets but it is a strongly typed data model. Every entity has a type and types are grouped into a type hierarchy with sub-types inheriting the attributes of their parent type. Types may be thought of as representing the set of all entities in the IB of that type. Furthermore, a sub-type may be thought of as a specialisation of its parent type, inheriting all the properties of the parent type but having some additional properties not shared by its parent type. For example, if type A is a sub-type of type B then all instances of type A are also instances of type B, but not vice versa. In other words, the type of an object acts as a constraint on its value and the additional requirement that an object's type should be a sub-type of its original type is a further constraint which is compatible with the original type constraint. Therefore, the value part of a binding may be represented by the surrogate of the type that the actual value denoted by the binding should have, and the binding may be refined by replacing the surrogate of this type with the surrogate of one of its sub-types.

This refinement of type to sub-type down the type hierarchy is not in itself sufficient to allow the binding to constrain the actual parameter to only assume a single unique value (unless of course the lowest sub-type in the refinement hierarchy has only one instance). However, since both types and instances of types are denoted in an RM/T database by the same mechanism, a surrogate, the value part of the binding may equally be used to represent either a type or an instance. It is therefore quite natural to allow a second kind of refinement from type to instance of that type, as well as from type to sub-type.

Binding to versionable objects

It is possible to extend the refinement of bindings still further. The version control facilities of the IBS define certain special entity types to represent objects which can exist in more than one version. This is explained in more detail in Section 6.5 of this chapter but the model is summarised here for convenience.

Two special entity types are defined, *component* and *version*. Components represent the logical objects which make up the whole software system and can exist in several versions. All the versions of a given component must be of the same type and this type is designated by the *component* entity type. The only versionable objects are those whose type is a sub-type of *version*. The *version* entity type characterises the component of which its instances are versions. Thus, a component A may designate the type program and have versions V1 and V2 each of which is an instance of a program. Versions are grouped into version sets of the same component and within version sets, versions are grouped into one or more sequences, representing development through time, known as variants. Variants are used to control parallel development of alternative versions of the component.

Given the existence of the version control mechanisms in the IBS and the two special entity types *component* and *version*, it is natural to allow two further refinements of bindings to versionable objects. A binding to a particular type may be replaced by a binding to a component of that type and a binding to a component may be replaced by a binding to a version of that component. Thus, with the example above (A is a component of type program with versions V1 and V2), it is possible to progressively refine a binding from the type program (meaning any instance of a program) to the component A (meaning any version of A) to a specific version of A such as V1 (which is of type program and is a version of A and therefore satisfies each of the previous stages in the refinement of the binding).

In principle, it would be possible to allow bindings to variants as well as bindings to versions and components, but in practice the lack of an explicit variant type causes implementation difficulties. These would have been resolved had the integration of the various prototype IBS facilities developed for the demonstration been continued.

To summarise, a binding may be refined in any of the following ways:

1. From a type to a sub-type of that type.
2. From a type to an instance of that type.
3. From a type to a component denoting that type.
4. From a component to a version of that component.

Each of these refinements may be interpreted in terms of narrowing a constraint expressed as a set of permissible values to a subset of those values.

Although in general a binding may be refined in any of these ways, for any particular binding only certain refinements will be possible. For example, if the value part of the binding is the surrogate of an entity type, then only the first three kinds of refinement are possible. Conversely, if the value part is the surrogate of a component then only the fourth kind of refinement is possible. Otherwise, if the value part is the surrogate of an instance or a version, no further refinement is possible because the binding already uniquely identifies a single object in the database. Thus, the binding may be thought of as being in one of four states (TYPE, COMPONENT, VERSION, INSTANCE) depending on the type of entity denoted by its value part, with this state governing the ways in which the binding can be refined. (Note that because not everything in the IB is versionable, it is necessary to allow bindings to instances of non-versionable objects. An instance of a versionable object is of course a version.)

The various ways in which a binding can be refined may be represented by a state-transition diagram in which the arcs are labelled according to the type of refinement they represent:

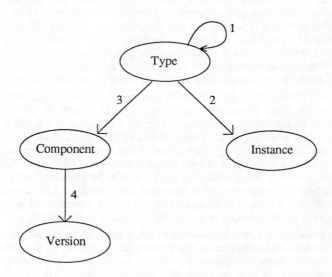

It is convenient to model the state of the binding in the IB as an attribute of the *binding* entity type. Thus, the complete definition of the *binding* entity type is as follows:

Binding			
binding_eatt	binding_name	binding_value	binding_state

In fact it is possible to deduce the state of a binding by examining the type hierarchy for the entity denoted by the *binding_value* attribute, this information being available in the RM/T catalog which is accessed like any other entity in the IB. However, this would be a time consuming and potentially expensive operation, involving several queries on the IB. The binding state is in fact a simplification (or indeed customisation) of the full RM/T type hierarchy, and may therefore be thought of as a binding type. Indeed this is how the operation to update (i.e. refine) a binding is implemented. Note that because the *binding_value* attribute of a *binding* can denote any type, it must be modelled as the most general RM/T type, namely *Root*. Bindings are thus polymorphic objects and all type-checking must be done by the program implementing the "refine binding" operation. The basic algorithm for this is to deduce the binding type of the object denoted by the proposed new surrogate for the value of the binding, check that the implied refinement is compatible with the current binding state and update the binding value and state if the refinement is allowed.

6.3.5.1 Interpreting the value of a binding

The value part of each binding is interpreted when the task definition as a whole (including associated bindings) is frozen and assigned to a role. This section discusses the mechanisms by which bindings are resolved to yield values for actual parameters and suggests various generalisations or customisations which go beyond the simple notion of binding to a single unique value. None of these proposals have been implemented because the integration of tasks, domains and the other elements of the IBS didn't get that far. However, these suggestions have been included to give some idea of the flexibility and generality of the binding mechanism.

The restriction that the binding must denote a single unique value (i.e. that its state is VERSION or INSTANCE) may be relaxed by the use of appropriate defaults. For example, a binding in the COMPONENT state might be interpreted as referring to the default version of that component. Even the interpretation of default could be customised. For example, the version control facilities in the IBS could be extended (perhaps by sub-typing the *component* entity type) so that every component could designate an optional default version of itself. Alternatively, the binding resolution mechanism could deduce the default automatically using some built-in rule (such as "most recent version" or "released version"). The rule for deducing the default might even be part of the context of the task instantiating the bindings of the customised task and assigning it to a role. For example, in a heterogeneous environment, the type of target system for which a task was intended to produce code might trigger the selection of the latest version of a particular variant as default.

Although it is possible to choose default objects in various ways and hence resolve bindings which might otherwise have been ambiguous, it does not necessarily follow that it is always appropriate that a binding should denote a single value. In certain circumstances it might be appropriate for the "single value" denoted by a binding to in fact be a set of values. An obvious example might be a binding to a programmer's tool kit. Rather than binding a task destined for a programming role to a whole series of individual tools, it is more sensible to bind to a single object representing a set of tools, in other words a tool kit. If new tools were added to this tool kit they would then automatically become available to all the tasks that were associated with a binding to the tool kit. It would not be necessary to add a binding for the new tool to each such task.

Integration with the version control system provides another opportunity for interpreting bindings as multi-valued. A binding to a component could make all the versions of that component available to a task. Similarly, if bindings to variants were implemented, such a binding could be interpreted as providing access to all the versions in that sequence. Furthermore, if the variant were published to the task with development permission, then this sequence could be locked against further development by other tasks.

These examples again illustrate ways in which indirection and late binding can be used to make the IPSE kit provided by the IBS more flexible. The default version or set of versions included when a component or variant is bound to a task is determined when the task is executed, not when it is defined. Similarly, the choice of tools in the tool kit is delayed until the binding is instantiated, i.e. until it becomes necessary to publish the contents of the tool kit to a domain associated with the task to be executed so that the tools are available during the task's execution. At this point, appropriate default versions of the tools may be selected using a combination of the various mechanisms for selecting defaults described above. Indeed, subject to the constraints of concurrency control, it might be possible to delay the choice of tools in the tool kit until after the task has started execution by publishing just a reference to the tool kit rather the contents of the tool kit to the task's domain. Binding would then occur whenever the tool kit was "opened" to examine its contents.

Such an extreme form of late binding is possible because most programming roles are concerned with developing an application rather than a programming tool. Although some tools are developed during the course of a project for special purposes, in general, tools such as compilers and debuggers are fixed at the start of the project. For this reason, such late binding would not be appropriate for a project which used experimental compilers with bugs where it was necessary to track which modules were compiled with which version of the compiler, because changing the bindings midway through a task execution would make this information difficult to determine.

There is another reason why it might sometimes be appropriate to bind to a set of values rather than a single value. For certain tasks it is appropriate to bind to a type rather than an instance of a type. Operations such as "create new instance" (as opposed to "create copy") should be applied to a type rather than an instance and it is therefore appropriate to treat types and operations as first-class objects in the IB which can be the subject of bindings like any other object in the IB.

A good example of this occurs in the demonstration. The Customer Services role may be thought of as "owning" the type *Customer Request* in the sense that tasks assigned to the Customer Services role with a binding to the type object *Customer Request* may have further bindings to operation objects which create new instances of customer requests or browse through existing customer requests. These operations require different interpretations of the binding to type *Customer Request* because creating a new instance of a type is simply an operation on the type object itself whereas browsing through all instances of a type involves treating a type object as the set of its instances. On the other hand, although the Project Manager role has access to the *Customer Request* type in the sense that tasks assigned to the Project Manager may (subject to appropriate bindings of course) read and act upon particular customer requests published to the Project Manager role by the Customer Services role, it does not make sense for the Project Manager role to be able to generate new customer requests or even to be able to browse through all existing customer requests.

In the same way, the Senior Programmer may "own" a particular component of the system and only allow the Junior Programmer to access particular versions of this component. Binding to a component for the Senior Programmer may mean binding to all versions of that component rather than to the default version (and similarly for variants).

If types and operations are to be treated as first-class objects in the IB, it is also natural to allow the arguments to operations to be partially bound to objects in the IB, thus creating closures which are themselves treated as first-class objects. For example, a general "publish object to domain" operator could be partially bound to either its object or domain argument (or indeed to both) to construct a restricted operator that could only publish a particular object to a particular domain for example. Such a closure could be created by a parent task and then published to one of its sub-tasks as a means of constraining what was done with the output of the sub-task.

These examples show that the choice of suitable bindings and the use of publication may be used to constrain the operations and the data available to the tasks assigned to each role. The Aspect model of binding is very flexible because it allows the interpretation of a binding to be customised either by building in rules to resolve ambiguities or by extending the binding state-transition diagram to allow different kinds of refinement and interpretation of bindings according to the needs of the project methodology being modelled in the IPSE. However, the difficulty with achieving the full generality that this approach allows is that often the interpretation of a particular binding will depend on the semantics of the operations allowed on instances of that binding (as illustrated by the two simple examples taken from the demonstration). To capture this in the IB requires a richer data model than RM/T. The ability to model the semantics of operations directly and to treat operations and their closures as first-class objects in the IB suggests a need for some kind of object-oriented data model with powers of abstraction beyond those provided by the relational model of RM/T. The requirements of such a model are a subject for further research.

6.4 People and Roles

This section describes the implementation of the project organisation part of the Aspect process model in the IBS. Entity types were created to represent users and roles. Two role hierarchies were created using a *roletype* entity and a *manages* entity although these were not used in the demonstration. The association between users, roles and tasks was modelled using appropriate associative entities.

People

For the demonstration people were modelled very simply using the following entity type.

User		
user_eatt	user_name	user_passwd

Each user has a name (*user_name*) and a password (*user_passwd*) which the IPSE recognises. In order for a user to log on to the IPSE, they must first type their name and then in response to a prompt type their password. The demonstration models two users of the IPSE by two instances of this *user* entity type. These have values for the *user_name* attribute of "freda" and "beatrice" with corresponding passwords "alpha" and "beta".

Roles

Each user will assume a particular role on each occasion that they use the IPSE. To allow similarities between roles to be captured in a role hierarchy, the following *roletype* entity type was defined.

Roletype	
roletype_eatt	roletype_name

For the purposes of the demonstration, several instances of this *roletype* entity type were created. Their names, given by the attribute *roletype_name*, included "Manager", "Programmer", "Services" and "QA". (Roletype "System" was also created but not used.)

Roles were modelled using the following *role* entity type.

Role		
role_eatt	role_type	role_name

Every role is an instance of some role type and similar roles are instances of the same role type. This is implemented in RM/T using a designation from the *role* entity type to the *roletype* entity type. Thus, each instance of a *role* designates a *roletype* entity through the attribute *role_type*. Roles also have a name attribute *role_name* giving their name. The roles created for the demonstration together with their role types are given below.

Role type	Role name
Manager	Section Manager
Manager	Project Manager
Services	Customer Services
Programmer	Junior Programmer
Programmer	Senior Programmer
QA	Archive
QA	Quality Assurance

Had the demonstration been developed further, the *roletype* entity type might have been used to enable a manager, say, to find out which roles were of type programmer.

Associating people with roles

Each person who is logged on to an Aspect IPSE will assume some role before performing any task. The possible roles that each user can play are modelled by a *user_role* entity type which associates an entity of type *user* with one of type *role*. This can be used to discover which roles a user can assume or to assign a role to a user.

User_Role		
user_role_eatt	ur_user	ur_role

In the Aspect demonstration there are two users, freda and beatrice. Freda can assume any of the roles Customer Services, Project Manager and Senior Programmer. Beatrice can assume any of the roles Archive, Junior Programmer and Section Manager. These are unlikely combinations of roles for real users but were chosen so that the demonstration could be carried out more easily by changing role rather than by repeatedly logging in as a different person.

The pop-up menu which appears in the demonstration when the *Role List* box for a particular user is selected is generated by querying the *user_role* entity type in the IB. Instances of this entity are created and deleted dynamically as users are given new roles or are no longer required to carry out old roles. Since the roles of users are not changed in the demonstration, the *Role List* pop-up menus do not change.

Note that in this version of the IBS, each role is associated with at most one user. Thus, when *user_role* instances are created in the IB, a check is made that the role is not already associated with a user. If it is, then the create operation fails.

Managing people

In any project there will be people in charge of others and people who are responsible to others; many people will be in both categories. In order to provide a means of modelling this, the *manages* entity type was created. This is an associative entity type linking two entities of type *role* since it was considered more appropriate to think of the hierarchy in terms of roles rather than people. The attribute *manages_parent* describes the managing role and the attribute *manages_child* describes the subordinate role in each instance of this relationship.

Manages		
manages_eatt	manages_parent	manages_child

This entity type was not used in the demonstration.

Assigning tasks to roles

The tasks that each role has to perform are modelled by the *role_task* entity type which associates an entity of type *role* (attribute *rt_role*) with one of type *task* (attribute *rt_task*).

Role_Task		
role_task_eatt	rt_role	rt_task

This entity type is queried when the *Task List* box for a particular role is selected. As tasks are assigned to roles or tasks are completed, entity instances are created or deleted dynamically.

The demonstration IPSE is set up so that users log into roles and then into tasks associated with those roles. This has blurred the rather subtle distinction between users, roles and users performing roles. Since in the demonstration each role is associated with at most one user, the *role_task* entity type is sufficient to establish which tasks a user logged on to a particular role has to do. However, if more than one user could be associated with the same role, then there would need to be some additional means of establishing which of the tasks assigned to that role were to be performed by which users. An obvious way of doing this would be to replace the *role_task* entity type with a *user_role_task* entity type which associated a *user_role* entity with a *task* entity. By joining this entity type with the *user_role* entity type, it would be possible to discover which tasks were associated with each of the project roles.

The *user_role_task* entity type would have been used to model the user/task relationship in the demonstration IPSE if the scenario had allowed several users to perform the same role. However, since for the demonstration scenario at most one user could play each role, *user_role_task* instances are effectively the same as *role_task* instances since *user_roles* are in 1-1 correspondence with *roles* (provided that each role has been assigned to a user). Thus, the simpler *role_task* entity type was used for the demonstration even though in real life tasks would be assigned to users not roles.

It is worth noting that the *manages* entity type described above could be used to check whether or not a given role was allowed to assign a task to another role since normally such an assignment would only be performed by a role managing the role to which the task was assigned. However, this was not implemented for the demonstration.

6.5 Versions and Configuration Management

6.5.1 Introduction

In the overview of the Aspect process model in Chapter 3 we presented the basic concepts central to the Aspect version control and configuration management systems. In this section we will discuss how those concepts are realised in the IBS using the RM/T IBE, both in the full model we would have ideally liked to implement, and in the restricted model which was actually implemented to support the demonstration IPSE described in Chapter 4.

The reader is advised to look through Chapters 3 and 4 to get a higher-level view of the functionality of the version control and configuration management systems before plunging into the technical details of the present chapter. The demonstration IPSE is used to illustrate the use of these systems and we hope that these examples will clarify the explanations given.

Although the version control system can be implemented without the configuration management system (and vice versa), many basic concepts are common to both.

6.5.2 Version control

We start with the RM/T implementation of components, versions and variants. This part of the system was almost fully implemented in the demonstration IPSE. The examples drawn from the demonstration therefore illustrate directly the RM/T structures and functions described.

Components and types

The Aspect process model makes a basic distinction between the logical and physical levels of the product. At the logical level, a software system with all supporting documents is described as a set of components. Components are typed and a software release will typically be made up of many different kinds of component (e.g. requirements analysis components, design document components, source code components, executable program components and so on). The physical contents of the components – the text files, source code etc. – are not held at this logical level. The only information the component need hold, therefore, is its type.

In the RM/T implementation, components are represented by the *component* entity type which designates the type of its instances. The component relation looks like this:

Component	
component_eatt	comp_etrep

The attribute *component_eatt* is the RM/T e-attribute. Every entity type has an e-attribute which holds a surrogate used by RM/T to identify tuples. The attribute *comp_etrep* designates one of the members of the *entity_type_reps* relation (the catalog relation of all entity types).

Components in the demonstration

In the Aspect demonstration, a user wishing to browse parts of the software system in the IB uses the Browse panel (see Chapter 4 for details of the functionality of different parts of the screen). On entry to a task the Browse panel displays a list of types appropriate to that task. For instance, Figure 6.4 shows the types available in task *Create Amendment Spec*.

Selecting a particular type with the left mouse button, for instance *Ada_packages*, and then choosing the *Open* operation retrieves the components which designate that type from the IB and displays them as shown in Figure 6.5.

The items appearing in the Browse panel for a particular task would ideally be determined by the view that the task had of the IB and the objects which had been published to its domain (see later sections on views and concurrency control in this chapter). However, since views and domains were not integrated with the rest of the IBS because of lack of time, the demonstration IPSE adopted a simpler approach. Associated with each task is a list of component types which determines which items appear in the initial Browse panel for the task. However, all components of a given type and all versions of those components are visible to every

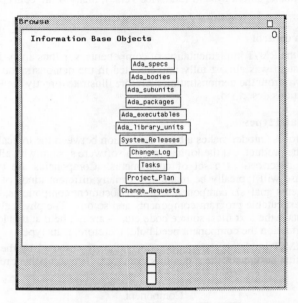

Fig. 6.4 Displaying component types in the Browse panel

task provided the type is visible to the task.

Components exist only at the logical level of the product. To browse the contents of a component, we need to select a particular version of it. This is the physical level of the software system modelled by the product.

Physical versions of components

Versions may be thought of as the physical instantiations of components, holding their contents (source code, text, or whatever) as they develop through time. Each component has one or more versions and these are entities of the entity type designated by the component. For example, the versions of one of the components in the *Ada_packages* list displayed in Figure 6.5 (say *car_package*) are entities of type *ada_package*.

Versions of all types of component need to record some basic information that is used by the version control system. Firstly, all versions must at least state the component of which they are a version. In the RM/T structure, the versions characterise the component, and have an attribute which holds the surrogate of the component. This design was chosen because versions are in effect extensions of the component; they cannot exist without a component. In the demonstration IPSE versions also hold their date of creation and a file for their "contents" (text, source code, etc.).

Since the entity types of all versionable objects have these attributes in

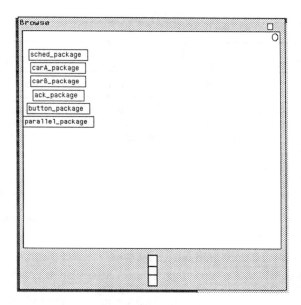

Fig. 6.5 Displaying components of one type (*ada_package*) in the Browse panel

common, a *version* entity type was defined to hold these attributes. Versionable objects are grouped into sub-types of this basic *version* entity type according to the type of component they represent. Information peculiar to particular kinds of component is held as type-specific attributes of these sub-types.

The implementation of the *version* entity type in the IB was as follows:

Version			
version_eatt	version_comp	date_created	contents

Note again the e-attribute *version_eatt* holding the identification surrogate.

The version control system ensures that when versions are created they are of the correct type. This type determines the information recorded in the version, i.e. the attributes of the entity. As well as the basic attributes that all versions have in common (the component of which they are a version, their date of creation and their contents), additional attributes may be used to hold type-specific information peculiar to a particular kind of component. In fact, only one of the types used in the demonstration held such type-specific information: the type *executable*, which represents an executable Ada program. One of the tools provided as part of the Aspect facilities for developing distributed target systems (see Chapter 10) takes the name of an Ada package and uses the package specification to work out a graph of dependencies between this and other compilation units. The resulting collection of required Ada units is known as a virtual node and can be used to build an executable that will reside on one processor. In the RM/T structures underlying the demonstration, the package specification from which the graph is derived is held as an attribute of the type *executable* called *virt_node*. The type *executable*, a sub-type of *version*, therefore looks like this:

Executable				
executable_eatt	version_comp	date_created	contents	virt_node

The information held in the *virt_node* attribute is not actually used in the demonstration but was simply chosen as an example of the sort of type-specific attribute which could be stored in the IB and accessed by users or appropriately designed tools. In a real-life situation, the IB structures required to support complex tools and queries would of course be much richer and there would be many such type-specific attributes.

The scope of version control in Aspect is defined with respect to the *version* entity type. Version control may be applied to all those objects in the IB whose type is a sub-type of *version*. Such objects characterise the component of which they are an instance and may be grouped into version sets accordingly. Objects of types which are not sub-types of *version* do not characterise components and are therefore not versionable.

The structure of versions within the component

The information held in the version itself makes it possible to group together versions of one component, but it is also necessary to know the relationship between versions – their order of development, which versions are alternatives (or variants) of others, which may be modified and which are frozen. This information is recorded in, or derived from, the *version_graph* association between versions. This models relationships between versions thus:

Version_Graph			
v_graph_eatt	v_graph_source	v_graph_target	rel_type

The *rel_type* attribute is used to model the kind of relationship which exists between the two versions denoted by the *v_graph_source* and the *v_graph_target* attributes. Relationships between versions arise as a result of the development sequence for versions of a given component as we will now explain.

Order of development – version sequences

In the scenario used for the demonstration, there is a component *ack.H* which designates type *ada_spec*. This is the specification of the Ada package which acknowledges requests for lifts. The first version of this component (an entity of type *ada_spec*) is called *ack.H:0* (the naming scheme is part of the customisation of the IPSE kit and is explained below). This version is subsequently revised, creating a new version *ack.H:1*, followed by *ack.H:2*, and so on. The relationship between the members of this sequence is called revision. *Ack.H:1* revises *ack.H:0* and is revised by *ack.H:2*.

This sequence of versions can be displayed in the Browse panel of the demonstration IPSE. Having opened the item labelled *Ada_specs* in the Browse panel of Figure 6.4 to obtain a list of the components of type *ada_spec* (c.f. Figure

6.5 which shows a list of the components of type *ada_package*), the particular component of interest *ack.H* may be selected followed by the operation *Show Versions* from the Browse panel menu. The resulting display is shown in Figure 6.6.

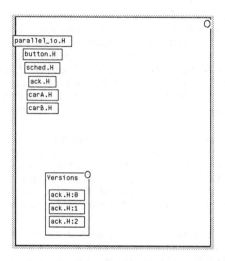

Fig. 6.6 The version display in the Browse panel

The revision relationship is held in an associative entity type, *version_graph*. The version sequence used in this example would be held as follows.

Version_Graph			
v_graph_eatt	v_graph_source	v_graph_target	rel_type
100	ack.H:0	ack.H.1	revision
101	ack.H:1	ack.H.2	revision

There is more than one sort of relationship between versions, so the fact that these versions are revisions of each other is recorded in the attribute *rel_type*. The e-attributes 100 and 101 are system generated − in reality the values of the *v_graph_source* and *v_graph_target* attributes (e.g. *ack.H:0* and *ack.H:1*) are also surrogates denoting the actual version entities participating in the relationship but such surrogates would not be very meaningful to the reader!

Once a version has been revised it is frozen (i.e. only the latest version can ever be revised). This can be expressed as a constraint on the version graph: a version cannot appear in the *v_graph_source* attribute of more than one tuple whose *rel_type* attribute has the value "revision". In the above example, only *ack.H:2* can now accept a revision.

The sequence may therefore only be added to at the end. Furthermore, permission to add to the end of the sequence is restricted to one task at a time. This "development permission", which effectively locks the sequence against any other attempted updates, is one of several Aspect-defined permissions and is further discussed in Section 6.6 on concurrency control.

Parallel development – variants

With the above restrictions, only one person at a time can work on updating a component, and then only in one task. Within a project it is often necessary for more than one person to work on variants of the software (and accompanying documentation) in parallel. This may, for instance, be for different sites, languages, or for experimental features to be offered as optional extras. Each variant develops through time and is subject to the above protection mechanisms, i.e. only one person in one task can work on updating a variant. In other words, a variant is a sequence of versions and there may be several such sequences in the version set of one component.

The RM/T structure used to support variants is the *version_graph* association which was described above as relating members of a sequence. Just as one version can be a revision of another, in a similar way it can be a variant of another, and this fact is noted in the value of the *rel_type* attribute. New paths of development can therefore branch off from the current path at any point. A given version can only have one revision, but there are no restrictions on the number of variants it may have.

Returning to our example of the component *ack.H*, we may decide to create a variant of one of its versions: *ack.H:0, ack.H:1* or *ack.H:2*. First we must create a new version, then an entry in the version graph to relate it to the existing versions. The new version is the head of a new sequence and strictly speaking it is the entire sequence which is the variant. The variant sequence will be added to as it is revised in time.

Suppose we create a variant of *ack.H:2*. The variant software represents a development path for a lift control system for four lift shafts, as opposed to two in the original software, and the sequence is given the overall name *fourcar*. In our customisation, the new version is therefore called *ack.H:fourcar:0* i.e. the first version of the *fourcar* variant. If the four-car software is then modified, the revised version is *ack.H:fourcar:1* and so on. After the *fourcar* variant has branched off, the original two-car software may continue to be developed. This will cause the version graph to form a tree as shown in Figure 6.7. If a merge facility was introduced, versions would form graphs rather than trees and "merge" would be another permitted value of the *rel_type* attribute of *version_graph*.

Naming schemes for version/variant structures

Since variants can be formed from existing variants at any point in their sequence, the resulting structures could be very difficult to display in a meaningful way on the screen. The naming scheme could also be awkward to handle if we wished the name of the version to hold all the necessary information to place it precisely in the development history of the component. In particular, names would have to be of the form:

<component name>:<version number>{:<variant name>:<version number>}

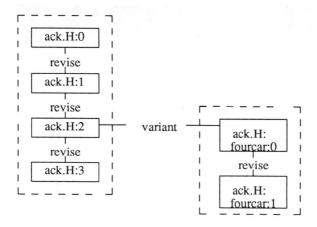

Fig. 6.7 Variant/version structure

where the trailing variant name and version number can be repeated indefinitely. However, this naming scheme is not built into the basic Aspect IPSE kit and consequently it is possible to introduce restrictions on the possible uses of versions and variants when this kit is customised and thus limit the forms that names can take.

For example, the customised IPSE built for the demonstration imposed the restriction that variants could only be made of versions in the original development path or main variant. Versions of the main variant are named as the component name followed by a sequence number. The names of versions from subsequent variants contain a variant name as well as their sequence number in that variant. However, they do not include the sequence number of the version in the main variant from which their variant was derived. Names therefore have the form

<component name>[:<variant name>]:<version number>.

where the variant name is optional. Some information has thereby been lost and variant names must be unique within a component to prevent ambiguity.

Displaying variants

In the demonstration system, the user can select a version from the sequence followed by the Browse operation *Show Variants* to display a list of variants (Figure 6.8). This operation queries the *version_graph* relation and displays any variants whose source is the selected version.

Selecting the variant *fourcar* and the operation *Show Versions* will cause the sequence of versions for that variant to replace the original sequence. Note that once the variant list is displayed, the screen design does not show which version was queried to produce it and this information does not form part of the version

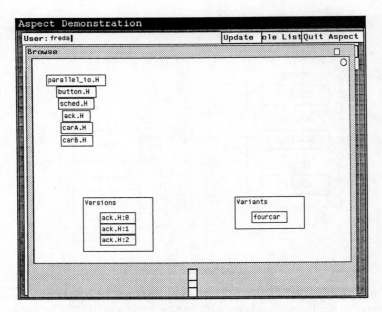

Fig. 6.8 Variants of a selected version

name as explained above.

Creating variants

The *Create New Variant* tool (Figure 6.9) may be selected if it is available in the Tool execution panel for the task. This is the only means of updating the version graph and of creating new versions given in the demonstration IPSE, and is thus an illustration of an environment where low-level operations are not accessible to the user (see Section 6.8 on views).

  The *Create New Variant* tool operates on a previously selected version or component. If it is applied to a component, then by default a new variant is created from the last version of the main variant of that component (c.f. the discussion of interpreting bindings using default values in Section 6.3.5.5). To create the first version of the new variant, the text file of the source version is read from the IB into the editable region of the *Create New Variant* tool. The user edits this, gives the new variant a name and selects the *Save* operation. A new version of the component is then created and an entry is added to the *version_graph* relation to link the new version to its source version.

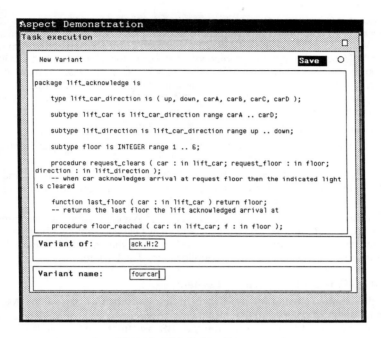

Fig. 6.9 The *Create Variant* tool

Constraints on updating and creating versions

In the demonstration, there was no restriction on the creation of variants other than the availability of the *Create New Variant* tool to the task. If a *Create New Version* tool had been designed to revise existing versions, then the appearance of this tool would have been very similar to the *Create New Variant* tool but its operation would have included a check that the source version was the latest version in a variant, and that the domain had development permission on that variant, as discussed in Section 6.6 on concurrency control.

Further controls could be introduced into a customised IPSE by extending the types of permission held by a domain on an object to include, for example, permission to create a variant of a version. If a version was selected for which the domain did not have this permission, the *Create New Variant* tool would be rendered inoperable or might not even appear in the Tool execution panel. Similarly, an apparently simple *Edit Version* tool could either update the selected version in place, or create a revision of it, or reject the selection, depending on the permissions held by the domain on the version in question.

6.5.3 Configuration management

So far we have considered relationships between versions of one component. It is also necessary to hold the relationships between versions of different components in the IB. We need to know the relationships between particular versions of source code and object code, and between versions of the user documentation and versions of the software. Some of this information is what is traditionally regarded as Configuration Management (CM), i.e. how one component is built from several sub-components. The Aspect concept of CM includes all dependencies between objects, whether these arise from:

- building one object from several objects, e.g. a thesis from chapters,
- developing several objects from one, e.g. several module designs from one functional specification, or
- translating one object into another, both automatically (e.g. compiling) and by a lengthy process of human judgement (e.g. developing a software release from the original requirements analysis).

This last example highlights another feature of Aspect configurations, namely that they should hold information about dependencies between any two stages of the life-cycle, not just adjoining stages. Such information should only be held if it is useful for specific tools, particularly to provide quick feedback loops.

The status of the demonstration CM system

In the ideal implementation of the CM facilities, described as part of the Aspect process model in Chapter 3, all the information necessary to trace dependencies and rebuild objects would be derivable from the IBS structures used to implement the task system described in Section 6.3. The CM system would then simply provide the tools needed to query these structures and link them to the version control system.

For the demonstration IPSE, only part of the task system was implemented and consequently a simple CM system was built independently of the task system. The information recorded by this CM system would in some ways be duplicated by a full task system were such a system to be available. This simple CM system is described, followed by a proposal for a more sophisticated system, although this would still not be fully integrated with the task system. Finally, a brief sketch is given of how our eventual aim might be achieved. This is a CM system fully integrated with the task system. However, the simple CM system implemented for the demonstration illustrates many of the basic features of any Aspect CM system.

The demonstration CM system

The dependencies between objects are the result of how they were derived in the first place. The task system models the derivation process dynamically whilst the CM system models the relationships between derived objects statically. Thus, the CM system holds a static view of information derived from the dynamic model of the development process implemented by the task system. Ignoring for the moment the problem of deriving that static information from the history of task executions, or the possible duplication of information between the two systems, the dependency relationship between objects can be held as a graph using an RM/T associative entity type. In the demonstration system this was called *configuration_graph*.

Configuration_Graph			
c_graph_eatt	config_parent	config_child	config_task

Config_parent represents the derived object and *config_child* represents the object from which it is derived. (This is perhaps counter-intuitive in that the parent is subordinate to its children – it means for example that a graphical representation of the configuration should be read from the leaves upwards to follow the development history chronologically.) *Config_task* points to the task execution which caused this dependency to exist.

There is an instance of a *configuration_graph* entity for every child object that a given parent object is derived from. Configurations form graphs rather than trees as a child object may be used in the derivation of more than one parent object, e.g. an object module could be included in more than one executable program. The attributes *config_parent* and *config_child* are both of type *version* (or a sub-type thereof) rather than of type *component* for reasons we will explain shortly.

Using configuration graphs, it is possible to hold configurations in the IB. For example, Figure 6.10 shows the structure of a particular Ada package (the scheduling package from the lift system) as it would be held in the demonstration IPSE. However, Figure 6.10 is an over-simplification because the version numbers have been omitted; it is actually a graph showing the relationship between versions not components.

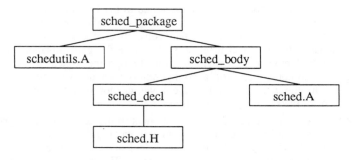

Fig. 6.10 The Scheduler Package configuration

The structure of the configuration shown in Figure 6.10 represents the order in which objects need to be retrieved or rebuilt in order to rebuild the whole. Each node in the graph represents a *version* object whose *contents* attribute denotes a source file or object file that the version may be said to contain. The sequence of operations necessary to rebuild *sched_package* from scratch is as follows:

1. The package specification *sched.H* must be compiled first. The version object *sched_decl* which is derived from *sched.H* therefore contains the result of this compilation, namely the object module *sched.O*. The task in which the compilation was performed is pointed to by the *config_task* attribute of the

configuration_graph instance which represents the dependency between *sched_decl* and *sched.H*.

2.   The package body *sched.A* is compiled to produce a version of *sched_body*. This depends on the results of compiling *sched.H* (i.e. *sched.O* which is represented by *sched_decl*) or in other words requires step 1 to have been carried out.

3.   The compilation sub-unit *schedutils.A* is compiled and combined with *sched_body* to form *sched_package*.

The graph in Figure 6.10 is only a section of the configuration graph for the entire lift system. The source modules here are leaves of this sub-tree − they appear in the graph as children, but not parents. They could be said to have no configuration of their own. Conversely, *sched_package* is the final end-product of this sub-graph and has no parents. In the larger graph, the source modules are derived from design documents and the package is used in the configuration of Ada executables.

It is worth explaining why the *configuration_graph* entity type presented above is an association between versions rather than components. If everything could only exist in one version, there would be no distinction. However, the presence of version control means that components can exist in more than one version and can therefore have more than one configuration. For example, suppose there are two versions of the scheduling package, and in the earlier version the source code of the package body has not been split into two parts, i.e. there is no sub-unit *schedutils.A*. The component *sched_package* now has two configurations, one for each version. So how should this be represented in the IB? For the demonstration system, we chose the simplest solution, which was to make *configuration_graph* an association between versions rather than between components. Configurations, therefore, exist at the physical level only. We lose the generalisation that would come from introducing a level of indirection through the logical to the physical, selecting the sub-components of a configuration then the version of each subcomponent. In the demonstration system we cannot therefore group together configurations of the same logical structure.

To browse the configuration of a component in the demonstration system, the user first selects a particular version of that component and then the operation *Show Configuration*. Alternatively, the user can select a component and then use the operation *Show Configuration of Latest Version*. Either way, the configuration stored in the IB is actually drawn as a graph linking components, not versions. The components displayed are derived by querying the versions in the configuration graph. This fitted in with screen design and seemed more natural, pointing to the need for configurations to also exist at the component or logical level as mentioned above.

Incorporating designs into the CM model

For the reasons discussed above, it is desirable for the CM structures stored in the IB to include a level for the logical structure, or design, of a configuration. A component may have, among its versions, more than one configuration, but the likelihood is that not every version of the component will be configured differently at the logical level. Several versions may share the same design, by which we mean the logical structure, or set of components, used in the configuration of those versions. To create a configuration at the physical level from a given design for a component, we must replace each sub-component in the design by one of its versions. Changes in the design of a component will occur at important points in the development of a component, and will often (but not always) coincide with the creation of variants for the component. Thus, this two-stage derivation of a version of a component via a design expressed in terms of its sub-components to a configuration expressed in terms of versions of those sub-components allows the IB to capture more information about the development process. Designs model the logical structure of components whilst configurations hold the physical instances of the objects going to make up a particular version of a component.

In the IB this could be modelled as follows. Each component has (designates) one design component. The *design* entity type is a sub-type of the *component* entity type and consequently designs can exist in one or more versions. Design instances (i.e. versions of designs) are the logical configurations described above, and are represented by the *logical_config* entity type which is a sub-type of *version*. There is an association *in_logical* between *logical_config* and *component* to represent the components used in each logical configuration (version of a design). The physical configuration of a particular version of a component is represented by the *physical_config* entity type. Physical configurations are derived from (i.e. characterise) logical configurations and designate the version for which they are a physical configuration. There is an association *in_physical* between *physical_config* and *version* to represent the versions used in that configuration. This is the equivalent of the *in_logical* association at the physical level

Figure 6.11 shows the inter-relationships between these entity types in an RM/T diagram.

With this scheme, a tool for creating a new version would need to be rather more complex than the simple *Create New Variant* tool described as part of the demonstration IPSE. All newly created versions would need to be placed in configurations, and their own configurations would have to be taken into account in order to create them. The user would first need to select a design from the existing designs for that component, or possibly create a new one, and then select versions of each component in the design. The new version would differ from previous versions of the component built using that design by using different versions of some of the sub-components required by the design. Some of these versions might not exist yet and would therefore need to be created. The *Create New Version* tool would therefore be invoked recursively until all the objects required for the creation of the new version were specified. The new version would then be built bottom-up in the order determined by its configuration. The creative process at any level (for new versions of sub-components, or for the end-product of the tool invocation) could be under human control (e.g. using an editor) or automatic (e.g. using a compiler).

There are two main points to note about this model. The first is the complexity of the above description of a procedure for what often seems to be a trivial task. In fact the difficulty with incorporating this sort of tool in the demonstration IPSE lay with the design of the user interface rather than with the required IB structures

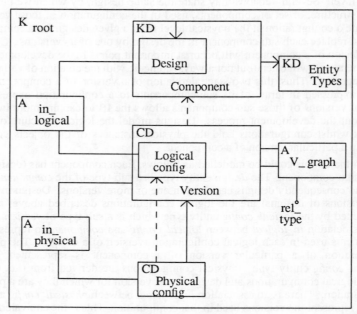

Fig. 6.11 The CM entity types

and operations. From this experience, it seems that this question – how to record the complex data required to control the development process without crippling the user with long procedures and unwanted information – deserves more attention in IPSE design.

The second point is the obvious similarity between the process just described and the task system. Both are concerned with a set of instructions that take some objects as input and produce something as output. These instructions may be general or specific, and so the objects mentioned may be general (in CM terms, logical) or specific (in CM terms, physical). The instructions may be broken down into nested sets of instructions. The set of instructions for the process is clearly equivalent to a configuration in the CM system or a task in the task system. The CM model records a subset of the information held in a task; there is no structural information such as selection or iteration as is held between tasks. Also the tools required to carry out the task to produce an object are missing from the configuration of that object, or, if tools are included in the list of objects from which the new object is configured, they are not distinguished from any other input data. The aims of the two systems are different. Configurations were designed to work out dependencies between objects and can be seen as complementary to the task system where the aim is to control the process by which objects are created, modified and derived from each other.

However, there are obviously problems of redundancy if both systems record what was used to create an object. The integration of that information would be desirable. The main barrier in achieving this was the complexity of the information structures that would be required, together with the attendant problems of tool design. However, some initial thoughts in this direction are now presented.

Binding and configurations

A configuration describes how a particular version of some component is constructed from particular versions of its sub-components using particular tools. If designs were to be introduced into the CM model in the way just described, then the logical design of a component (which sub-components it is made up of) would be distinguished in the IB from the choice of physical versions of those components. Building a version of a component would then involve selecting a version of the design for that component and then selecting versions of the sub-components required by that design. This same CM functionality could be achieved using the task structures described in Section 6.3 (namely bindings and reusable task templates) in the following way.

Designs would be represented by sets of generic COMPONENT bindings indicating the sub-components required by the design. These COMPONENT bindings would be refined to VERSION bindings in order to select particular versions of the sub-components they denoted. The refined bindings would then be associated with a task description derived from the design and the result would be a package of work describing how to build a particular configuration of a component that could be assigned to a role and performed in the usual way.

These ideas have not been implemented but they indicate a possible way in which the IBS facilities supporting tasks and configuration management could be integrated using bindings. The use of generic COMPONENT bindings would allow designs to be re-used, separating the logical and physical aspects of configuration management by making it possible to model the structural part of a configuration directly.

6.6 Concurrency Control

Concurrency control proved to be one of the most difficult parts of the IBS to design and implement. In this section, we will explain why this area is so difficult by discussing the issues involved and some of the trade-offs. We will then describe a solution based on the concept of domains, discuss the problems with this approach, and finally show how a simplified model of concurrency control could have been implemented and integrated with the demonstration IPSE.

Unfortunately, although this implementation was completed, it was not possible to integrate it with the other parts of the IBS and consequently it was not possible to evaluate the ideas described here in practice. Nevertheless, there is some evidence to suggest that they would have worked since other IPSEs (in particular Perspective from which some of these ideas were imported) have successfully demonstrated concurrency control mechanisms based on the domain concept.

In order to include some form of concurrency control in the demonstration IPSE, a rudimentary mechanism was incorporated by which tasks were only able to see instances of those components whose component types appeared in their initial

Browse panel. However, tasks had access to all the versions and configurations of components of which they were aware. Permission to create new versions was limited to those tasks which had access to the *Create New Variant* tool. A mechanism for publishing change requests between roles was also incorporated.

6.6.1 Introduction

Aspect is a multi-user system and consequently many users will want to access the objects in the IB simultaneously. It is important that these users are presented with a consistent view of the IB and that different transactions do not interfere with one another. In traditional database management systems, control of concurrent access to objects in the database is frequently done either by employing some form of locking of objects in the database or by proceeding on the optimistic assumption that transactions will not interfere with one another. If it is subsequently found that they did interfere, then one or more of the transactions involved is rolled back.

While these approaches may be quite satisfactory for short lived transactions such as might be found in a banking system, they are not at all suitable for a software engineering database because typically the interactions which occur with the data items that would be stored in such a database take place over extended time periods which may last for hours, days, weeks or even months.

If, for example, locking is used as a means of concurrency control, then this will result in some objects being locked for intolerably long periods during which time other transactions will be unable to access the objects and will have to wait. In addition to the attendant annoyance, long periods of waiting will also increase the chance of deadlock among the transactions.

Alternatively if an optimistic approach to concurrency control is adopted then, because transactions last for a long time, there is an increased chance that there will be interference between them. Transactions will frequently have to be rolled back because they cannot obtain the resources that they need or because they are found to have made changes which conflict with other transactions. This could involve undoing a considerable amount of work and is clearly unacceptable.

Despite these problems, it is still desirable to treat transactions with a software engineering database as atomic in some sense. Thus, a more acceptable form of controlling concurrent access to objects in a software engineering information base is required than either locking or optimistic concurrency control can provide.

In addition to ensuring that concurrent access to the IB does not give rise to an inconsistent state, it is also necessary to ensure that the creation of new objects does not similarly cause inconsistencies. For example, the development of a particular piece of code may involve the creation of a number of versions of it before it is considered satisfactory. It is important to ensure that that only one user at a time has permission to create a new version. In other words it is important to ensure that only one user at a time has permission to develop the piece of code: development must be controlled as well as access.

6.6.2 Controlling access to the IB

To overcome the problems of concurrent access to shared data the following approach has been adopted in the implementation of the IBS. When users are logged into an Aspect IPSE, they are associated with a domain and associated with this domain is a set of objects together with permissions on these objects. The objects associated with the domain determine the objects of which a user of the domain can be aware. The permissions on these objects (for example "read" and "write") determine what a user can do with them. The majority of the objects of which users will be aware will be versions of components. Each of these versions will be an instantiation of a particular component which has different contents from another version of the same component. Versions can be grouped into variants as explained in Section 6.5.

In many ways the Aspect concept of a domain is rather like a workspace. The objects of which users are aware and the operations that they can perform on them are determined (indirectly) through the domain with which the users are associated at the time. However, there are some important differences. Because of the need for users to share objects, domains do not partition the IB but instead overlap. However, the permissions on shared objects are carefully controlled to prevent conflict.

The domain with which someone using the IPSE is associated may be based on a variety of things. These include the user themselves, the role they are playing, the user/role combination, the task on which they are currently engaged while playing a specified role or something else. Each project can choose for itself how it wishes to base this association during the customisation phase of the IPSE.

If the association is based on the user, then an individual will always be associated with the same domain. If it is based on the role or user/role combination, then the associated domain will probably, but not necessarily, change when the individual changes role. If it is based on the task then, again, the associated domain will probably change with each task. Concurrent access is controlled by ensuring that only one user is associated with a domain at any one time and by ensuring that the permissions on an object in different domains do not conflict.

Permissions on objects will be such things as "read" and "write" but the semantics of these permissions will vary with the type of object being considered and might not even be applicable in some cases. For versions, such as a version of a C program, "read" and "write" permission will have their normal meaning of allowing the right to access and the right to modify the contents of that version of the program. However, for variants, the meaning of "read" and "write" permission is not so obvious and indeed further permissions are required.

In the case of a variant, which is a set of versions that form a sequence tracing the development, "read" permission could mean that a user was allowed to discover the sequence of versions. Note however that "read" permission on the variant would not give permission to access the contents of these versions, This would require the domain to have "read" permission on the versions themselves.

This interpretation of "read" permission for variants is analogous to the interpretation of "read" permission for directories in Unix. "Read" permission is required in order to list the contents of a Unix directory (i.e. see the names of the files it contains). "Search" permission on the directory is required in order to make use of these names (e.g. to obtain more detailed information about the files such as their size, ownership, creation date, etc.). However, in order to access the contents of the files named by the directory, "read" permission is required on the files themselves.

"Write" permission on a variant could be used to mean that a user was allowed to extend the version sequence by adding a new version at the end. Another name would be needed for the permission to develop a new variant from an existing version in the variant. Alternatively, words other than "read" and "write" could be used to denote the permission to know the version sequence of a variant, the permission to extend this sequence, and the permission to start a new variant from a given version in the sequence. This would be more sensible in that it would avoid overloading the meaning of familiar terms. Thus, in what follows we shall use the term "development permission" to mean the permission to develop the next version in a variant.

Objects which are and have only ever been associated with only one domain are referred to as private. The user of a domain is responsible for controlling concurrent access to private objects. In other words, he or she must either take care that concurrent transactions do not conflict or, alternatively, take appropriate action to resolve any conflicts which do arise. Since the Aspect system allows only one user to be working in association with any particular domain at any one time, this allows users to work independently of one another and without interference.

However there is obviously a need for users to be able to share data such as versions. This is achieved by having a publication mechanism which enables the user of one domain to allow users of other domains to access (read) versions which are private to it. As a result of this publish operation, a version becomes public and cannot be updated (written) at any future time by the user of any domain whatsoever. This restriction is imposed to preserve the version history. If the user of a domain wishes to modify something that has been published, this can only be done by publishing a new version. However, this is only possible if the domain has permission to create a new version in the first place. There is a strict level of control over which domains can access which versions since, when an version is published, explicit mention is made of the domains to which it is published. No interference between users of different domains is possible since only versions which are private can be updated and these can only be accessed from a single domain.

The essential points about private and public (published) versions are summarised in the following table.

Type of Version	Relationship with Domains	Mod. Possibilities
Private	May be associated with 1 domain	May be modified
Published	May be associated with many domains	Cannot be modified

In summary the problem of concurrent access to versions and the sharing of versions is solved through the notions of:

- Domains.
- Versions which are private to those domains and which can only be updated from those domains.

- Public versions which cannot be changed.
- The publication mechanism.

However, users of an IPSE will want to share more than versions. They will, for example, want to share the information that a particular set of versions makes up a variant. This set will vary over time so the information will not be unchanging and for this reason the simple dichotomy into "private modifiable" objects and "public unchanging" objects is too simple if we want to include variants among the objects.

A version is created in one domain, and when it is finished it will usually be published so that other domains are made aware of it. A variant, in contrast, is never finished in that the possibility of adding another version to it always exists. In addition, although successive versions in a variant would normally be created in the same domain, this is not always the case. Development permission could be transferred to another domain and this could happen several times in the course of a project. Consequently, a variant is rather like a "public modifiable" object

Finding the versions that constitute a variant is a query on the version graph associated with some component. The ability to do this can be provided by giving domains suitable permissions on the versions in this structure such as the permission to know the existence of a revision or variant of a version or the permission to know its parent version. This would enable domains to reconstruct part of the version graph. (Note that since the version structure changes over time, some of these queries will give different answers at different times unlike the answer to the query "what is the value (content) of version 4.2?")

An alternative to this would be to give all domains permission to browse the version graphs associated with any of the components of which they are aware. By browsing this graph, a domain could discover what versions there were of the component and how these versions were interrelated – i.e. whether or not they were variants or revisions. However, the domain would not be able to read the contents of any of the versions unless it had the appropriate permission on them. This is the approach taken in the demonstration. Similarly, in the demonstration no additional permissions are required for a domain to be able to find out the configuration of a version or the component of which it is an instance.

6.6.3 Controlling development

In addition to preventing inconsistencies which arise as a consequence of concurrent access to the IB, the concurrency control mechanisms must also prevent inconsistencies consequent upon an object being developed in more than one domain. A typical object in this context would be a variant of a component. If users in two domains each try to produce the next version of a document or piece of code then, depending on how the creation of the next version is implemented, this could result in scrambled text or code or in one version overwriting the other. To prevent problems of this nature, a restriction is imposed to ensure that an object which can be developed can only be developed from one domain. In the case of the variant of a component, only one domain has permission to develop it and consequently create a new version which is a revision of the last version in the sequence.

This permission to develop an object can be transferred from one domain to another. The mechanism or operation by which this transfer is achieved is known as allocation and is similar to the publication mechanism described above except that it transfers development permission rather than access permission.

To summarise, development of objects is controlled by:

- Only allowing an object to be developed from one domain.
- The allocation mechanism which transfers the permission to develop an object from one domain to another.

6.6.4 The implementation of publication and allocation

The original design of the IBS envisaged that an element of user control over the objects accessible to each domain was required. It was not felt to be desirable that the objects in a domain could be changed without the participation of the owner of that domain. This element of control over the contents of domains was achieved by implementing the passing of objects and their associated permissions between domains using double handshake protocols. Thus, publish and allocate were not implemented as atomic operations but rather as double handshakes between the publishing domain and the domain to which the objects were being published.

With the revised ideas about the IBS in the final year of the project, it is by no means clear that such a mechanism is still appropriate. It depends very much on what domains are associated with (a granularity issue), and the degree of autonomy that domains (or rather the agents associated with them) should have. For example, if objects are only published to domains as part of the binding process before a task begins its execution, then an atomic publish operation is more appropriate (not least because until the task has begin its execution, there is no agent associated with it that can respond to the other half of a double handshake protocol). However, if objects can be published to domains during the execution of the task associated with them, then some form of handshake is required to prevent the contents of the task's workspace from changing unexpectedly.

Another difficulty with the handshake mechanism is the implementation of the asynchronous notification required in order to inform a domain that an object's availability has changed in some way. What form should this take? Is a domain expected to examine the list of published objects periodically or should there be some mechanism to seize its attention? Under what circumstances should a domain be allowed to refuse the handshake and under what circumstances should the publishing domain be allowed to force it to accept the published object?

A difficulty with the whole concept of publication and allocation is the question of granularity. At what level of abstraction are objects published or allocated? The original specification of publication for the IBS operated at the level of the basic RM/T entity types. This required the introduction of many rules to ensure the internal consistency of what was published and guarantee that every domain always contained not only a consistent set of entities but also a consistent subset of the RM/T catalog describing those entities. Thus, whenever an entity was published, the things that had to be published with it (or published already) included its type, attributes, the type of those attributes, the type of any entities any of those types designated, characterised or were associated with, and so on, recursively, until the transitive closure of all those relationships had been formed.

Even if the basic set of entity types required to guarantee the internal consistency of the RM/T database plus the entity types required by the IBS and the customisation of the Aspect process model to suit a particular project are always published to a new domain, this still represents a considerable overhead. Indeed, in the original implementation of the IBS, a new domain was associated with every activity execution and a key operation was the binding of an activity definition and a view to a new domain in which the execution of the activity could take place. This was implemented by publishing all the objects required by the view and the activity definition to the domain. The performance of this operation was critical to the usability of the activity model but because publication was defined to operate at too low a level of abstraction, the overheads of this operation caused considerable problems, especially when a distribution layer was added to the IB.

But even if publication and allocation operate at a higher level of abstraction such as versions and variants by effectively excluding some of the basic IBE and IBS catalog structures from the scope of domains, there are still difficulties. Where should the boundary be drawn? How should relationships between those entities which are published be made visible? (i.e. what is the visibility of version graphs and configurations if versions and variants are the basic units of publication?). In particular, if the end user of the IPSE is to be presented with an extensible set of objects and relationships (in other words, if the underlying database implementation of the process model is allowed to show through and the user is allowed to define new types of object and relationship in a further customisation of the IPSE kit), then the concurrency control mechanisms must themselves be made extensible and capable of capturing whatever semantics are appropriate for the new models of the software development process defined by the IPSE user. The basic mechanisms of publish and allocate could be used as models for such extensions.

In the demonstration, simplistic solutions to these problems were adopted. The visibility of a component (or indeed the visibility of a component type) in turn made visible all versions of that component and all relationships between those versions in version graphs or configurations. Extensibility was not an issue because the user of the demonstration IPSE was presented with a fixed set of tools and objects (and indeed a fixed scenario). The rudimentary forms of publication that were implemented were effectively atomic and there was no double handshake involved. However, in general these issues and the various trade-offs involved are difficult and the solution is by no means clear cut. More work would have to be done on the integration of the various IBS facilities in order to resolve these questions. Despite this and in the interests of completeness, the implementation of the original double handshake mechanism is now described in the context of the version control system implemented for the demonstration. This represents one possible way of integrating a domain based concurrency mechanism with the demonstration IPSE. The implementation of an atomic publish operation which would have been used in the demonstration had time permitted is described later.

Publication

The principle underlying publication is this: while an object is visible to any domain other than the domain which created it, it cannot be modified. This also includes the case where the object is part of a configuration (e.g. released system) which is visible to other domains, even where the individual object (e.g. module specification) is no longer in use. In other words, an object on which anything else depends cannot be modified or deleted.

A domain owns a set of data items. In the simplest case, a domain would own only those data items it created and a user working within that domain would only be able to access those data items in the database. However, if a domain wishes to share any of its data items with other domains, it can invoke the *publish* operation. This prevents the owning domain from performing any further updates on the published item, ensuring that shared information is not updated. The published entity still cannot be read by the domain it was published to, but that domain is aware of its availability. In other words, the publish operation makes the entity published visible outside the domain which owns it.

In order to acquire read permission upon a published entity, a domain invokes the *acquire* operation. Acquire brings the entity into the domain's set of readable entities. The reason for this two step process to share data is that a domain user should have control over the data accessible within that domain. When a data item is published to a domain, it is up to the domain user to decide when it is appropriate to acquire that data item and make use of it.

At some point a domain may no longer wish to keep a published entity. The *dispose* operation cancels the effect of having acquired the object, and makes it no longer readable by the disposing domain. However, at this point the disposing domain is still able to re-acquire the entity should it wish to be able to read it again.

The original publisher of the entity may wish to regain write permission upon the entity. This is achieved by invoking the *withdraw* operation at any time after publication. As long as the published entity is not within the readable set of any other domain, the withdrawn entity is re-introduced into the writable set for the domain which originally published it. However, if the entity is readable by some other domain (i.e. it has been acquired but not yet disposed of by that domain), then further acquisition is prevented, and the re-introduction is deferred until the entity is disposed by all domains reading it.

Withdrawal cancels the effect of the publish operation, permitting the owner to perform updates on the contents of the object. However, updates are only permitted if the object had not yet been incorporated into any configurations. Once an object has been used in the development of others (by being designed, compiled, or linked, for instance), it has been included in a configuration and may therefore not be withdrawn. Using a version control system, updates are therefore usually performed by creating revisions, not by modifying versions in situ in the version graph.

Allocation

Publication imposes the restriction that an object visible to other domains cannot be modified. The allocation mechanism is used to allow permission to develop objects to be transferred between domains

Like the publication mechanism, allocation involves a double handshake, passing on development permission. The unit over which development permission is held is the variant. As there is no variant entity type in the IB, only a sequence of versions, this permission associates the domain with the entry in the version-graph which marks the start of the sequence.

The following primitives make up the allocation mechanism.

(a)   *Allocate* – a domain allocates an object (i.e. a variant to be developed) to another domain. The allocating domain cannot develop the object further.

(b)   *Accept* – a domain to which an object has been allocated accepts the object, permitting it to develop the object further.

(c)   *Return* – a domain which has accepted an object returns it to the domain that was responsible for its allocation.

(d)   *Accept Return* – a domain which originally allocated an object accepts its return. This domain can now develop it again.

6.6.5 Permissions on versions

Publication and allocation can be seen as particular examples of operations in which permissions on objects are passed between domains. In the case of publication, one domain gives the other domain permission to read a version (and presumably permission to know of its existence) and at the same time permanently removes its own permission to update that version. In this section we consider some of the issues involved in implementing a more general mechanism for passing permissions between domains by considering the kinds of permission which exist and the rules which restrict when particular permissions can be shared.

The basic permissions on a version are summarised below. For most of the permissions described here, there is no limit on the number of domains that may have the permission simultaneously. However, two of the permissions can be held by at most one domain at a time and these are indicated by "(at most 1 domain)" following the description.

- Permission to know of its existence
- Permission to examine its contents, i.e. read it
- Permission to update its contents, i.e. write it (at most 1 domain)
- Permission to create a revision of it (at most 1 domain)
- Permission to create a variant of it
- Permission to know the existence of any revision
- Permission to know the existence of any variant of it
- Permission to know its parent

Only one domain may have the permission to update the contents of a version – update in place – but once the version has been published, then its contents can no longer be changed

Similarly, only one domain is allowed to create a revision of a version and once a revision of a particular version has been created then no domain may create another revision of that version. In principle, there is no need to restrict the number of domains that can create a variant of a version, but in practice a project may want to impose restrictions in order to prevent chaos. In order to do this, suitable rules would be incorporated in the IPSE at customisation time.

In addition to the basic permissions described here, there are also the permissions to give all these permissions. Consistency of the database is maintained if each domain is allowed to give any permissions that it has itself on a version to another domain. In each case it can retain the permission itself except if the permission is to update or create a revision. Indeed, the permission to update cannot be transferred at all because of the way that "private" is defined with respect to a single domain. However, there is no reason in principle why update permission should not be transferrable. The permission to create a revision must be transferred using the allocate mechanism so that there is still only one domain able to create the next revision of a version sequence.

Rules relating to permissions to give permissions will depend on the management style that the project wants to adopt. At one extreme, a project may have a management style in which, apart from update and revision, each domain can propagate permissions freely. At the other extreme, it could have a style in which one domain – a project manager like domain – could control all these permissions except, possibly, those relating to private versions. Deciding on appropriate rules to fit the management style is part of the customisation of the IPSE. More research is needed in order to establish what are good rules for controlling permissions and this would include the study of different styles of project management.

For simplicity, in the demonstration domains were allowed to propagate freely any permissions they themselves had on versions subject to the rules outlined above which avoid problems of concurrency control. For the most part, this meant giving other domains "read" permission on versions, i.e. publishing them. In addition, all domains had permission to scan the version graph and configuration associated with any version and to know the component of which it was a version.

Although the various permissions could be given to domains independently, a sensible policy would link related permissions and grant them simultaneously. For example, it would be foolish to grant a domain permission to create a revision or variant of a version, without also giving the domain permission to examine the contents of the version and permission to know of the version's existence

In the preceding discussion, the permissions described were those that a domain could exercise if it wished. A domain should also be able to suppress some of the permissions that it has in order to protect itself from mistakes. For example, it could temporarily make a private version read-only. Alternatively it could temporarily make a version not readable for some time.

6.6.6 The relationship of domains with the process model

Earlier it was stated that it was during the customisation phase of the IPSE that it was decided with what domains should be associated. It was suggested that this could be a user, a user in a role, a task that a user was performing while assuming some role, or yet something else. Some of the implications of these choices are outlined below.

user   Each user is associated with the same domain whatever role is being played or task is being performed. Since at most one user can be associated with a domain at any one time, a user cannot play two roles or perform two tasks at the same time. Provided that different users are associated with different domains then users are able to work without interference from each other.

role   Each user is associated with the same domain while playing a particular role. Provided that the domains for different roles are different, a user may play several roles simultaneously but only one task may be performed in each of these roles at any one time. However, if more than one user is associated with any role, this could lead to conflict unless only one of them is allowed to play the role at a time.

user/role   This is similar to the previous case except that, provided that different user/roles are associated with different domains, there should be no conflict between users.

task   Each task is associated with a domain. A user may work simultaneously on several tasks provided that they have different domains.

In the original implementation of the IBS, domains were associated with tasks. Furthermore, this association was one to one in that each task was associated with one domain and each domain was associated with one task. This had the disadvantage that when a task finished it was no longer possible to access its domain. It could not be accessed through the task that had finished nor could it be accessed through any other task. Consequently any objects which had been created in it and which had not been made known to any other domain were lost to users of the system for ever.

Ways around this problem include:

- Associating a domain with something which is more persistent than a task.

- Associating additional permanent tasks with each domain.

- Not allowing a task to complete until all objects of which it is aware are made known to at least one other domain.

 This could be achieved by publishing objects to, for example, the task that created the completing task, some task or tasks named in the task description or some permanent task which kept track of objects in the system which were temporarily in limbo. It is in any case desirable that any task description should state what should be done with the objects produced by the task and to what domains they should be published.

- Not allowing a task to finish unless the domain with which it is associated is empty.

 This would require some mechanism for the transfer of objects to other domains and a mechanism for deleting objects that will not be required again. Appropriate checks would have to be made that objects really will not be required again.

More research and experiment is needed to establish the best thing with which to associate a domain. Something more permanent than a task seems to be desirable and a suitable compromise appears to be the user/role. This gives users flexibility to do several tasks at once − provided they are done in different roles − and should not lead to conflict between users if each user/role is associated with a separate domain. For each task it is desirable to restrict the view that the user has of this domain to those objects that are relevant to the task. In terms of a task's description, this would be those objects specified with the *uses*, *produces* and *requires* relationships. A task to write a program would only require to see the particular modules involved and the tools to do the job. A task to check out how many modules were in the domain would require a wider view. The view would filter out objects that are not relevant to the task in hand with the advantage that:

- The screen was not cluttered
- The possibilities for accidental concurrent access and modification of objects in the domain were reduced. Remember that the user is responsible for making sure that concurrent access of objects in the same domain does not lead to inconsistencies, or if it does then recovering from any mistakes.

6.6.7 A simplified implementation of domains and publication

For the purposes of the demonstration, a simplified model of domains together with a generalised mechanism for publishing objects with arbitrary permissions between domains was implemented. This publication operation occurred atomically rather than with a double handshake and was therefore intended to be used when parameterised task descriptions were instantiated by supplying values for their bindings. Once a task had been instantiated in this way, and the objects specified by its bindings had been published to a suitable domain, then its execution could begin.

In keeping with the philosophy of indirection used in the implementation of the task system (described in Section 6.3.2), simple entity types were used in the implementation with the intention that they would be integrated later. In the event, there was not time to complete the integration and thus demonstrate the mechanism outlined above. Instead, a rudimentary form of publication was used to illustrate change requests being published between roles in the demonstration.

Domains were modelled very simply as follows:

Domain
domain_eatt

In other words, *domain* was just a dummy entity type to be used in association with other entity types.

From a domain, various objects will be available with specified permissions. Any user performing a task will be associated with a particular domain by virtue of being a user, a user in a role, a user in a role performing that task or some other criterion and will have displayed on his or her screen in some form those objects that are associated with that domain. The operations that it will be possible to perform on these objects will be determined by the permission associated with the object in the domain.

The association between objects and domains was modelled by the associative entity type, *public*.

Public				
public_eatt	public_ent	public_ent_et	public_dom	public_perm

(Note that the name "public" given to this entity type is possibly misleading in that objects that are private to a domain are also included in it.)

The attribute *public_ent* gives the surrogate of an object (entity) which is associated with the *domain* whose surrogate is given by *public_dom*.

The attribute *public_ent_et* is the type of the entity *public_ent* and does not need to be here as it can be discovered by querying the catalog. Indeed, duplicating this information in the *public* entity type goes against the principles of good data modelling. However it was included to speed up the operation of the system.

The permission associated with each entity in the domain is given by the attribute *public_perm*. This permission is a binary encoded number (or bitmask) of the form

$$0+1+2+4+8+16+...$$

where it is to be understood that each of the plus signs represents an optional addition. The interpretation of this permission will vary with the entity type of the object and it is for this reason that the entity type of each object is included as an attribute of the *public* entity type.

The ability to publish variants causes complications because there is no explicit *variant* entity type or instance that may be used to represent the variant. The permission to develop a variant should be associated with the variant in some way. A variant is a set of versions but it can be represented in a variety of ways. One possibility is by the appropriate variant link in the version graph. Other possibilities are the first and last versions in the version sequence. (Note that the last version in the sequence will not always be the same.) The permission to develop the variant could be associated with any of these representations. It was hoped to experiment with different ways of representing variants for the purposes of publication in the course of preparing the demonstration but there was not enough time to do so. Had work on the IBS been continued, the IB structures used by the version control system might have changed to include a *variant* entity type because of this difficulty (and a similar difficulty described in Section 6.3.5.4 which prevented binding to variants in task descriptions).

Since the *public* entity type is only intended to provide information about the sorts of objects that would have meaning for someone performing a task and that could therefore be displayed in some way on the screen during the performance of the task, only certain types of object will occur in instances of this entity type. A user of a domain will also have access to other objects of which he or she is unaware. Many of the objects of which a user is aware will be versions of entity types such as C programs and Z specifications. As versions are created and published to other domains, instances of the *public* entity type will be created to record this.

When the prototype IBS was being developed for the demonstration, it was not known with what is was best to associate domains; whether this should be user, role, user/role, task or something else. In order to facilitate experimentation with different ways of doing this, various associative entity types between *domain* and entity types such as *task*, *role*, *user_role* and *user* were created. The intention was that the actual association would be hidden by an operation to get the domain associated with a user by querying the appropriate IB structures to discover the *role*, *user_role* or *task* to which that user was assigned and then querying the appropriate association with a *domain*. Since all these associative entity types are essentially the same, a single example will be used to illustrate all of them, namely the *role_domain* entity type which associated a *role* with a *domain*.

Role_Domain		
role_domain_eatt	rd_role	rd_domain

In each experiment, only one of these entity types would be used. For example, if the experiment involved associating a *domain* with a *role*, then the *role_domain* entity type illustrated above would be queried to find out which domain corresponded to the role that the user was playing. The *public* entity type would then be queried to establish the objects that that domain knew about and these would be displayed on the screen. The operations that would be possible on these objects would be determined partly by their types and partly by the permission with which they were published to the domain, described by the *public* entity instance. C programs for example can be edited, compiled and debugged but a particular program might only have been published with read permission, effectively limiting the available operations to compilation. Operations would be presented to the user in the form of pop-up menus at appropriate times.

6.7 Rules

Rules (and views which are described in the next section) formed part of the original IBS. However, for reasons explained in Section 6.2, they did not form part of the revised IBS implemented for the demonstration, although it was always intended that they should be integrated eventually. Thus, they are described here for completeness and because they formed a considerable part of the original IBS concept.

The rules mechanism was intended to be used in conjunction with the activities mechanism which also formed part of the original IBS. The tasks described in Section 6.3 are a simplification of activities and do not make use of the rules mechanism in the same way. Thus, in order to put the rules mechanism into context, it is necessary to describe the original activity concept first.

6.7.1 Rules and activities

Activities represent pieces of work that must be carried out to further the progress of the project being modelled by the Aspect IPSE. As such, they are tasks which managers can allocate to their staff. An activity description must describe the purpose of the activity and what it is supposed to achieve. Activities are the only way in which tasks can be performed within the IPSE and consequently the Aspect notion of an activity must be capable of capturing every task associated with the software engineering project modelled by the IB. This means that the description of what an activity is supposed to achieve must be very flexible. For a low-level well-defined clerical task, the description can be very specific, whereas for a high-level managerial task it should be much less constraining to allow freedom of action. Different degrees of control may be appropriate for different parts of the project and different degrees of freedom may be appropriate to different roles within the project. An activity description could therefore be very rigid (specifying that certain actions should be carried out in a precise sequence) or very flexible (providing a list of possible actions but allowing the person performing the activity complete freedom to choose whichever action was most appropriate). Indeed, at its most general, an activity might have no purpose as such but might simply provide a framework in which a person could carry out actions to further the project. Such an activity would allow a manager to define more specific activities to be carried out by other members of the project but would not seek to control the actions performed by the manager.

The need for a general purpose mechanism to describe what an activity can do has resulted in Aspect providing several ways of expressing such constraints. However, this is not inappropriate since Aspect is intended to be a customisable IPSE kit that can be used to build many different specialised IPSEs, each embodying a particular project management strategy or methodology.

Using rules to describe the purpose of an activity

The most flexible way of expressing constraints on what an activity can do is to use a declarative approach, describing what the activity must achieve but not how it is to be achieved. Such constraints may be expressed in the form of pre- and post-conditions or rules describing what must be true before and after the activity is executed and how the final state of the IB after the activity has been executed is related to the initial state of the IB before execution of the activity begins. This relationship describes the transformation of the IB that the activity is designed to effect in order to further the project but not the mechanism by which this transformation is to be brought about.

Executing an activity involves invoking tools and operations on objects. Tools are prescriptive in the sense that the implementor of the tool has prescribed in detail the sequence of more primitive tools and operations which the tool will invoke on its operands in order to achieve the action that it is designed to achieve. However, the person who invokes the tool is only concerned with the transformation of the IB that the tool will effect and not the mechanism by which this is achieved. In this sense, tools may be thought of as being declarative.

Each tool invocation achieves a certain transformation of the IB and by composing tool invocations it is possible to build up a greater and greater transformation until eventually the transformation specified declaratively for the activity as a whole is achieved. An activity description can declare the transformation it is supposed to achieve and prescribe the tools by which this transformation is to be achieved without specifying the order in which the tools are to be invoked or the operands on which they are to be invoked. Unfortunately, it is therefore possible to define an activity whose declared purpose cannot be achieved with the tools prescribed for the activity, and it is the responsibility of the person defining the activity to ensure that this cannot happen. In practice, this is unlikely to be a problem because an activity with a specific purpose will be prescribed specific tools for that purpose, whereas a more general purpose activity may not be required to achieve any particular purpose (in other words, its post-condition may be very weak or even trivially satisfied, i.e. "true"). Such an activity may not be required to terminate or may simply act as a framework in which more specific activities are defined and executed.

Using rules to constrain the execution of an activity

A purely declarative statement of what an activity is supposed to achieve does not of course provide any guidance as to how the person performing the activity is to achieve the declared goal of the activity. Aspect therefore provides two mechanisms for constraining the actions performed in the execution of an activity. These mechanisms provide guidance to the person performing the task modelled by the activity whilst allowing the person who defined the activity to maintain some degree of control over the course of its execution.

The first mechanism is again based on the notion of rules and is therefore very general purpose. Just as the designer of an activity may specify rules that must be satisfied before and after the activity is executed (its pre- and post-conditions), so also is it possible to specify rules that must be satisfied during the execution of the activity. These rules serve to constrain the actions which may be performed in the process of carrying out the activity and achieving its declared goal. As such, they serve more as a control mechanism than a guidance mechanism, although obviously such rules could be so precise that at each stage of executing the activity, only one action was possible.

Imposing constraints on the execution of an activity introduces the problem of granularity. At what stage should such rules be checked? Are they at least conceptually always in force, or is it possible for them to be relaxed temporarily? Are rules checked between each action (tool invocation) or during each tool invocation? Conceptually, such rules should be checked continuously which in practice would mean that rules would be checked every time a primitive operation was invoked on the IB both before, during and after the invocation to ensure that the constraints expressed by the rules were not violated. However, continuous rule checking might well prove impractical for performance reasons. A more realistic compromise would be to analyse the content of the rules and deduce from knowledge of the structure and semantics of the IB and the operations allowed on it which operations were capable of violating which rules. In this way rule checking could be optimised so that each rule was only checked when there was a possibility that it might have been broken. These issues are discussed further in a later section.

Relaxing the constraints expressed by rules

A rule-based system that only allowed constraints to be imposed and never relaxed would be too inflexible to be useful in practice. Consequently, Aspect makes a distinction between those rules which act as invariants of the IB and can therefore never be broken, and those rules which are only appropriate at a certain level of abstraction and may usefully be violated within that abstraction (and indeed in some cases must be violated in order to achieve the ends of that abstraction). For this purpose, the rules in an activity definition that express constraints on the execution of the activity are divided up into two sets. The given rules are those rules which must be true at all times (the invariants of the model) and the applicable rules are those rules which may be temporarily relaxed in a controlled fashion. If an activity delegates some of the task it is intended to perform to a sub-activity, then although the applicable rules for the parent activity must be satisfied at the end of the execution of the child activity, some of the applicable rules may be relaxed during the execution of the child activity. In this way, the applicable rules for an activity act as post-conditions for any child activity which the activity may spawn but do not apply within the child activity. In contrast, the given rules of an activity must be satisfied not only at all times during the execution of that activity but also during the execution of any child activity associated with the activity (and recursively within any child activities associated with those children and so on).

Using plans to prescribe the execution of an activity

The ability to express the constraints on an activity in the form of not just pre- and post-conditions but also given and applicable rules to be enforced during the execution of the activity gives the designer of an activity a fine degree of control over the activity being defined. However, since such rules are purely declarative, they do not provide much guidance for the person responsible for executing the activity as to how best to go about their task. Such guidance requires a more prescriptive approach, in effect a plan to govern the execution of an activity. This is the second mechanism for guidance alluded to above.

Just as a programming task may be broken up into sub-tasks and structured using constructs such as sequence, choice and iteration, so does Aspect provide facilities for an activity designer to provide what is in effect a very high level program describing the execution of the activity in terms of sub-activities structured using the same constructs of sequence, choice and iteration. Although each sub-activity is purely declarative, the plan which describes how the sub-activities are joined together and executed to achieve the goal of the parent activity is prescriptive, providing a rigid framework in which the execution of the various sub-activities is to be carried out. However, although this framework constrains the person responsible for executing an activity to perform various sub-activities in a certain order, it is still flexible enough to allow the designer of the activity to change his mind and provide a different plan for any part of the overall activity which has not yet been completed. Thus, activities may be recursively decomposed into sub-activities according to some plan but at any level of the hierarchy the plan for executing a particular activity may be modified dynamically whilst that activity is in progress. The ability to modify the plan for some or all of an activity is something that the designer of the activity may choose to pass on to the person responsible for executing the activity. Some parts of the activity may deliberately be left undefined so that no pre-defined plan is imposed. Alternatively, the way to perform some task may be rigidly defined in terms of performing some fixed sub-tasks in a particular order with no scope for variation.

As with any general purpose mechanism, the extent to which the structure of an activity is prescribed with a plan in this way will depend on the purpose of the activity and the abilities of the person carrying out the activity. However, the mechanism allows a plan to be provided to whatever level of detail is felt to be necessary or appropriate. For an activity whose course cannot be predicted in advance or an activity whose nature is such as to preclude computerised guidance because a high degree of human judgement is required in its execution, it may not be appropriate to supply a plan at all. On the other hand, for a very mechanical task or a task whose execution is specified by the particular methodology embedded in the customised Aspect IPSE, it may be appropriate to define a completely rigid and inflexible plan in advance which will neither require nor need any modification during the execution of the task it describes. In practice, the plan for an activity will lie somewhere in between, providing an appropriate degree of guidance but leaving some of the details unspecified. Consequently, the order in which sub-activities and actions are performed in pursuit of some overall goal will in part reflect a predefined plan and in part reflect the exercise of free will by the person responsible for executing the overall activity.

Using plans to satisfy the goal of an activity

The plan for an activity serves to guide the execution of that activity by dividing it up into a series of smaller executions of sub-activities. The combined effect of executing these sub-activities is to achieve the goal of the parent activity. The plan may provide guidance in achieving this in two ways. Firstly, it may serve to enforce some methodology or project management strategy adopted by the project modelled by the IPSE. If this methodology or strategy requires certain tasks to be broken up into sub-tasks or certain steps to be followed in the correct order, then this can be reflected in the design of the plan for an activity representing these tasks. For this reason, the ability to supply a plan to guide the execution of an activity is a vital part of the mechanism for customising the Aspect IPSE kit to support a particular methodology. This degree of control is necessary in order to ensure that an IPSE is truly integrated, containing a set of cooperating tools rather than a bunch of competing utilities.

The second way in which a plan can guide the execution of an activity is by providing a way of satisfying the post-condition describing the goal of the activity. In the same way that it is possible to derive a correct program formally from its pre- and post-conditions, it is possible to derive an activity plan that will decompose an activity into sub-activities in such a way that the combined effect of achieving the post-conditions of each sub-activity will guarantee the post-condition of the overall activity. By decomposing this post-condition into its constituent predicates, it is possible to construct a plan which decomposes the execution of the activity into sub-activities whose post-conditions match one of these predicates. For example, if the post-condition is of the form "A or B" then an appropriate plan might be to decompose the activity into two sub-activities, one to achieve A and one to achieve B. The person responsible for executing the activity and carrying out this plan would then choose to execute whichever of these sub-activities was most appropriate. Similarly, if the post-condition of the activity represented a strengthening of its pre-condition, then an iterative plan might be appropriate, decomposing the activity into a sub-activity whose iteration could progressively strengthen the pre-condition of the parent activity until its post-condition was met. The fact that the techniques used in the formal construction of programs may also be used to construct activity plans should come as no surprise as activity plans are themselves just programs (albeit at a very high level of abstraction).

Summary

To summarise, an activity description describes the purpose of the activity using pre- and post-conditions, imposes constraints on the execution of the activity with given and applicable rules, and provides a plan to guide the execution of the activity through a series of sub-activities. The activity description also describes which objects in the IB the activity is allowed to access or modify during its execution. The rules and constraints that govern the execution of the activity are written in terms of these objects which therefore serve to parameterise the activity description. Activities are central to the IBS because they provide the framework about which all the other components of the IBS are integrated.

6.7.2 The use of rules in the IBS

Unlike many existing databases or project support environments, in addition to a set of built-in rules which are always applied, Aspect allows users to define new rules appropriate to organisational or personal needs, and provides a number of mechanisms for applying these rules. This rules system is used to perform a number of functions:

(i)   Rules which are built into the system have as their primary purpose the maintenance of the referential integrity of the database (as described in the previous chapter on the Information Base Engine);

(ii)   User-defined rules can be used to impose other **integrity constraints** on the state of the IB. In Aspect, such integrity constraints are handled as part of the definition and execution of the high level **activities** governing all work carried out in an Aspect system.

(iii)   As pre- and post-conditions, user-defined rules are also used to define the activities mentioned in (ii) above.

Hence, the full functionality of the rules system can only be understood in relation to Aspect's process model which governs the way activities are defined and executed. Functions (ii) and (iii) of the rules system were described in more detail in the previous section. In the following sections, the discussion of rules will be confined to describing:

● The types of rules which can be defined in Aspect;

● How rules are actually defined and enforced using RM/T's relation algebra query language.

6.7.3 Classification of rules

Two broad categories of database rule can be identified [40]:

1.   Domain rules;

2.   Relation rules.

Domain rules are those which specify the legitimate value sets which may be associated with particular domains, whereas **relation rules** can be used as a flexible way of further constraining the set of values permitted by the domain rules.

In the reference quoted above, Date further classifies relation rules depending on whether they are:

(i)   **record vs set**, i.e does the rule refer to one record or a set of records;

(ii)   **state vs transition**, i.e. does the rule refer to a particular state of the IB or does it involve a comparison of one state with another;

(iii)   **immediate vs deferred**, i.e. must the database be in conformity with the rule at all times or can there be periods (until the end of a transaction, say) during which integrity is not maintained.

Aspect caters for all these different types of rule. However, the rules mechanism described here as part of the IBS only deals with relation rules. Domain rules are tied in with the facilities for defining value sets provided as part of the database operations in the IBE.

An important category of relation rules are those associated with referential integrity. In the previous chapter describing the IBE, it was shown how referential integrity constraints are built into RM/T. This section will not concern itself with built-in referential integrity but concentrate on relation rules which can be user-defined.

The Aspect rules mechanism makes a clear distinction between state and transitional rules and allows both **static** and **transition** rules to be defined. However, no distinction, in terms of definition, is made between rules which are immediate and those which are deferred. Instead, in Aspect, it is left to the process model to provide the facilities which determine whether rules will be applied immediately or whether they will be deferred until the end of a particular activity. Also, no distinction is made between rules which concern one record (or tuple) in the database and those which reference sets of records.

6.7.4 Informal description of rules mechanism

Defining rules

At the most abstract level, rules in Aspect are functions, and as mentioned above are of two types:

1.   Static – those rules which map all possible states of the IB onto TRUE or FALSE.
2.   Transition – those rules which map all possible transitions of the IB from one state to another onto TRUE or FALSE.

We term the definitions given above as **extensional** in that they associate a Boolean value with every possible state of the IB. (This is analogous to defining a set by explicitly listing every one of its members.) Clearly, in practice rules cannot be defined in this way, but rather more conventionally using some form of Boolean expression. This is termed the rule's **intension**. Later, in Section 6.6.4, some examples will be given of how the intension of a rule is defined in Aspect using RM/T's relational algebra.

Enforcing rules

As mentioned above, the full functionality of rules in Aspect can only be realised in their association with the process model. Rules which must be enforced during the execution of an activity to ensure the integrity of the IB are called **applicable** rules. Every activity has associated with it two sets of applicable rules: one composed of static and the other of transition rules. Both sets of applicable rules are enforced whenever atomic changes are made to the IB during the course of the activity in question. The fact that all activities can be started within the context of a higher level activity means that the sets of applicable rules can also be changed. It is this facility which allows the application of particular rules to be deferred – in other words, switched on and off. Applicable rules which cannot be deferred but must be enforced at all times are called **given** rules.

Rules may also be used to define activities in terms of pre- and post-conditions. Each activity is defined by means of:

- One set of pre-conditions which are all static rules;
- Two sets of post-conditions, one of which is composed of static and the other of transition rules.

Before an activity can start, its pre-conditions must be enforced and likewise before the activity can be successfully completed, both its sets of post-conditions must be enforced.

Aspect provides automatic mechanisms to enforce all these different sets of rules. But, in addition, it also provides a mechanism for the user to check a set of rules, either static or transition, at any stage during the course of an activity.

Consistent sets of rules

An important consideration when defining any of these different sets of rules is that they be **consistent**. By this we mean:

(i)   In the case of a set of static rules, that there is at least one state of the IB, common to them all, which maps to true;

(ii) In the case of a set of transition rules, that there are transitions which map to true in all the members.

Consistency is an easy property to specify for a set of rules. However, in practice, it is much more difficult to guarantee that a set of rules has this property.

Operations on rules

Aspect provides a number of operators with which to manipulate rules. The operators allow the user to:

- Create and delete rules;
- Create and delete sets of rules;
- Include and remove rules from various sets of rules such as the set of applicable rules, a set of pre-conditions, etc.

6.7.5 The intension of a rule

In this section, we show how an intensional definition of rules is implemented in a running Aspect system.

The query language of RM/T is based on the relational algebra. As a query language this allows the user to retrieve a tuple or sets of tuples which satisfy various conditions or constraints. But looked at another way the language can also be used to specify the conditions which a tuple or sets of tuples must always satisfy. For example, given a relation, PROGRAMMER, which lists all programmers and their ages, we can find all those who are over 18 by using the relational algebra expression:

select(PROGRAMMER, (age > 18))

However, suppose we wish to have a rule that all programmers in the relation must be over the age of 18. This could be specified in the relational algebra by writing an expression which selected all programmers of 18 years or younger and then stipulated that this set of tuples should be empty. Adopting the convention that, if a relational expression returns a relation containing at least one tuple, it is TRUE, otherwise if the result is empty it is FALSE, and adding the syntax that NOT changes TRUE to FALSE and vice versa, the rule can be written as:

NOT select (PROGRAMMER, (age <= 18))

To understand this rule, it is helpful to follow the steps the system would perform when enforcing it. First of all, the relational expression in brackets selects all programmers aged 18 or less. The set of tuples returned by this expression should be empty. But according to the convention referred to above this would cause the rule to return FALSE. However, the NOT reverses this and so the rule will return TRUE if there are no tuples, which is what we want.

Technically, this use of NOT is a simple way of obtaining universal quantification. In the example rule above, we wanted all programmers to satisfy a certain condition. This is equivalent to saying that there should not exist any programmers who do not fulfill the condition.

Another example assumes the existence of an EMPLOYEE relation having two attributes, 'sub_emp' and 'sup_emp' representing an employee and his/her supervisor. We can express the rule:

every manager is also an employee

as follows:

NOT difference(project(EMPLOYEE, sup_emp),
project(EMPLOYEE, sub_emp))

This rule can be explained as follows: the relation obtained by projecting EMPLOYEE onto the attribute 'sup_emp' must be a subset of the same relation projected onto 'sub_emp'. In terms of the relational algebra this means that if we take the difference of the first relation with the second, the resulting relation should be empty. Hence the use of the NOT.

Another rule stating that

no employee should have more than one manager

can be written as follows:

NOT select(product(EMPLOYEE, EMPLOYEE),
sub_emp = sub_emp1 & sup_emp != sup_emp1)

This looks complicated but merely expresses the fact that if the relational product is taken of the EMPLOYEE relation with itself (with suitable renaming of attribute values not shown here), then there should be no entries in the resulting table for which the 'sub_emp' attributes are the same but the 'sup_emp' attributes are different. This condition is checked for by selecting out those tuples which satisfy its inverse and applying NOT to the result which should be empty if the rule is true.

So far we have only given examples of static rules. Transition rules are defined in exactly the same way. However, their implementation relies on a mechanism for recording the 'before' and 'after' states when changes are made to the IB. Since changes will be made to an Aspect IB using a nested activity structure, this mechanism would be extremely complicated to implement.

The following points concerning the implementation of the Aspect rules mechanism should be noted:

(i)   By using the query language for the IB as the basis for defining rules, there is no need to implement a complicated new mechanism for checking rules. To check a rule, all the software needs to do is:

* run the query associated with the rule;
* check whether the resulting relation has tuples in it or not;
* then return TRUE or FALSE depending on whether or not the query is proceeded by NOT.

(ii) Not every rule has to be checked when changes are made to the IB. For example, referential integrity constraints only need to be checked when data is added to or deleted from the IB. Other rules may only be relevant when existing data is updated (See [40]). The Aspect system does not provide this level of sophistication. As described above, the rules system, in the context of a nested activity model is already highly complex. At this stage, it was not considered prudent to add another level of complexity.

(iii) Rules for a database system are often specified to contain an action which should be carried out if the rule is not satisfied. At present, the Aspect system does not offer this level of functionality. All that happens is that the operation in question fails and the user is informed which rule or rules have failed.

6.7.6 Summary

In this section we have described in outline some of the facilities which can be offered by the Aspect rules system. This was done informally.

The main points to note about this rules system are as follows:

(i)   Rules are categorised as built-in or user-defined, static or transition.

(ii) They can be used to:

* specify integrity constraints (applicable rules) on the state of the IB, which are enforced whenever this state is changed;
* define activities using pre- and post-conditions.

(iii) Applicable rules and pre- and post-conditions are automatically enforced by the system.

(iv) However, a mechanism is also provided to enable the user to check a set of static or transition rules.

(v)   Operations are provided to create and delete static and transition rules as well as include and remove rules from a set.

(vi) An actual Aspect system uses the relational algebra associated with RM/T as a basis for defining rules. This means that the mechanism for running queries can be used to check rules.

The full significance of the rules system can only be appreciated in terms of the Aspect process model which is driven and controlled by the use and application of the rules mechanism.

6.8 Views

One of the consequences of maintaining data in a shared database is that all applications which access the data must work with a single, pre-defined set of data structures and operators. However, in some database applications, and particularly software engineering, a large and diverse group of users and applications will wish to make use of the data. For example, it is expected that a complete IPSE would be used by project managers, quality assurance groups, clerical and administrative staff, as well as software engineers and programmers.

Another problem concerns the porting of existing development tools to an IPSE. Such tools may need to be rewritten to use the database facilities provided by the IPSE. The interface to which tools are written, often known as the Public Tool Interface (PTI), needs to be stable, but if it cannot be extended, the following observations can be made:

- Data structures and operators suited to one application, or class of user, may be inefficient, unnatural, and time-consuming to other users;

- The level at which database interaction occurs through the PTI may be too abstract for some users (e.g. programmers), while too low-level for others (e.g. project managers). The working requirements of these users are very different;

- There will be some data which is of relevance to only a subset of users, and we may want to restrict access to such data to other users so that they are not confused by this unnecessary information;

- Often databases contain sensitive information which we may not wish to be generally available. Many different levels of security may exist, and we need a mechanism to control access to data at different levels. For example, if an IPSE is used in the development of a large, real-time application, we would need to record data about project costings, security procedures used by the application, and intimate details of working practices. It would not be desirable to allow all IPSE users access to this information;

- For similar reasons, we may want to restrict the operations different classes of user are allowed to perform on data. For example, at the lowest level, a user may be given read-only access to certain information.

Early in the development of conventional database systems the need for such functions became apparent and solutions were devised. A mechanism often used to tackle some or all of these problems is the creation of external **views** of the underlying database.

A view mechanism allows the creation of abstract interfaces to a database. Each interface can be tailored to a particular class of user's needs, at an abstract level suited to those users' style of interaction. The view mapping, which defines the interface in terms of the underlying database, filters out unnecessary or sensitive data, and may derive new abstract data and operators. Each user is working at an abstract level suited to their particular role, and as a result, may make quicker progress with their task, interfere less with other users, and consequently produce more accurate results.

In a software engineering application, the ability to provide abstract tool interfaces to the PTI, and in this way extend the PTI, is particularly useful. Clearly tools which access the data will interact with the database at different abstract levels, which a view mechanism can support. More importantly, it is expected that existing tools will be ported to new IPSEs, potentially requiring a great deal of rewriting. A view mechanism, however, could be used to define abstract interfaces to the database which allows tools to run in the new environment with a minimum amount of change.

An attempt at designing and implementing such a views mechanism is discussed below within the context of the Aspect IBS. It is expected, however, that many of the ideas described here are independent of the IPSE used.

6.8.1 The basis of a view mechanism for an IPSE

Having discussed the need for a view mechanism, it is necessary to examine existing mechanisms which have been used in similar situations in order to provide the kind of functionality we are seeking. In particular, we can look at the traditional database notion of a view to see how it can be adapted to an IPSE. In fact, we will see that the extension of a view mechanism towards abstract data types is required.

Traditional database views

In existing database systems, views are used in a very simple way to provide abstractions of the data [96,6]. Through the definition of a view, a new abstract data object can be created which is some combination of existing data objects. In this way, a view is synonymous with a stored query, defined (for relational databases) using the relational algebra or calculus provided by the database system. Whenever access to a view is required, the stored query is evaluated within the context of the current state of the database. Hence, a database view can be thought of as a "window" on the database.

Nesting of views to any level is also possible, by using one view object in the definition of another view. When a nested view is evaluated, we can envisage a tree of stored queries being evaluated in an interpretive fashion (as an optimisation this interpretive process is often pre-compiled).

Though the simplicity and elegance of this approach are attractive, there are a number of drawbacks to this when we wish to design a view mechanism for an IPSE that provides environments in which tools and users access data.

1. Providing a closed environment.

We would like tools and users to operate in an environment which is closed in the sense that the only access to data is through the objects provided in that environment. We do not want users to be able to access lower-level objects, by-passing the interface that has been provided. In existing database view mechanisms, however, the view objects that are defined are used to extend the set of data objects available to users, and access to all objects is possible.

2. Defining abstract operators.

Existing database view mechanisms only allow abstraction of data via stored queries, not the ability to define new abstract operators on the data. For an IPSE view mechanism, we need to be able to create environments in which users work that include abstract operators to manipulate the available data objects. Such operators are an essential component of an environment.

3. Updating view objects.

A well-documented problem with database view mechanisms is the issue of updating view objects [72, 8]. The usual approach is to devise an algorithm which decides by examining the definition of the object whether it is possible to insert, update, or delete elements of that object. When it is not possible to uniquely determine the inverse of the object mapping, then updates to the object are not allowed.

For an IPSE view mechanism, this approach is unsatisfactory as we wish to have the choice of whether or not to allow updates to all view objects, irrespective of their definition. Only in this way will we have the necessary generality to allow the possibility of creating arbitrary interfaces to the data. In the traditional database approach, the decision as to whether an update of a view object is allowed is made as a consequence of the way the object was defined. In IPSE databases a more flexible approach is required, so that the view definer can have greater control over which objects are updatable. For example, we may want a restricted "read-only" environment for some users, even though update of the data objects is possible for others.

Views and abstract data types

The approach we have taken to designing an IPSE view mechanism is to extend the traditional database notion of a view by incorporating ideas used in programming languages that allow the creation of abstract data types (ADTs) [88].

Like the "package" concept of Ada (and similar constructs in other languages), an ADT allows us to create abstractions of the basic data structures and operators available in the language, and provides strict support for enforcing those abstractions [15]. An ADT basically consists of two parts; a set of data structures, and a set of operators which manipulate those structures.

The data structures provided are derived from existing lower-level data objects by a re-definition using the constructs available in the programming language. This is analogous to defining a view object from lower-level objects using the relational algebra or calculus as the host language. However, with ADTs, a hierarchy of data structures is enforced. The new structures are derived from a set of parent structures, without any knowledge of other lower-level structures. Hence, a strict hierarchy of abstract data objects is constructed.

The other component of an ADT is a set of operators which manipulate the defined data structures. These operators are expressed in a host programming language, and make calls to the defined parent operators, which manipulate the parent data structures. A strict abstract operator hierarchy is constructed, similar to the hierarchy for abstract data objects.

An advantage of this approach is that manipulative and update operators are both similarly defined. This means that all the update operators required for an ADT have pre-defined effects on the data structures. No changes to the data structures are possible other than through these operators.

Therefore, we can view the definition of an ADT in a program as the creation of an abstract interface to the data structures of the program, with both data and operators tailored to the needs of a particular application. The view mechanism needed for an IPSE can be seen as the use of an ADT mechanism on top of the IPSE database. The first steps toward this have already been taken in existing database systems, using a simple view mechanism to allow abstract data objects to be defined and accessed. What is proposed here is to extend that mechanism to more closely resemble the ADT approach.

However, an important distinction between the programming language approach to ADTs and the view mechanism needed for an IPSE concerns the support given at a project level, as opposed to a programming level. In most programming languages, data is not persistent between program invocations other than through very simple file-based mechanisms. The ADT mechanisms are provided for use with transitory data in the execution of a single program. Clearly, in an IPSE application it is necessary to provide a project level view mechanism which acts on data that is both structured and persistent. The data should be available for many different programs, users, and tools to operate on, in the same way that traditional database systems allow many diverse groups within a large enterprise access to the same set of data.

We now describe how an IPSE view mechanism based on these principles has been specified as part of the Aspect IBS.

6.8.2 The Aspect view mechanism

Recognising the arguments presented above, an important feature of the Aspect PTI is that it includes facilities for its own extension through a view mechanism. This means that a set of primitive functions are available at the PTI to enable users and tools to define and make use of abstract data and operators in a structured and controlled way.

The approach taken in Aspect is to insist that all users of an Aspect system work within an **abstract environment** (**AE**) which provides an abstract interface to the Aspect system built upon the facilities available at the PTI. The AE provides a set of data objects and operators tailored to that particular class of user's needs. The user cannot access the IB other than through the facilities offered in their AE. Thus, when a user is assigned an activity to be carried out in the Aspect system, that user is also given an AE in which to execute the activity. This will provide the data and operators necessary to perform the activity at an abstract level which is appropriate to the task.

Similarly, Aspect can support 'foreign' tools that have not been written to use the primitives specified at the Aspect PTI by providing them with an AE that emulates their native operating environment. The data and operators seen by this tool will be mapped to underlying Aspect PTI operations by this AE, which in turn will make controlled calls to the Information Base.

By way of an example, we will examine the approach used in Aspect to allow Unix tools to operate within an Aspect IPSE. The tools provided by Unix are written to use a set of primitives which allow access to the Unix operating system and file system facilities. For example, data is presented as a collection of files related in a tree structure, and operators exist to open files, read data from a file, and close files. If Unix tools are to be made available in an Aspect system, then there are three possible ways in which they could be integrated:

1. As Aspect is hosted on a Unix system, these tools could be allowed to by-pass the Aspect PTI and directly interact with the operating system;

2. The tools could be partially rewritten to make Aspect PTI calls instead of Unix system calls;

3. A view of the Aspect PTI could be defined that closely resembled the Unix system call interface. With minimum modification, the tools could then run within this view, and still access the Aspect services through the PTI.

The first of these alternatives was rejected as it destroys the desired uniformity of approach to tool integration that Aspect intends to provide, it side-steps the semantically-rich interface offered at the PTI, and it binds Aspect to the Unix operating system as its host. The second possibility is unattractive as it requires a great deal of redundant work rewriting tools that already exist. The third alternative, which has been adopted by Aspect, means that all tools, written to any interface, can be uniformly integrated into an Aspect system by defining a suitable view of the Aspect PTI. By insisting that all data access and manipulation is ultimately performed through the PTI, the integrity constraints enforced there are consistently applied. This special Unix view of the PTI is known as the Aspect Open Tool Interface (OTI).

Hierarchies of AEs

It is intended that the Aspect view mechanism will be used at a project level, with the definition of AEs taking place in a hierarchical fashion mirroring the traditional project structure. Hence, all the objects available in one AE will be defined purely in terms of those in its parent AE in the hierarchy. The lowest level AE at the root of this hierarchy, known as the Base Environment, is the complete Aspect PTI itself, available to manipulate all the data maintained in the IB with the operators provided at the PTI. As each AE is created, and the AE hierarchy is extended, interfaces to the IB will be provided at increasingly higher abstract levels.

Operating within a particular AE in this hierarchy, the evaluation of a data object, or execution of an operation, will result in this call being interpreted at successively lower levels, until a sequence of calls to Aspect PTI functions is made on the lowest level data items. These operations will then be executed to create the effect requested by the single high level operation.

6.8.3 A simple example

To illustrate the Aspect view mechanism in use, consider the simple example given below.

Suppose data is held in the IB concerning programmers, change requests for software components, and assignments of programmers to carry out these change requests. Represented in simple relational terms, the IB may contain the following data:

PROGRAMMERS		
PROG_ID	NAME	AGE
p1	fred	32
p2	joe	21
p3	jane	26

CHANGE REQUESTS			
CR_ID	DESCRIPTION	REPORT DATE	STATUS
cr1	fault in output	12-10-85	outstanding
cr2	crashes on input	8-11-85	completed
cr3	update documentation	23-6-86	outstanding
cr4	add new option	15-7-86	outstanding

ASSIGNMENTS		
PROG_ID	CR_ID	DEADLINE
p1	cr1	18-3-86
p2	cr2	20-8-86
p2	cr4	7-10-86

Coupled with this data will be a set of operators to insert, delete and update individual tuples of each relation.

This lowest level view, or Base Environment, will be used by the project controller who is responsible for all project data, and for initially setting up the AE hierarchy. For example, the project controller may wish to define an AE for the chief programmer which shows all assigned change requests with the programmers assigned to them, and also includes an operator to change the status of a change request to "completed" when the change has been carried out by a junior programmer.

To do this, the project controller, who is working within the Base Environment, will define the data objects and operators necessary for the chief programmer's AE in terms of the data and operators available in the Base Environment. When the chief programmer works in this AE, it may contain the following data:

CR_ID	DESC.	REPORTED	STATUS	NAME	END
cr1	fault in output	12-10-85	outstanding	fred	18-3-86
cr2	crashes on input	8-11-85	completed	joe	20-8-86
cr4	add new option	15-7-86	outstanding	joe	7-10-86

Also, an operator "change-status" will be available, which, given the identifier of a change request in the data object, will change the status of that request from "outstanding" to "completed". This operator will have been defined by the project controller as a sequence of lower level operations to insert, delete, and update individual tuples of relations using the operators provided in the BE.

Now suppose the chief programmer wishes to define an AE in which a junior programmer can work that only allows that programmer to see their own outstanding change requests, and does not give them any operators to amend those change requests. The chief programmer would do this by defining the junior programmer's AE in terms of the data and operators available in his own AE. In effect, the newly defined AE would be a further abstraction of what the chief programmer has available.

For example, the AE defined for programmer p2 (who has been assigned change requests cr2 and cr4 of which cr4 is still outstanding) would contain the data shown below. However, no operators would be defined to manipulate or update this data.

CR_ID	DESCRIPTION	DEADLINE
cr4	add new option	7-10-86

The final result, then, will be a simple hierarchy of AEs with the Base Environment at the root, and the chief programmer and junior programmer AEs at subsequent levels.

Clearly, this is an over-simplified example to give a flavour of the Aspect view mechanism in operation. Without much difficulty, it is possible to envisage how this example could be extended to support a much larger project.

6.8.4 Views and domains

The concurrency control mechanism described in Section 6.6 provides each user with a partition (not necessarily disjoint) of the data in the IB which reduces the possibility of interference between users. In Figure 6.12 an IB is shown divided between three overlapping domains.

In a simple way, this provides each user with a view of the IB appropriate to the work they carry out. In effect each user has been provided with a restriction of the data available.

The view mechanism just described is a way of providing tailored interfaces to the IB which are most appropriate for the users interacting with the data. This must be integrated with the concurrency control mechanism.

In fact, there is no conflict between these two mechanisms, rather they complement each other. A user assuming a particular role will work within a domain associated with that role. This provides a restricted set of IB data, notably limiting the user's access to only those versions of data which are appropriate. Then, to perform a task, the user's access to data is further constrained by having to work within a view of that domain. The view may not only further restrict the data visible, it may also provide an abstraction of it to allow the user to carry out the task by interacting with abstract data items which are appropriate for the job in hand. Thus, where more than one task is assigned to a role, there may be a different view

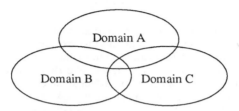

Fig. 6.12 Overlapping domains in the IB

associated for each of the tasks. For example, within a customer services role there may be a different view associated with the task of logging customer requests than with the task of producing an outstanding requests report, although the tasks share the same underlying domain. This is illustrated in Figure 6.13.

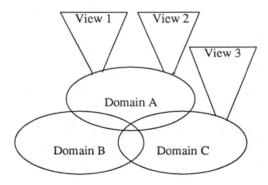

Fig. 6.13 Different views of domains

6.8.5 Views within the Aspect demonstration IPSE

In this section we describe some of the features of the Aspect demonstration with regard to its support for different user views. As described in the earlier sections of this chapter, all work carried out in an Aspect IPSE is through the execution of a task. The task acts as the context for a user to perform work within a particular role. Hence, the definition of a task not only defines pre- and post-conditions which bound the task, but also includes the definition of which operations can be performed on which data objects. For example, a user who is responsible within a customer services role for the task of logging complaints from users will require access to a limited amount of data, and will require a minimum of operations on that data. Perhaps the only operation available is to create amendment requests which are sent to the appropriate project manager. The definition of this task must include the specification of the view which is appropriate for the task. With a graphical user interface, the interface which is appropriate for interaction with this view must also be defined.

For example, Figure 4.4 shows the interface to a *Log Customer Contact* task within the customer services role. Within this task execution a minimum number of operations are available, and a form-fill style of interaction seems most appropriate. In contrast, consider the very different view of the IB required by a programmer when source code needs to be amended to affect some change. Here a number of source code tools will be needed which help in the task. An example of such a view is shown in Figure 4.12. The tools available allow compilation, testing, and debugging of the source code. The operations available are completely different to those for logging customer requests but are just as appropriate to the task which needs to be performed.

6.9 Summary

The vital services required by IPSE tools for large-scale software development are, in Aspect, provided by a number of individual support mechanisms collectively known as the Information Base Superstructure (IBS). These may be thought of as a customisable IPSE kit. The IBS facilities are built upon an RM/T database providing a set of general data structuring and manipulation primitives known as the Information Base Engine (IBE).

In this chapter, the services provided by the IBS have been defined with particular emphasis on the need to support not only the software product as it is developed within the IPSE, but also the development process itself, and the personnel assigned to the individual project activities. We have argued that in this way a more accurate model of the project can be maintained.

More specifically, the Aspect models of tasks, people, version control, configuration management and concurrency control have been explained within the context of a prototype demonstration IPSE which has been used as the focal point of this chapter. This has provided a concrete realisation of many of the concepts we have developed.

The final sections of this chapter considered some additional mechanisms of the Aspect IBS which were not included in the demonstration IPSE. These included facilities for controlling data integrity through the definition and enforcement of user-defined rules and the ability to provide customised end-user views of the IPSE. In particular, the relationship of these facilities with the Aspect demonstration IPSE was discussed to indicate how such services could be included in further extensions to the prototype system.

Chapter 7

HCI Perspectives

I.D. Benest

7.1 Introduction

It is difficult to predict the type of user-interfaces that will be designed in the future; and difficult to predict what graphical functions will be needed to make those user-interfaces visible and simple to design. For the human-computer interface designer there has been little direction given by the software engineering community as to the future requirements for software design environments.

It seems that the dumb (or only semi-intelligent) terminal, keyboard oriented style of user-interface has been widely adopted. There has been a general lack of exploitation of the developments in computer graphics as that discipline has progressed. Furthermore, an attitude which is also prevalent in electronic and mechanical engineering disciplines is the tacit agreement that the user-interface is very important to get right, but a general reluctance to devote the same time and resources to its design as, for example, with the design of the data and internal software structures. These points combine to make it difficult to predict quite precisely what user-interfaces will be designed in the future for software engineering environments.

Two points should be clear. First, the manipulation of the design environment is not an end in itself, rather it is a means by which a product evolves. Software engineers of the future will wish to concentrate on the task of designing the product rather than having to remember: precise commands, location of and paths to information, and exact design procedures, all of which impede the route from

Requirements to Product. Second, the software engineer will need to have access to hundreds of drawings, hundreds of thousands (or maybe millions) of lines of code; they will need to access reports, documents, letters, memos, specifications, etc., a huge quantity of information. But, in this context, it is not the technical storage and access mechanisms that are important, it is the ease with which the information can be casually found and the satisfaction that the user feels that he has arrived at the information he requires.

7.2 Computer Graphics – an Historical Perspective

Software engineers, unlike their electronic and mechanical engineering counterparts, have in the past shunned the use of computer graphics; and as a result have not exploited it for program specifications and general input and output to and from their products. Hopgood et al [64] remarks that computer graphics appeared almost at the same time as the first general purpose computers. It is recognised that many of the important interactive graphics techniques were pioneered by Sutherland [99]; that the ubiquitous mouse was developed in the mid-1960s [47]; and that by 1965 [11] menus had been found to enhance the ease-of-use of computer programs. Though recent years have seen the development of diagrammatic specification tools on small single user workstations, it is chastening to realise that this equivalent activity for electronic engineering emerged in the mid-1960s [70].

Much of the pioneering work in computer graphics was supported by the aerospace and automative industries where the cost of computers with high performance graphics displays was quite small compared with the cost of developing new mechanical or electronic products that were superior to those of their competitors. Now that it is becoming widely accepted that the creation of software is a necessarily separate engineering discipline, and that software will control safety critical systems, greater financial support may be forthcoming than has hitherto been the case.

However, this has meant that the output graphics primitives which are now well understood (such as are available in GKS [64] have been developed primarily for the mechanical and electronic engineers on vector displays. These output primitives, though they would be useful to programs which support informal (drawing) specifications, are not ideally suited to the software engineer whose requirements are orientated to swift handling of text and mathematical equations rather than the rotation of artifacts (though translation and re-scaling of text is an important requirement).

Fortunately, ten to fifteen years ago, XeroxPARC [104] began experimenting with high performance, single user, bit-mapped graphics displays that had graphics primitives which seem to be more suitable. The concept of the window (in their terms) and its supporting and necessary hardware raster-operations (bitblt) was a major innovation, because it allowed for multiple processes to be visually multiplexed on the screen, and those processes could be quickly moved to another screen location. Processes not immediately required may be tucked out the way by closing to an icon, moving the window off screen or simply (partially) hiding it with another window. This provides a basic means for a software user to handle his work environment.

7.3 User-Interface Design Perspective

Unfortunately, it is often the case that window-managed environments merely provide multiple dumb terminal interfaces, thus reinforcing the view that careful interface design may be important, but is not the job of the software engineer (and perhaps it ought not to be).

If a dumb terminal style of interaction is adopted then the underlying approach to the user-interface design is one of the computer interrogating the user. Though this can be partially hidden by using menus, underneath, the computer is only reminding the user of the limited set of choices available at each stage and inviting the user to make a selection. This in some senses is a characteristic of machine-centered design where the system has been designed for the ease with which the computer can accomplish a function rather than the ease with which the user can assimilate progress and results. Such systems are serial in the order in which the user is interrogated, and where path decisions have to be made, the system becomes hierarchically structured. Once the user is meant to navigate up and down the hierarchy, the user can quickly become lost, he is unable to find screen pages which he knows exist, but cannot remember the path from the current location. Systems whose paths are networked (particularly if the user can establish those networks himself) are even worse.

This contrasts with direct manipulation systems where the user is given an impression that he is interrogating the computer or commanding that it carry out some computation. This style is more characteristic of human-centered design and such systems attempt to meet the needs (human and functional) of the user. It is in this style that tools which support a creative activity can encourage innovation in, for example, a design system, or provide insight into the behaviour of an artifact.

What is not so readily understood is that retro-fitting user-interfaces to software designed for dumb terminals (and even quite intelligent displays) is not generally advisable. Programs have to be designed for the input and output devices that are going to be used in the final product; a fact which those enthused by the idea of device independence will not readily accept. The point is that if, for example, a program is designed to accept cursive script input via a stylus on a general purpose tablet, then replacing the stylus/tablet combination with a mouse will not be satisfactory, although the odd free hand cross or circle could still be drawn (awkwardly) with a mouse. If the physical input and output devices are fixed early in a system design then this imposes a limitation on the freedom of the interface designer (which is sometimes gratefully accepted). So if a program is to be designed for the widest range of devices possible, then the interface is restricted to driving a dumb terminal with a keyboard, a configuration to which most devices will sink. This should not be taken to mean that device independence is unimportant; indeed device independence does increase the range of devices that can be used by a particular program provided the interface designer is aware that technical device independence does not automatically generate user-interfaces which are independent of device.

Certainly, if an interface is to be retro-fitted to a program then it seems to be simpler if that program were designed originally to be run in a batch mode of operation (with no user-interaction at all). When there is a dumb terminal interface it will probably have defined the internal structure and that will probably make its porting to, and full exploitation of, a more sophisticated environment, very difficult and time consuming to perform. (A program which was menu driven on a dumb terminal and which is changed to utilise the pop-up menu package on a high performance workstation has not been changed to fully exploit the workstation.) In many cases full exploitation (to the benefit of the end user) can only be achieved by changing the inherent interface style.

7.4 User-Interfaces in the Future

The high performance workstation offers the capability for providing interfaces that are tailored for humans to use, though precisely what those interfaces will look like, is very much open to conjecture. Assuming that whatever is designed will be capable of emulating dumb terminals, it is necessary to assess the current level of graphical interface available from the perspective of the resulting user interface, in order to predict how they will develop in the future.

Current window managers perform an integrating role at the user-interface level and are suited to multiplexing dumb and intelligent terminal driving software components. However, the overall user-interface resulting from this level of integration is one of: **chaos** – requiring the user to fiddle with the environment by resizing, moving, closing and opening windows; **inconsistency** – each tool has its own rules and 'feel', even if the designers have 'obeyed' a set of guidelines; **an imposed 'operating' system style** – for manipulating the window environment that is technically unsatisfactory (reaching and pointing at a thin line, then searching and selecting from a menu); **irritation** – when the overall task demands frequent changes of input device.

Whatever overall style of interface a software attempts to impose on its toolset, there will be a style imposed by the window manager, and that style may conflict with that of the toolset. If every software house adopts the same window managed environment, then it will be more difficult to impose what might be described as a 'designer label' that visually and instantly identifies the toolset as distinct from its competitors. For a system to be truly integrated, window manipulation should be performed implicitly by the user through the task and not explicitly by the user through the window manager; by this means, system style is imposed by the task and not by the computer system.

The window, like the dumb terminal, offers a 'tunnel-vision' view on to a data space, a view that is often made worse by a query language which displays a degree of reticence of divulging information not specifically requested. The use of windows to represent sheets of paper stacked on top of each other while satisfactory for small information systems, becomes inadequate and unwieldy for larger systems. Using hierarchies to 'contain' large quantities of information leads to users experiencing difficulties in knowing their own location in, knowing the location of information in, and navigating through, such systems. There is a need to linearise those hierarchical systems to enable the user to browse properly, and a need to provide the user with implicit cues so that he is aware almost instinctively how to reach the information he requires.

In short, it seems necessary to provide a mechanism which expands the physically constrained view on to the information space offering an improved 'look and feel' more orientated to the task being performed and providing implicit cues to aid navigation. There seems to be a need to browse the equivalent of many hundreds of windows in order to open up the otherwise constrained view through one window.

One approach may be to develop a small number of high-level user-interface objects. Together they will impose new metaphors; consistency at the user-interface will be imposed by the interface objects themselves both separately and together. By grouping tasks into user roles, the role controller (a high-level user-interface object tailored for that role) would organise the display according to the tasks being performed. The objects would be self-contained processes capable of independent behaviour and of passing messages between each other, and to and from 'hidden' application processes. They would exploit the graphical input and output facilities of a window manager but would remove the need for the window manager itself to have a user interface. This would mean that the task and role that the user performs, controls the graphical environment.

7.5 Graphical Interface Implications

The foregoing implies the development of a graphical interaction management system which replaces the conventional window manager and provides highly interactive functions normally relegated to the application. This system must be interposed between the user and the application tool to provide a computer-managed multiplexed display; it must be essentially device independent, impose little overt style on any final user interface, and provide graphical output which closely matches the needs of software design environments. The Presenter provides these facilities. It is a constituent part of the public tool interface; its design retains the conventional window manager ability to multiplex tool output, but this has been generalised to provide, in principle, an infinitely deep hierarchical set of screen regions and a more general and extended mechanism for manipulating those regions than is conventionally provided for windows, in a window manager. The display and all its interactive and dynamic attributes are saved in a device independent structure for use by the application tool, thus removing the need to generate automatically large software modules of graphical manipulation procedures.

An interesting trend has emerged from this work. While graphical user interaction has in the past, been quite distinct from the user interface, it is becoming clear that the new graphical interaction mechanisms now in place, are at such a high level that they could quite properly be regarded as user interface mechanisms; thus the distinction between the user interface and the graphical interface is becoming blurred, to the benefit of the end user. But internally, by segregating the lower level user-interface functions from the application, enables the interface designer to concentrate on providing the functions which support the requirements of the task.

7.6 Designing Graphical User-Interfaces

Designing graphical user-interfaces, particularly the aesthetic presentation and dynamic behaviour, is very time consuming if conventional graphics libraries need to be bound in with the application. The edit, compile, debug loop is repeatedly traversed in order to produce a pleasing display and pleasurable tool to use. Unless the designer has tremendous powers of intuition, no amount of formal specification will define the aesthetic appearance of the tool unless the appearance is already defined by a high-level user-interface object. To design such objects or application specific interfaces, a rapid prototyping tool is desirable.

Doubleview is a rapid prototyping tool which provides designer access to the very large number of attributes available to screen objects in the Presenter. No evaluation on human and computing time saved has been undertaken, but experience in designing without such a facility indicates that the resultant increase in designer productivity must be quite substantial.

Chapter 8

Constructs for Interface Generation and Management

R.K. Took

8.1 Basic Requirements

An interfacing system, in the sense of this chapter, mediates between the aspirations of the application designer and the I/O capabilities of the raw machine (and, through these, with the end user). Whatever application behaviour can be achieved via an interface system can clearly also be implemented directly on the raw machine, so what are the advantages of and requirements for an interface system?

An ideal interface system should not cut the application programmer off from any of the capabilities of the raw machine. However, one requirement of applications may be portability between machines, and in theory this may constrain the functionality of the interface to a virtual machine which is an intersection of the capabilities of a number of real devices. In practice, in contrast to character-mapped terminals where the repertory of control-character driven operations varies widely from machine to machine, current bitmapped workstations, about which this chapter is concerned, have a high degree of consistency in their fundamental capabilities, usually restricted to the standard raster operations and event streams. It may well be that future bitmapped workstations will have higher level I/O operations built into the hardware: it is precisely as to what these could be that this chapter is about. At the moment on bitmapped workstations, however, machine exploitation and portability are not usually in conflict (the number of mouse buttons is a notable exception).

An ideal interface system should equally not cut the application programmer off from any design aspirations. In practice, of course, some restrictions are necessary: I have found no way to get voice input and colour on my monochrome Sun! But in the domain of possible screens the interface system should not restrict but rather support and inspire the construction of interesting and useable ways to convey application functionality. The essential requirements are that the interface be easy to use on the one hand, and powerful on the other. Ease of use implies a single intuitive model from which the primitives are derived. Power implies that the model have strong generative capability.

8.2 Options for Interface Constructs

In the sense in which I am using it here, constructs are features of the single model which unifies interaction at the interface. Thus the 'window' and the 'icon' can be considered constructs within the standard WIMP interface. Primitives are operations which invoke, or depend on, the constructs. 'Create a window', 'move an icon' would be examples. At this level we need not distinguish whether it is the end user or the application which invokes these primitives.

8.2.1 The static-dynamic axis

There seem to be two axes along which one can make decisions affecting the style and level of constructs offered in an interface system. Firstly, there is a clear distinction between static and dynamic constructs. Standard graphics packages (like GKS [46]) offer mainly static constructs consisting largely of imaging facilities such as line and polygon drawing, area filling, clipping, scaling and rotation. The functions are usually bound in to the application code from a library, or invoked by interpretation of a script, as in Postscript [109]. Responsibility for the minutiae of control, such as the handling of low level events and echoing, remains with the application, even though the cost of coding may be reduced by binding in logical input devices (like LOCATOR, VALUATOR, and CHOICE in GKS). In a window-managed environment, although some filtering of the input stream may take place (to capture window manager specific commands, for example) this situation does not radically change. From the application's point of view it has a low level input stream, and entire control over a logical bitmap. In-window primitives offered by the window manager are usually static facilities to print text, draw lines etc., although 'toolkits' of objects with minimal functionality (such as menus or sliders) may also be provided.

At the dynamic extreme, in an object-oriented system the application is in danger of relinquishing control altogether to an assemblage of objects, each of which encapsulates its own behaviour. The task of the application is to muster relevant objects, possibly modifying behaviour specifically or generally through an inheritance mechanism. The dynamics of the interaction, however, are largely taken over by communication between objects and their responses.

Constructs which formulate dynamic behaviour like this have two distinct advantages. Applications are relieved of the grind of low-level interaction, with its associated problems of coding cost and device dependence, and are free to operate at a more abstract level, notified of only the essential events in the interaction. Secondly, such a model reinforces the dynamics of those interactions which are likely to be common over a number of applications, like editing and selection highlighting, and so a bias towards interface consistency is built into the system. The fully object-oriented paradigm, however, risks obscuring global control issues in the welter of local events.

8.2.2 The lexical-syntactic-semantic Axis

The second axis for decision is orthogonal to the first, and lies along the well established lexical – syntactic – semantic continuum. In the sense of this chapter, the lexical level will govern the appearance of the interface: whether text is highlighted by underlining or by inverting, and what the mail icon looks like, for example. A 'house style' may well be specified at this level.

At the syntactic level, constructs will govern the structuring of screen objects, and this itself will range from simple partitioning of the display space, through layered coordinate spaces and clipping rectangles, to notions of persistent screen objects, and thence to their structuring from simple two layer models to hierarchies and to networks.

At the semantic level, finally, constructs may govern meaning and functionality, either for simple stimulus-response behaviour (like opening or closing an icon), or at a more abstract and programmable level. Class-type hierarchies may be employed as a means of generating object instances. The semantics may control relatively minor issues like input packaging (of characters into strings, for example) or may cover more important concerns like command parsing and interpretation, or even the running of a whole interactive session as in a UIMS.

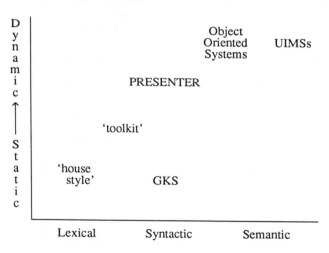

Fig. 8.1 A classification of some interface systems

The decision as to where in this space to construct useful interface primitives will be influenced by a number of other considerations. Device capabilities and implementation efficiency may be one (3D may be abandoned, for example, as a real time graphic capability). Application domain may be another (CAD may have different priorities from the paperless office). An important issue will be the nature of the invocation language required by the constructs. A verbose invocation language (like Postscript) may pose problems if the channel between the construct manager and the application is constricted by inter-process communication or distribution. Also, the class of the language may have implications for the power or useability of the constructs themselves. A simple finite language may seem to imply a limited capability, but may ensure ease of use and efficiency. A Turing-equivalent grammar (again like Postscript) implies power, but places the onus of definition back on the application, and is likely to entail the overhead of run-time interpretation. Finally, for the purpose of application porting or hardcopy generation, some abstract and device-independent representation for the resultant screen objects is desirable.

8.3 Presenter

Presenter, the interface system to the Aspect IPSE, has taken the deliberate design decision to limit its concern to the optimal management of screen objects within a geometric, manipulable domain, and to provide powerful generic abstractions over the structuring, representation, and manipulability of these objects. Presenter constructs are therefore dynamic, but without compromising application control – the application (used here in its broadest sense) may elect to intervene at any level of interaction. The constructs therefore also have no intrinsic semantics – it is entirely up to the application to interpret user action. Presenter screen objects can thus be said to have *behaviour without functionality*. That is, their response to user manipulation changes only their own visible state (e.g. size, position, highlighting) – only then may an application function be triggered to change the state of some other domain.

This classification of Presenter's constructs as dynamic and syntactic distinguishes it on the one hand from UIMSs (there is no dialogue management), but on the other puts it firmly into the arena with the many window-based interface systems.

8.4 The Window Manager Model

The obvious advantage of a high-resolution, high-bandwidth workstation screen over a character mapped terminal is greatly increased informational content. Whereas on a glass teletype processes must be laboriously switched between like turning the pages of a book, each one obscuring the last, on a bitmapped screen there is enough informational room to spread these processes around like loose sheets of paper on a desk. Furthermore, raster operations are inherently suited to handling overlapping rectangular graphical areas. Add a pointing device like a mouse, and window manager functionality is inescapable. However, there are a number of reasons for arguing that the window manager model represents only a rudimentary stage in the evolution from glass teletype interaction to exploiting in full the capabilities of a bitmapped workstation. A fundamental criticism of window managers is the division of functionality presented to the user between window management operations, and application operations. Unless there is a well defined and generalisable model for the semantics of the mouse buttons, for example, and the application is well-behaved, there is no guarantee that interaction with the window manager and with the application will be consistent – the window boundary often represents a discontinuity in the interface. More specifically, a window is a binding between a process and a contiguous area of screen. The coralling of application functionality to strict rectangular areas can in some cases lead to inefficient and unhelpful use of the overall screen space.

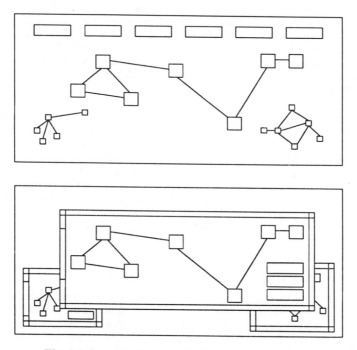

Fig. 8.2 Non-windowed and windowed presentation

Consider the two (fictional) screens in Figure 8.2. The first is a representation of a Presenter generated screen showing three graphical views (differently scaled) of a database schema, notionally produced by separate processes. The second is the same information in window format. In the windowed presentation:

- it may not always be possible to organise the information so as to optimally fill the rectangular space. This may lead to unnecessary obscuring of other information where empty portions of window overlap lower windows;

- extra visual clutter is involved in the borders and backgrounds of the windows themselves against the screen background, and this is exacerbated in many window systems by scroll bars, title bars, selection frames, and other hot spots duplicated within each window border;

- application control functions must be displayed within the assigned window, and so in some cases windows may have to be popped before they can be used. In the Presenter screen, the user is able to move buttons and control panels about arbitrarily to maximise their accessibility;

● controls for generic functions (if there are any) or for functions common to a number of windows may be difficult or impossible to display without duplication;

● the dominance of the window as a display surface may lead to problems if controls for associated application functions are clipped or scaled away by sizing operations on the window as a whole. In general, there is no real-world analogue for overlapping, clipping windows (try simulating these on an overhead projector, for example!). It is thus also possible to 'lose' clipped objects (i.e. when they are moved outside the window) in some virtual dimension.

This is not to say that the window model is not appropriate in many cases. Text, for example, is usually rectangular in format: a window is an ideal frame. The window model is also an efficient way of indicating a locus of functionality: there may be many cases where it is important to know the scope of an operation, and to have this limited to some immediately perceivable area.

The contention in Presenter's design is that there exist interface models from which window-manager-style functionality may be derived, if desired, but which are also capable of generating a wider range of interactive scenarios. To a certain extent this possibility is borne out by the plethora of window fragments that abound in window-managed systems: subwindows, panes, panels, frames, tiles, regions, icons, etc. It seems that the window is too gross a construct to act as a fundamental construct for an interactive interface.

8.5 The Presenter Model

It is fundamental to Presenter, however, that the most important consideration in deriving constructs for an interface system is the nature of the manipulable domain itself. This domain is presupposed by the capabilities of a bitmapped screen and a pointing device, and the design of Presenter emphasises the notion that the most effective constructs within it are those which have physical analogues, since these are intuitive to the user.

A screen and a pointing device are the raw materials for tool-making: are there any *a priori* qualities of potential artifacts in this space that can be abstracted, so that the task of construction is simplified?

The manipulable domain consists fundamentally of *objects* which are *identifiable, persistent,* and have *behaviour*. Objects are identifiable in the sense both that they are perceptual items recognisable by the end user, and that they have a logical identity that can be referenced by the application programmer. Identity is useless without persistence over operations: an object which disappears when touched has minimal usefulness (a textual character which can be typed but not moved is a more specific example). Equally important is the object's response to operations: this should be consistent with the object's perceived state and environment (for example a textual character which can be edited in one window but not in another fails this criterion).

8.5.1 Structure

Presenter has a single basic construct: the 'region'. In itself, the region is just an abstract coordinate space, but it may represent groups of other regions, and it may have content. There is no higher built-in construct than the region – there is no notion of 'window', for example.

In general, fundamental and intuitive structuring constructs are hierarchical grouping (tree structures), and paths (representing connectivity or sequence). In Presenter, complex regions may be built up by composition of simpler regions, without restriction. Only leaf regions in the hierarchy have displayable content, which may be text or graphics. There is a single system tree, which comprehends all regions of all applications (applications own immediate children of the root and their subtrees). The tree is ordered, and the sequence of leaf regions maps to screen layering. The tree does *not* represent a type hierarchy.

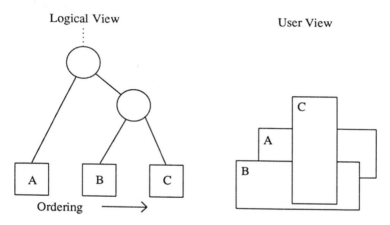

Fig. 8.3 Screen layering

Although the tree is the primary structuring construct, regions may also be arbitrarily threaded by paths into a networked structure. Presenter maintains such links logically (to be queried by the application) and on the screen, where linked regions are dynamically connected by other regions whose appearance can be determined by the application (to be a line or an arrow, for example).

Visually, perspective varies with point of view. In Presenter, each region has its own coordinate scheme, in which its children are situated. A change to the size or position of the parent therefore affects all descendants. In a number of other hierarchical systems [83,87], children are constrained to be *contained* within the extent of their parent. In Presenter, there are no constraints on the relative positions and sizes of any regions. Size and position are expressed in real coordinates, and the coordinate origin is the top left of all regions. A region of size (1.0, 1.0) is the same size as its parent in both dimensions. When a region changes size, it does so round a pivot point in its coordinate space (which may be set anywhere). The pivot

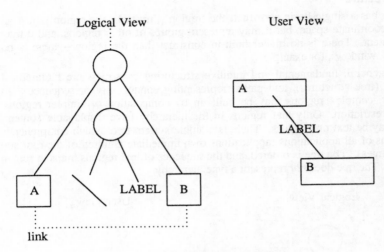

Fig. 8.4 Screen linking

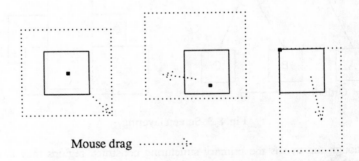

Mouse drag ············

Fig. 8.5 Sizing round the pivot point

point also serves to site the region in the coordinate space of its parent. Thus a region at position (-3.0, 0.5) will have its pivot point at the same horizontal level as its parent's origin, but three parent widths to the left. The actual position of the region will be determined by the siting of the pivot point in its own coordinate space. The relative coordinate schemes allow global or local changes in size or position to be carried out by sizing or moving a single node on the hierarchy. In Figure 8.6, region B is the same size and at the same position as its (undisplayable) parent. The relative sizes and positions of regions A, B and C remain the same whatever the size and position of the parent.

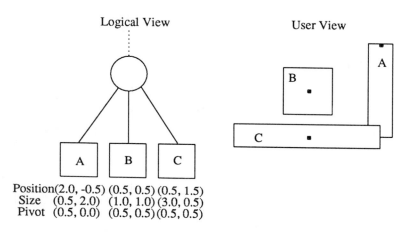

Position (2.0, -0.5) (0.5, 0.5) (0.5, 1.5)
Size   (0.5, 2.0) (1.0, 1.0) (3.0, 0.5)
Pivot   (0.5, 0.0) (0.5, 0.5) (0.5, 0.5)

Fig. 8.6 Hierarchical, relative coordinate schemes

8.5.2 Behaviour

In contrast to a constraint-oriented system like Borning's ThingLab [16], the behaviour of Presenter's regions is not immediately programmable, but is defined by a set of attributes. In general, these attributes govern *transformation* or *representation* of regions. They are not inherited, as in a typing system, but their effects may propagate to descendant regions.

Selection

Before any manipulation, its subject must be designated. Enabling users to select simple or compound screen items (that is, leaf or higher regions on the grouping hierarchy) is achieved by setting or clearing the 'selectable' attribute on regions. An act of selection (mouse click, say) will be passed up the tree from the leaf region under the cursor until a selectable region is found. Thus, for example, a small button can be constructed through which large groupings may be selected by the user. Multiple clicking jumps selectable regions.

In Figure 8.7, a mouse click in the user view of region A results in a selection of that region. A mouse click in regions B or C results in a selection of their parent, and so both regions B and C would be highlit on the screen. Double clicking in any of the regions would result in selection of the root of the group, and all regions A, B and C would be highlit. All the regions could then be moved or sized as a group.

Regions may also be set 'permeable' to selection (as region B in Figure 8.8 below). In this case a coincident region underneath would be selected.

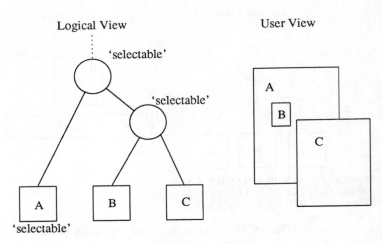

Fig. 8.7 Selection

Transformation

Physical manipulation

Constructs over manipulation are important in the design of Presenter. The basic interactive capability which Presenter provides is movement and sizing of regions and their descendants in the coordinate space of the parent region. Useful properties emerge, however, when successive constraints are applied to this freedom (just as useful information is a restriction of chaotic noise). Via attributes, regions in Presenter can be set moveable or sizeable in one dimension only. Together with the adjustable pivot point, this gives the potential for the creation of a wide range of sliding and expanding regions. The manipulability of regions may also be influenced by their content: it is a useful facility to allow the size of a text region to expand or contract dynamically so as just to enclose the contained text. Such a region may not also be changed in size manipulatively, since the constraints conflict. (This has been specified but not yet implemented in Presenter).

By the physical analogy, however, constraints on manipulation are as much inter- as intra-regional. Objects in the real world have restricted movement not only through inherent properties, but also because they abut other objects. In Presenter, regions can be set to contain or exclude a subset of their children. Thus sliders can be created, for example, which have a restricted range of movement.

In addition, subsets of grouped regions may wish to secede from manipulations applied to the whole group. Regions thus may be set not to scale when higher regions change size, or not to move when higher regions change position. Thus a sizeable and moveable box can be given constant-size panels or appendages.

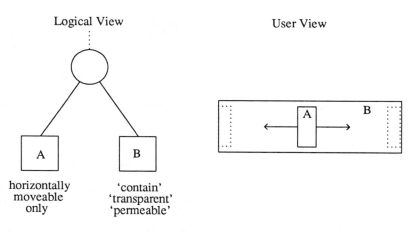

Fig. 8.8 A composite, manipulable object

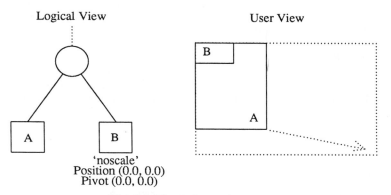

Fig. 8.9 Fixed-size regions

In Figure 8.9, region B will remain the same absolute size, and at the same position (in top left corner of A), irrespective of changes to the size (or of course position) of its parent.

Logical manipulation

Presenter provides primitive operations which cut and paste the region tree, and by means of which regions may be regrouped (to pop a group of regions to the front of the screen, for example). However, these operations must be invoked by an application on behalf of the user – there is no direct invocation mechanism.

Representation

A number of attributes control the displayed appearance of the content of regions, principally opacity and image 'not'ing. 'transparent' regions may be set to 'and', 'or' or 'xor' with their background. It is therefore possible to perform the full sixteen RasterOp modes within Presenter. Regions may also be 'hidden' altogether from the screen, although they remain on the logical tree. This is useful for items that appear only temporarily.

With the same scope as containment, it is possible also to set regions to 'clip' a subset of their children.

8.6 Presenter Control

Presenter is in sole charge of the whole screen and the input devices. The benefits of this centralisation, particularly in a multi-processing environment, are well known: applications deal with virtual spaces, while inter-application conflicts for screen space are handled rationally and efficiently by the screen manager. In design (although not yet in implementation) Presenter is a server process with which applications communicate. Basically, the user interacts with Presenter, which passes on relevant messages to the appropriate applications. Applications may choose their level of involvement with the interaction – having set the behaviour of their regions, they may simply be interested in selection. Equally they may elect to be informed of low-level events (character insertion, mouse movement) and take their own action. The default Presenter interpretation of the mouse for selection, sizing, and movement may be overridden.

8.6.1 Generic services

User-accessible operations to edit content (either text or graphics) are provided within Presenter. As should be expected, it is possible to edit across regions (that is, text can be cut or copied from one region and pasted into another). These operations are only allowed on regions with the 'editable' attribute set.

8.7 Discussion

8.7.1 Application/interface separation

The problem of the semantic separation of application and user-oriented front ends is still being examined [33, 101]: Presenter deliberately avoids this issue by restricting itself to the relatively delimited domain of geometric, manipulable objects. It takes no part in dialogue management – it is a screen manager pure and simple. Since no state other than regions and their structure has to be maintained, Presenter can be an 'open' system, in that its operations are available at any time to any participating process. It might also be called an 'equal access' system, in the sense that the same operations are available both to applications and to the end user: a user moves a region with the mouse, whereas an application makes a Presenter call referencing the same region.

Experience with applications so far has shown that this leads to two entirely different ways of constructing the components of a particular interface. Either these can be built up analytically, using a script of Presenter primitives which is invoked during or prior to the interaction, or they can be constructed manipulatively by the designer, and loaded in as a Presenter subtree at run time. A Presenter tool, DOUBLEVIEW, has been developed by Sylvia Holmes at York which allows the application designer to control most features of his creation interactively. The analytic approach leads to greater precision and easier global modification. The manipulative approach is suited to rapid prototyping and iterative design, where placement by eye and experimentation is preferred.

8.7.2 Genericity vs. convenience

In intention, Presenter is a generic I/O management system for convenient generation of application interfaces. Certainly the simplicity of the basic model (the tree of regions) makes for both genericity and convenience. Even though the tree structure is overloaded (part-whole grouping; relative coordinate schemes; screen layering), the relation between these interpretations is exclusive and intuitive. In addition, the avoidance of concrete atomic entities like points, lines or rectangles (as are fundamental to GEGS [102] for example) makes graphical presentation very general – the region is simply a blank coordinate space. Even text handling is generalised, since the concrete image of a character can be replaced by any other image (a diagram, for example), which will then be formatted as if it were a character. Certain imaging primitives are of course supplied (currently line drawing and pixel operations) but these are an extensible set.

Genericity may conflict with convenience, however, when it comes to the allocation of control. All participants (application, interface, and end user) want a slice of the action. In general, claims for control may come at very different levels of granularity: an application may wish at one time to track the mouse for the purpose of drawing some shape, while at another it may wish simply to be informed of a menu selection irrespective of where the menu is situated. On the one hand, genericity requires access to all events, while on the other, convenience requires that certain transactions be packaged. Presenter resolves this conflict by allowing applications knowledge of all events, but also power to delegate action to the default Presenter operations.

8.7.3 Attributes vs. program

The use of attributes rather than a program to express region constraints is justified for two reasons.

Firstly, it is convenient for the application, since a small set of atomic constraints is capable of generating a very wide range of manipulable behaviour which can form the basis of sliders, scroll bars, pan boxes, icons etc. The major question that remains for research is: can a domain be defined over which a set of manipulation constraints can in any sense be said to be complete? For example, where is the boundary between the sort of constraint that restricts a region to horizontal movement, and the sort that converts a top hat icon into a rabbit icon? Clearly, the first is a geometric transformation whereas the second involves semantics. But what about a region that can only move at 23 degrees to the horizontal?

Secondly, since applications have access to all events, any functionality that requires programming (to convert a top hat into a rabbit, for example) can be performed using the language in which the application is written – there is no point in duplicating this power at the interface level.

8.8 Conclusion

Presenter's model is an attempt at a set of constructs unified by implicit reference to the domain of manipulable objects and their operations. The universe of objects generated is governed by simple, intuitive laws which, it is hoped, optimise ease of use for both application designer and end user.

Chapter 9

Doubleview – A User Interface Design Tool

S.J. Holmes

9.1 Introduction

9.1.1 Overview

When developing the end-user interface for a particular system or application, designers must, at some point, make commitments to certain styles of appearance and interaction. Doubleview is intended to reduce the cost of making those commitments by supporting the rapid prototyping and testing of easily reconfigurable, application independent user interface components, within the context of Aspect's screen operating system, Presenter [105], described in Chapter 8.

Doubleview is an editor, providing an interactive interface to Presenter functionality, and supporting the construction of mouse-driven graphical user interfaces. As the name suggests, it offers a user two orthogonal representations of user interface components being edited. These two representations contrast structure against surface, logical against physical, and the application programmer view against the end-user view.

As described in the next section, Presenter relieves the application of many user interaction support tasks and in this way, by centralisation of user interface functionality, it defines a boundary between application and user interface concerns. Doubleview reinforces this separation by encouraging the construction of autonomous interaction objects which persist outside of any application. These objects can be reconfigured and reused in many different applications with the help of

Doubleview, thus encouraging quick and easy user interface construction, and consistency between user interfaces.

Doubleview supports a structured 'design by composition' approach, in which small interaction objects are composed into full scale application interfaces. Using Doubleview, interaction objects can be designed, constructed and modified *interactively;* the designer receives immediate feedback on changes to the design, and avoids the compilation overheads imposed by a code-based user interface.

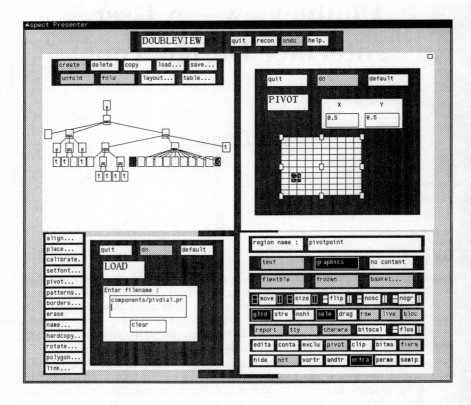

Fig. 9.1 Doubleview

9.1.2 How Doubleview relates to Presenter

A brief introduction to Presenter follows, in order to establish a context for discussion of Doubleview's design and development.

Presenter provides and manages an environment of hierarchically organised areas of the screen (known as 'regions'), whose appearance and behaviour can be defined, using a set of primitives, to produce user interfaces for applications. Leaf regions of the hierarchy may contain text or graphics, while regions *within* the hierarchy simply represent coordinate spaces.

All regions are positioned and sized within the coordinate space of their parent. Regions within the hierarchy thus also represent groupings of the visible leaf regions, so composite objects can be treated by the end user as single entities under scaling, moving, and selection operations.

Each region has behaviour, which is determined by a set of attributes. The behaviour a region is capable of includes movement and sizing (in either dimension), selectability, editability, and its response to mouse input. (There are approximately fifty attributes in all.)

Presenter provides a set of operations on regions, with a C-code interface [106]. These include operations to construct the tree of regions, operations to insert or delete content from leaf regions, operations to change the size, position or attributes of regions, and operations to inquire the state of regions. Via a default interactive interface, Presenter also allows the end user to carry out some of these operations by direct manipulation. Regions can be selected, sized, positioned, and edited (both text and graphics) in this way.

Using the above Presenter primitives, Doubleview provides interactive access to all Presenter operations on regions, and to both the logical and physical structure of Presenter subtrees. It also has a region-state display panel and a set of higher-level functions appropriate for the task of graphical user interface design. Using Doubleview, an application programmer can design, construct and modify user interfaces *interactively*, receiving immediate feedback on changes to the design, and avoiding the disadvantages of the blind 'edit/compile/execute' design cycle which is imposed by a code-based user interface. (These disadvantages are particularly intrusive during the design of graphical user interfaces, where the programmer/user is forced to perform difficult mental mappings back and forth between one-dimensional textual descriptions and two-dimensional graphical objects, displayed on the screen only after an intervening compilation process).

Using Doubleview, the appearance and behaviour of newly designed interaction objects can be tested within the design tool, at any stage of the design process. This is because one of the two views that Doubleview provides is a view of the designed object as it will appear and behave when fronting its application.

If satisfactory, the component is saved to an external file. This file may then be loaded into an application program running within the Presenter environment, which can navigate the structure and identify named regions as necessary. The application may then invoke its own application specific functions, when these identified regions are (for instance) selected by an end user. Interaction components saved in external files can be copied back into Doubleview, and modified for use with different applications.

The mouse is a major point of contact between a user and an interactive system. It is also a point at which Presenter and application must negotiate for control of interaction in the current version of Presenter. Doubleview makes use of Presenter's default interactive interface: this maintains highlighting on a single selected region, and binds selection, moving, sizing, and editing of regions with content to particular mouse button events. Doubleview extends the Presenter default selection mechanism to handle three concurrent 'selections', and the highlighting mechanism to handle two different types of highlighting. Also, the default move and size interfaces are extended to provide demonstrative cut and paste, zoom and pan facilities.

The environment Presenter manages is conceptually simple yet very powerful because of the homogeneity of the Presenter region tree structure. It is difficult, outside of a truly object-oriented system, to carry such simplicity through into task-oriented interactive interfaces designed to support the user in achieving a range of high-level goals, e.g. document preparation, Ada debugging, general database access etc.

To make the task of designing (and describing) Doubleview easier it has been useful to make a conceptual distinction between two sorts of basic object which appear in task-oriented direct manipulation user interfaces. These categories are 'controlled objects' (this term refers to the objects Doubleview is used to create or modify) and 'control object' (the interactive means by which a controlled object is created or modified).

Doubleview has been designed and developed in parallel with the design and implementation of the Presenter programming primitives. This concurrent development has been mutually valuable and demonstrates the benefits to be gained from user involvement at an early stage in any design process. Doubleview has been used continuously for testing and debugging Presenter primitives, and various modifications and extensions to the Presenter specification have sprung from seeing and using Doubleview while the primitives were still flexible.

9.2 Design and Development of Doubleview

9.2.1 Specification

In the field of software engineering, formal specification of systems prior to implementation is becoming normal practice, and formal specification lies at the heart of the Aspect project. However, in important but ill-defined and poorly understood areas of software engineering such as human-computer interaction, formal specification techniques are still very much research topics rather than tools for practical application.

Semi-formal methodologies for the specification of interactive user interfaces exist, although even these are thin on the ground and rarely used, as yet. Doubleview was specified [63] using a linguistic methodology devised by Foley and Van Dam [51] where an interface is defined first at the conceptual level, then in turn, at the semantic, syntactic and lexical levels.

Overall, this breakdown of the design process into levels was found to be helpful for exploring the results of making different controlled/control object partitionings, and the use of Augmented Transition Network diagrams at the syntactic/lexical levels clarified several issues. James Foley has recently been working on an interactive tool [52], which is intended to support, formalise and evaluate the conceptual and semantic stages of user interface specification.

Although such techniques can be extremely useful, graphical user interface design remains very much an iterative process which must be carried out in the concrete rather than in the abstract. It is absolutely necessary to *try out* interaction to test its effectiveness and useability, as a part of the design cycle, and to *look at* the appearance of the graphics components of such interfaces. Thus attempting to produce a complete yet abstract specification of graphical user interfaces prior to implementation is difficult, if not impossible, and is a strong justification for the development of rapid prototyping design tools such as Doubleview.

In the case of Doubleview's own user interface, a complete specification before prototyping began was not possible because the functionality to which it supplies an interactive interface was under simultaneous development. From the start, therefore, Doubleview was designed to act as a bootstrap for its own future development.

Before the semi-formal specification of Doubleview could begin, one important design decision had to be made. This was the decision to use Foley's 'Currently Selected Object' interaction syntax model.

Basically, interaction follows the pattern select 'noun' object, select 'verb' object. The noun (usually but not always a controlled object) is persistently highlit, and becomes the 'Currently Selected Object'. More complex tasks require sequences of noun-verb pairs, or noun,verb,enter parameter,verb...sequences etc. The CSO model is a restriction of the 'Currently Selected Set' model of selection in which multiple *non-contiguous* display objects may be selected and invocation of a function on the whole set is possible.

9.2.2 Definition of objects

Data and operations

The distinction made earlier between control and controlled objects is similar to the familiar one made between data and operations. However, a control object in a demonstrative user interface is not an operation itself, rather it represents or *provides access to* an operation via an application; similarly a controlled object represents or provides access to data via an application.

Within the Presenter environment, both control and controlled objects are in fact implemented as region subtrees, but for a tool user engaged on some specific task, it seems that some perceptible distinction between control and controlled objects is a prerequisite of useful work. Even fully object-oriented systems retain such a distinction in their graphical user interfaces, though conceptually such distinctions do not exist, and therefore should not be represented if the object-orientation metaphor is to be preserved.

In Doubleview, the representation of controlled and control objects is clearly differentiated on the screen, both statically and dynamically, so that the user can demonstrate to the system what actions are required by the simple selection sequences outlined above, and can receive immediate feedback from the system. To achieve this differentiation, Doubleview overlays the homogeneity of the Presenter region structure with a simple 'typing' mechanism which constrains, extends or overrides the Presenter default interactive interface appropriately for each kind of application entity (controlled or control object).

The object type hierarchy used in the design of Doubleview is as follows: at the top is the category 'Object'. This subdivides into 'Controlled Object' and 'Control Object'. In the case of Doubleview, controlled objects can be further subdivided into state dependent region or subtree 'types'. Control objects are further subdivided into three categories: 'Function Objects', selection of which directly invokes some operation, 'Parameter Objects', which provide parameters to qualify operations, and 'Information Objects'. Function objects can be further differentiated according to the domain (in terms of the object hierarchy) of the operation they represent.

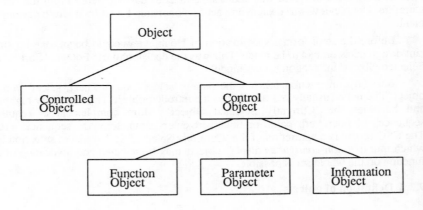

Fig. 9.2 Object type hierarchy

The boundary between object types frequently seems blurred because of Doubleview's application area. For instance, one instantiation of an object as controlled object can be modified using another instantiation of the same object as control object within Doubleview.

Controlled objects

Doubleview offers a user two representations or views of its controlled object. One is the physical or surface view, the other a visual interpretation of the Presenter display model, a structural or logical view, displayed in Doubleview's tree-editing component. To achieve this, Doubleview maps each Presenter region in the underlying construct to a second subtree representing the equivalent node in the tree diagram. The two views can be seen as equivalent to two of the roles which a user of Doubleview must play, of application programmer and end-user.

The underlying unity of the two representations is largely expressed to the tool user through dynamic feedback. Thus, when a part of the tree representation is highlit as a result of user selection, the equivalent part of the physical view is also highlit. Mappings which might cause confusion (for instance, left to right ordering in the tree representation mapping to back to front layering in the physical view) are quickly comprehended from user feedback during demonstration.

Fig. 9.3 Physical view of an interaction object

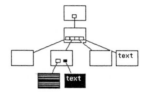

Fig. 9.4 Logical view of the same object as Figure 9.3

If a user makes changes to the logical structure of the tree representation these are reflected in the physical view, but any change made to the physical layout of the tree diagram does not affect the physical view. Similarly, changes to the graphical appearance of part of the physical view (altering size or position, for instance) do not affect the tree representation.

At present, neither view is presented to the user as dominant, and free movement is allowed between the two representations so a pattern of movement between structural and presentational design phases which seems natural and productive can be developed.

Doubleview's two views are both graphical representations; this is because of the particular task for which the tool is designed. There are very many other application areas where multiple graphical views would be useful, for instance, VLSI design where the physical layout of components is orthogonal to logical structure. There are also many applications where a textual representation would be useful component in a multiple-view tool, for example, a database browser/document editor. A possible extension to Doubleview itself would be a component which generated an editable textual representation of Presenter subtrees and their contents. This might be useful when, for instance, extreme precision in the positioning of interaction components is required.

Presenter regions in a controlled object acquire 'type' within an interactive application such as Doubleview, in that the set of operations that can be performed on a particular region depends on which of six mutually exclusive states the region is in:

- Non-leaf region with children
- Leaf region containing graphics
- Leaf region containing text
- Leaf region of type 'graphics' currently without content
- Leaf region of type 'text' currently without content
- Leaf region currently without type or content (empty)

Any region may be returned to the empty state directly, from which any other state is reachable. The state, and therefore appearance and behaviour of a region in the physical view is further determined by that region's current attribute settings.

Doubleview's controlled object is made accessible to users at the above atomic level via the tree diagram; through the mapping between the two views, any region in the physical view can be selected and have its state changed. The need for such a mechanism is made clear when considering changing the state of regions in the physical view which, for instance, do not currently have the attribute 'selectable' set, or of regions which are currently completely hidden by others.

In the physical view, a controlled object is also accessible for manipulation within Doubleview at the level of granularity the application programmer or designer deems appropriate for end users, as determined by the current attribute settings of the object.

Control objects

Doubleview's control objects are of course also hierarchies of regions, but their atomic structure is not apparent to an end-user of the tool. Their appearance and functionality are described in detail in Doubleview's User Guide [63].

A control object is a visible interaction component which permits the interactive modification or presentation of part or all of a controlled object. A control object may consist of one or more control objects grouped together (spatially, temporally or conditionally) by design, to aid in the fulfillment of some task or subtask. Simple examples are the familiar 'dialogue box' or menu.

The main two subtypes of control object used in Doubleview are function objects and parameter objects. 'Function objects' are represented as buttons in Doubleview, and stand for some function which is invoked when the button is selected. The domain of the function object may be a controlled object, or it may act on other control objects, for example by generating an functional extension to the interface, or by setting a parameter for some operation.

'Parameter objects' qualify a controlled object/function object pairing, usually by enabling the input of some numerical value or name by the user. An example of a parameter object often used in Doubleview are objects which permit the input and display of values based on the relative positioning of other control objects.

A blurring between object types occurs with the use of switches, which are

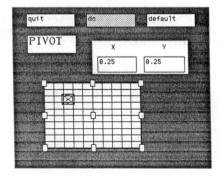

Fig. 9.5 Example of a control object containing a parameter object

function objects in that they invoke a toggle operation, and also parameter objects in that they represent at the same time the variable which is to be toggled.

9.2.3 Composition of objects

This section describes the reasons for the various groupings of controlled and control objects used in Doubleview, and the mechanisms behind those groupings.

Doubleview is most often used to create control objects for applications; controlled objects (representations of data) often need to be generated and composed dynamically by applications themselves. Doubleview can be useful however for designing simple formats into which an application can insert controlled objects dynamically, for instance fixed size tables or forms, or the basic units of some more complex representation.

Doubleview's own controlled objects are generated dynamically and maintained in an internal data structure. This structure permits the dynamic mapping between the two views previously mentioned, and also reduces search time when a user makes a selection. Dynamic generation of controlled objects is necessary in this case because they are of arbitrary size, and interactively extensible by the user.

Static composition

At first glance, Doubleview is comprised of five major components, which are :

- Title area
- Tree editor component
- Physical view component
- Sub-tool component
- Region-state component

These components are dynamically composed from external files into a default spatial relationship on tool invocation, and are designed to group together lower level control and controlled objects in such a way as to support a user in the high level task of user interface design.

In contrast, the contents of these components are largely static compositions of control objects. Often what relates control objects at this level is simply a shared domain; see for instance, the buttons in the set of horizontal attribute menus which form Doubleview's region-state component.

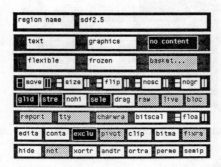

Fig. 9.6 Region-state component

All of these control objects are function objects, which have the domain 'region', and one menu is further constrained to a 'text region' domain. However, these are special function objects in that they are also switches, at the same time representing a variable and a 'toggle variable' operation. Therefore another reason for grouping them together is that they all display and toggle region attributes; they invoke the same type of operation. The composition mechanism is a simple spatial one in this case.

Although the actual domain of two function objects may be quite different, they may in fact appear to operate in the same domain from the users' point of view. For instance, the tree editing menu groups function objects whose domain is part or parts of the controlled object (create,delete etc) with function objects whose domain is another control object or subtool (layout,load,save, etc).

Fig. 9.7 Tree editing menu

What lies behind this grouping is that it is the *tree-diagram representation* of the controlled object which is the conceptual domain of all these function objects. The tree editing menu with its associated subtools, and the tree diagram representation of the controlled object, are grouped together to form a stand-alone tree-editing component. The composition mechanism for the tree-editing menu itself is again a simple spatial one, however, the compositional relationship between function objects in this menu and related subtools is dynamic and conditional.

An example of more complex static spatial composition is the positioning of the subset of control objects referred to as subtools in Doubleview. This grouping is based on the principle of positional consistency [94] in user interfaces. The subtools appear by default at the same position (referred to as the subtool component) on the screen, but in effect, at different times. This grouping is made because they share a common format and have some common functionality irrespective of their domains.

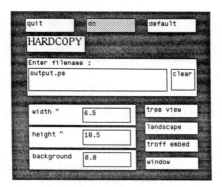

Fig. 9.8 Example of a subtool

They are all extensions of Doubleview's basic control structure, and permit the input and display of one or more parameters which qualify some operation, such as inserting specific contents into a region, generating a particular region-tree structure etc.

Dynamic composition

As remarked earlier, from the point of view of Presenter, Doubleview always consists of one very large undifferentiated tree of regions.

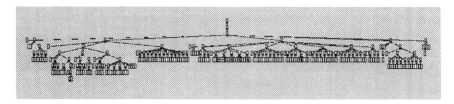

Fig. 9.9 Representation of Doubleview's logical structure

On invocation, control objects are composed from external files, and each control object is simply identified within Doubleview by name. When Doubleview is empty (does not contain a controlled object), the Presenter tree consists only of control objects, some visible, some not, including two 'hook' nodes, one in the tree editor component, and one in the physical view component. The hook is visible in the tree editor component as the root of the tree, but not in the physical view.

A controlled object loaded from an external file for editing, or such an object created using Doubleview, is attached at the above mentioned hook nodes, which are the articulation point between Doubleview's controlled and control structure. External Presenter files used by Doubleview (by convention, with the suffix .pr) are data files, and contain the logical structure of objects. Doubleview dynamically generates its own graphical tree representations from this logical structure.

Once the tool has been invoked in its initial default layout, conditional composition is used to provide access to many of the tool facilities. This mechanism is necessary because of limited screen space, the need to reduce on-screen visual 'noise', and to keep the tool memory requirements as low as possible.

The sequence 'selection of layout button in the tree-editing menu, loading and display of layout subtool in the subtool component' is a simple example of *conditional* composition of control objects. There are many examples of such composition techniques in graphical user interface design; hierarchies of pop-up menus are a common example.

The management of error messages gives a simplistic example of the part *temporal* composition can play in user interface design, in that in Doubleview, error messages are displayed for a finite length of time. A more subtle example of temporal composition, as yet unimplemented in Doubleview, is where objects newly added to or removed from the display appear and disappear gradually, via a zooming or fading mechanism, with speed under the control of the designer, rather than simply 'as fast as hardware constraints allow'. The possibilities of control of such rhythms of interaction are as yet largely uncharted territory.

9.3 Designing with Doubleview

The basic philosophy underlying Doubleview's support of the user interface design process is covered in more detail in [63].

The design by composition approach is closely associated with the principles of software configurability and reuse. Doubleview is intended to support the rapid construction of user interfaces through the composition of interaction components into well defined spatial, conditional or temporal relationships.

As it stands at present, the tool directly supports interactive spatial composition. Thus interaction components may be related spatially within a single plane, or in overlapping layers. The *execution* of conditional or temporal composition must be handled by the application, but Doubleview can still be used for the design of interface to be partitioned in this way. Some of the conditional groupings used in Doubleview's own user interface are described in Section 9.2.3.

A structured approach involving the use of small, conceptually discrete, easily configurable and reusable interaction objects is encouraged because of the interactive nature of the design tool. Naturally enough, performance degrades somewhat as Doubleview's controlled object gets larger, and it is easier to manipulate small Presenter subtrees (of, say, twenty or less regions) within Doubleview, rather than monolithic structures, although the latter is by no means impossible. Interactive fold, zoom and pan facilities have been incorporated into Doubleview so that large trees can be handled speedily, but at a reduced level of detail, or with a partial view of the overall structure.

Dynamic conditional composition has a larger part to play in broader ranging applications, e.g. the example IPSE system illustrating this book. In this case, very many large and structurally complex interaction components need to be designed in isolation using Doubleview. Checking how those parts fit together into the whole by composing them within Doubleview is done at regular intervals as a separate design activity.

9.3.1 Doubleview in relation to Aspect

There are several ways Doubleview might be used to form part of a kit for building IPSEs. Firstly, it might be used to design and develop a set of interaction objects, generic enough to provide interaction facilities for all applications on all IPSEs that might need to be built. These objects, along with tools for configuring and composing them (a restricted version of Doubleview), might be distributed to IPSE builders to build user interfaces for individual IPSEs. The set of objects might include control objects such as windows, menus, scroll-bars etc. and controlled objects (representations of data) such as tables, trees, graphs etc.

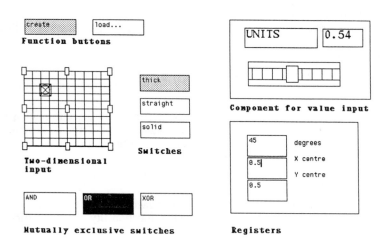

Fig. 9.10 Some general purpose interaction objects

The advantages of this sort of approach are:

1. A high degree of visual and interactive consistency is guaranteed between user interfaces on a particular IPSE, and also between Aspect IPSEs.

2. A considerable amount of time-consuming design work has been done, and need not be repeated by every system/application developer using the IPSE kit, or particular IPSE.

Balanced against this is the difficulty of designing a set of interaction objects which can be guaranteed to cover every user interaction requirement for a system, unless the objects are of such generality as to seriously reduce the productivity gains from the foregoing advantages.

Another point to bear in mind is that the graphical appearance of software systems is often required to reflect some proprietory company image, therefore similarities between IPSEs' user interfaces may be a thing to be avoided rather than pursued in the context of IPSE kit marketing.

Another approach is for IPSE builders to use Doubleview as it stands to help in the rapid prototyping and development of entire system and application user interfaces from scratch, within a particular IPSE. In this case, Doubleview is simply providing interactive access to the underlying Presenter primitives, with all the benefits of genericity and flexibility this implies. This is the way the tool has been used on the Aspect project to date, largely for developing demonstration software.

9.3.2 Building large scale application interfaces

Doubleview has been used for user interface development with applications of various sizes and complexity, from simple tools to Core and JSD workstations. The design and development of the user interface to the example IPSE illustrated in this book is now described, and role of Doubleview in such a design context is outlined.

Requirements

The user interface to the demonstration IPSE was required generally to illustrate and integrate the ideas and issues of Aspect. In particular, it was expected to provide:

- an illustration of one of the many ways in which the information base can integrate high-level project management and software engineering concepts such as tasks, publication, and configuration management to form a practical working environment;

- an illustration of integration of the human-computer interaction thread of Aspect with the IB;

- a useable but very flexible user interface, so that different ways of expressing and accessing underlying functionality could be tried out easily and cheaply by the system developers.

General design issues

It was decided at an early stage to implement Foley's Currently Selected Object (CSO) model [51] of interaction syntax in the demonstration IPSE. This model was used in Doubleview's user interface, and the previous experience was very useful for the rapid development of the demonstration interface. The CSO model provides a simple basic method for end-users to specify which function is to be applied to which object (Select Object which becomes CSO-Select Function). There are many ways in which the user can be provided with the means of making such specifications, some of which imply that an object-oriented system underlies the user interface: this is not the case in Aspect, where data and operations are distinct at the user interface.

Some major advantages of the CSO model are:

- it is adequate for both simple and very complex applications;

- it is easy to extend the syntax to allow for parameterised function invocations, without producing confusingly deep hierarchies of menus;

- Dynamic error prevention can be implemented easily, as in Doubleview.

A disadvantage is that graphical access to both data and functions must be provided simultaneously, which can prove expensive in terms of screen space.

A simple display object type hierarchy was implemented, again similar to that used in Doubleview. This breaks down as follows: display objects are either control objects or controlled objects (loosely, operations or data). Control objects can be further subdivided into: function objects selection of which directly invokes some function; parameter objects selection of which qualifies the invocation of some operation; or information objects.

Function objects can be further distinguished from each other by their domains of operation, which may be other control objects, controlled objects, or both. As an example of these distinctions, some function buttons become ineffective if a controlled object has not previously been selected, i.e. the CSO is null. The above organisation into types is visually expressed by screen layout, font and border weights.

Screen designs

All of the screens, tool fascias and data displays in the demonstration IPSE were developed using Doubleview, independently of the underlying application or information base development. The difficulties of providing a consistent user interface increase as the the number and variety of people involved increase, both as application developers and as projected system users. In this context a rapid prototyping design tool is invaluable as a discussion aid during the design process.

Doubleview was designed as a rapid prototyping user interface design tool. Because it is interactive, and promotes a high degree of separation between user interface and application, screen designs can be drawn up quickly and easily. Such designs can be tested interactively throughout the design process, and there is no compilation overhead to restrict an iterative design process. When the designs have been agreed upon, precise refinements and modifications can easily be carried out in Doubleview; again there is no need for recompilation, or any dependency on functioning application code.

Before going on to describe the demonstration IPSE user interface it should perhaps be stressed that the implemented format is just one of a multitude of possible designs.

There is an overall framework, available to all users/roles. The framework permits a user to display and interact simultaneously with as many role and/or task environments as are made available to that user in the information base and provides an integration mechanism for the different displays fronting work by different application developers. All work is carried out within task environments, and all task environments have a similar structure.

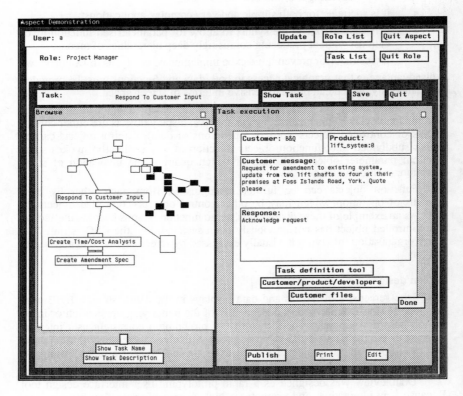

Fig. 9.11 An example task environment

Further illustrations of demonstration screens are included in Chapter 4. Each task environment is split into two parts; a browse tool which is used to display, select and navigate data appropriate to the current task from the information base, and an execution panel which provides access to tools and operations appropriate to the current task, which can be used to modify data selected from the browse tool. The execution panel can also display modifiable views of data, usually within the context of an editing tool of some sort.

The presentational separation of data and operations reflects the structure of the display object hierarchy described above, and is designed to promote consistency between displays for different roles and tasks while not sacrificing the flexibility necessary for handling their differences.

It is expected that most differences between task environments can be expressed by the provision of task-appropriate tools and operations (and sometimes a task-appropriate view of data within a particular tool). This will provide the flexibility necessary to supply user interfaces for very different roles and tasks.

At the same time, the browse tool can be used to provide a consistent interface to the information base whatever the current role or task, by using the same methods of data presentation, although the instances of data displayed using these generic formats will, of course, be task dependent.

Application framework

As well as the design of generic and task-specific screens, a framework application program was built to handle user interactions and the dynamic changes to the screens required as a result of these interactions. Some examples of the functionality required of this framework are:

- Identifying and invoking appropriate functions on appropriate objects when function buttons are selected;

- Loading in and initialising new task environments and tools;

- Obtaining and formatting for display, role and task information from the information base;

- Obtaining and formatting for display in the browse tool, data from the information base;

- Functions such as screen tiling, and enlarging/deleting of parts of the task environment;

- General purpose menu-generation, tree-layout routines etc.;

- General user feedback (highlighting, function enable/disablement etc.).

Despite the large size of many of the IPSE's display objects, Doubleview proved essential for experimenting with inter-screen relationships. As each tool interface was developed independently, it was necessary to check and modify how tools and screens would fit together at run time. Doubleview's 'folding' facility was very useful here, allowing easy experimentation with the relative positions and sizes of display objects and sub-components. Figure 9.12 shows the logical structure of the task environment illustrated in Figure 9.11, and gives some idea of the size and complexity of these user interface components. Designing, developing and maintaining such objects without any automated means of diagramming their logical structure would be a formidable task.

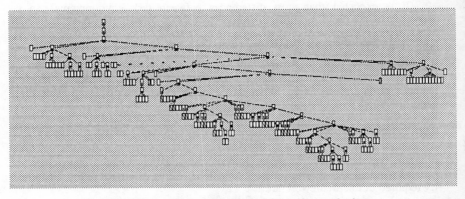

Fig. 9.12 Illustration of the size and logical complexity
of a single task environment in the demonstration IPSE

Chapter 10

Programming and Debugging Distributed Target Systems

A.D. Hutcheon, D.S. Snowden and A.J. Wellings

10.1 Introduction

Although the raison d'etre of Aspect is to support the development of real-time distributed* embedded computer systems, this has had very little direct influence on the design of the information base or the HCI primitives. Instead the support for distributed target systems is viewed as a set of application tools. These tools may have their own view of how target systems should be designed and debugged, but it has been found that in practise the general infrastructure provided by Aspect gives a sound base on which they can be built. It is this set of tools along with their underlying philosophy which is the subject of this chapter.

Although the Ada programming language is becoming increasingly popular for programming embedded computer system, there are (and will continue to be) other languages which are extensively used. For this reason we have tried to provide a set of tools whose underlying philosophy is language independent. It is our intention that our approach should be applicable to C, variants of Pascal (such as Perspective Pascal), Modula-1 and Modula-2, as well as Ada [66].

The chapter first considers our underlying approach to designing and

---

* We use the term distributed system to describe a multi-computer network where there is no common memory.

implementing distributed target systems in imperative programming languages. This approach is then applied to Ada. The debugging of distributed targets is then considered. To maintain continuity we consider our overall approach applied to Ada.

To test out our ideas we have implemented a set of tools to support Ada in a distributed environment. These are described and we show how they can be used to implement and debug an example system. Finally we consider performance issues and how the target tools can be integrated into the database.

10.2 Designing and Programming Distributed Target Systems

Very few programming languages provide direct support for programming distributed systems. However, as such systems become more widespread, many languages, particularly concurrent languages like Ada and Modula, will be employed for this purpose. Restrictions must be placed on the use of these languages so that processes executing on one machine do not have access to the memory space of processes executing on another. Furthermore, languages which do not support concurrency require extensions to facilitate their distribution. Unfortunately, there is no agreement as to which concurrent programming language facilities are best [4], and very little chance that any extension will be compatible with those provided in a language like Ada or Modula.

In this section we present a language-independent approach to designing and implementing distributed systems. This approach is formally specified in Z [95].

10.2.1 Design issues

There are many issues associated with distributed system design and implementation. We have concentrated on how distributed programs should be structured so that they can be partitioned for execution. Two basic approaches may be identified [28]:

(i)   distribute fragments of a single program across machines, and use normal intra-program communication mechanisms for interaction;

(ii) write a separate program for each machine and devise a means of inter-program interaction.

In this section we consider only (i) as it is more within the 'spirit' of distributed programs than (ii). The basic characteristic of this approach is that the application software is viewed as a single program, distributed across the target system. The main advantage of this approach, over (ii) above, is that all interfaces between the distributed program fragments can be type-checked by the compiler. Therefore, the type checking of the distributed program is that of the source language. Within this approach two general strategies can be identified [28]: *post-partitioning* and *pre-partitioning*.

Post-partitioning. As the name implies, this strategy is based on partitioning the program after it has been written. The program is designed without regard to a target architecture: the programmer produces an appropriate solution to the problem at hand and has the full language at his/her disposal. It is left to other software tools, provided by the programming support environment, to:

- describe the target configuration (which may be chosen by the designer or forced upon him/her);
- partition the program into components for distribution; and
- allocate the components to individual nodes.

The argument behind this strategy is threefold. First, most languages provide no facilities for configuration management so it is considered inappropriate for a program to contain configuration information. Second, the strategy promotes portable software – the same program can be mapped onto different hardware configurations. Third, no restrictions are placed on the way the language is used. However, a consequence of this approach is that the run-time system must support remote variable updates, distributed termination, remote inter-process communication, remote procedure calls, and distributed exception propagation. Furthermore, it is difficult to provide general support for post-partitioning.

The Honeywell Distributed Ada Project [38] uses the Ada Program Partitioning Language (APPL) to express the partitioning of Ada code onto different processors of the target system. To produce the object code for a distributed application the programmer submits an Ada program and an associated APPL program to the distributed Ada compiler. The compiler checks that the Ada program and the APPL program are legal and mutually consistent, and then produces an input to a linker along with a distributed run-time support package. The linker then produces an executable object module for each processor in the distributed target.

Pre-partitioning. The pre-partitioning strategy is to select a particular language construct as the sole unit of partitioning to be used throughout the design and programming process. The programmer is obliged to accept any constraints the choice of construct entails. The notion underlying this strategy is that of a *virtual node,* which is an abstraction of a physical node in the distributed system. A virtual node consists of one or more tasks (which may share memory) communicating with other virtual nodes via some form of message passing over a communication subsystem. More than one virtual node, however, can be mapped onto a single physical node. Note, that although the granularity of distribution must be built in at the design of the program, the ability to map more that one virtual node to a processor gives a degree of target independence.

The notion of virtual node is found in most languages which have been designed with the specific intent of supporting distributed programming (e.g. the 'guardian' of Argus [75], the 'group module' in Conic [90], and the 'processor module' of Starmod [37]

For a language construct to be effective as a virtual node it must be supported by [69]:

- separate compilation and library units;
- exception handling facilities to cope with communication failures; and
- dynamic instantiation without reinitialising the entire system.

It can be argued that for embedded computer systems this last requirement may be relaxed as such systems tend to be static, stand-alone, and purpose built. However, reliability requirements may imply some dynamic reconfiguration.

10.2.2 A language independent approach

We have adopted the pre-partitioning approach to programming distributed targets because we believe:

- potential distribution should be clearly visible to the programmer as it may affect the interfaces to be provided;
- post-partitioning is difficult to implement especially in a language as sophisticated as Ada; and
- adopting virtual nodes potentially allows a distributed system to be built from nodes written in different languages.

It is our view that units of encapsulation (we shall use the generic term *module*) such as the *package* in Ada and the *module* in Modula are one of the most important features of a programming language and that programs should be constructed, wherever possible, by linking together pre-written library modules. This has the significant advantage that programs are easier to construct and that software modules can be re-used effectively between programs. For this reason we have chosen the module as the basis of our Virtual Node; distributed programs can be constructed by linking together virtual nodes. However, in many languages modules are static and are not treated as first class objects; by adopting this approach we are accepting that there may be some limitations imposed on dynamic reconfiguration. If a variation of the module construct is not present in a language it may be possible to use some other form of encapsulation.

We have also decided that all virtual node communication will be via remote procedure call (RPC), for the following reasons:

- the procedure call is common to most imperative programming languages as a mechanism for transferring control;
- RPC's allow the possibility of easy communication between virtual nodes written in different languages; and
- techniques for reliable remote procedure call implementation are now fairly well understood [13,80,89] compared to that of implementing, say, a reliable remote Ada rendezvous [28].

We have indicated above that restrictions must be placed on the use of a programming language if it is to be employed in a distributed environment. Here we introduce the notation which will be used to specify formally our restrictions. The specification is written in Z [95], and consists of both a simple model of imperative programming languages and a collection of restrictions, expressed within that model, which ensure that a program can be distributed.

10.2.3 The Z specification notation

This section is intended to serve as a brief introduction to the formal notation used in the sections which follow.

Z is a formal specification technique developed by the Programming Research Group at Oxford University. The notation is a mathematical one based on strongly typed set theory and predicate logic. It is beyond the scope of this introduction to explain the theory of sets, functions, predicate logic and the like. Instead, some familiarity with such mathematical ideas is assumed and an overview of the facilities for structuring specifications given.

Much of the power of Z is gained from the schema language, which provides facilities to structure and reuse sections of mathematical notation. The basic building block is the schema itself, a construct used to enclose and name sections of mathematical specification. The form of a schema is shown here:

```
NAME1 ─────────────────────────────────────────────────
  signature1
  ─────────────────────────────────────────────
  predicate1
```

The signature provides the variables of the schema, consisting of a collection of names and their types. The predicate asserts properties which must hold upon the variables in the signature. The schema language provides several facilities for structuring and combining sections of specifications. The most frequently used of these is schema inclusion:

```
NAME2 ─────────────────────────────────────────────────
  NAME1
  signature2
  ─────────────────────────────────────────────
  predicate2
```

This has the effect of including the signature and predicate of NAME1 in NAME2, so allowing specifications to be developed in stages without having to repeat earlier material and so produce potentially large sections of unwieldy mathematics. Thus, the above schema is a shorthand for:

```
NAME2 ─────────────────────────────────────────────────
  signature1
  signature2
  ─────────────────────────────────────────────
  predicate1
  predicate2
```

Note the convention that the trailing 'and' of each line of a multi-line predicate is elided.

Z provides many more facilities than have been described here, but this should provide some familiarity with the notation when it is first used.

10.2.4 General specification of distributable programs

The intention is to distribute programs as collections of virtual nodes, with communication between these nodes by a remote procedure call (RPC) mechanism. This mechanism should be applicable to any imperative programming language which provides some unit of encapsulation and allows transfer of control by procedure or function invocation, examples being Ada, Modula and C. Certain assumptions underlie the specifications which follow.

- A distributed system should consist of a single program in the chosen implementation languages. This program will consist of a collection of virtual nodes, these being the logical units of distribution.

- Where the language provides separate compilation facilities it should be possible to compile virtual nodes separately. If such facilities are not provided it may still be possible to distribute programs by means of a preprocessor which splits the source into one program per virtual node.

Certain restrictions must be placed to allow the program to be split into virtual nodes using RPC communication. These prevent the sharing of memory between nodes and force all communication to be by procedure or function invocation.

We first give a general specification of the conditions which must hold for a program to be distributable, using a simple model of the sorts of object which occur in programming languages. These object have been chosen because their access or definition in a program must be constrained if that program is to be distributed. We then apply this specification to the concurrent programming languages Ada, Modula, and then the sequential language C.

There are several points which should be borne in mind when examining this specification:

- Although it attempts to remain general, the model given here cannot be applicable to every (current or future) imperative programming language. It is however intended to represent a common class of such languages.

- In order to remain general, certain parts of the model are left incomplete. These holes will be filled with specific details when the model is applied to particular languages.

- Some semantic details are missing from the model – these will be supplied by the connection of the parts of specific languages to the objects within the model, an action which effectively imports the semantics of the language under consideration.

10.2.5 The general language model

Before beginning the formal specification it is necessary to introduce a pair of functions which will be required later. Each of these maps a function from an object to a set of objects to a new, related, function from an object to a set of objects. They are generic in the type T of the objects mapped by the function parameters.

[T]

---

reflexive : $(T \rightarrow \mathbb{F}\, T) \rightarrow (T \rightarrow \mathbb{F}\, T)$
non_reflexive : $(T \rightarrow \mathbb{F}\, T) \rightarrow (T \rightarrow \mathbb{F}\, T)$

$\forall\, f, \text{rtof} : T \rightarrow \mathbb{F}\, T \mid \text{rtof} = \text{reflexive}(f)$ •
    dom f = dom rtof
    $\exists\, \text{rl} : T \leftrightarrow T \mid$ dom rl = dom f •
       $\forall\, t : T \mid t \in$ dom f •
         $f(t) = \text{rl} \,(\!\!(\, \{t\} \,)\!\!)\, \wedge \text{rtof}(t) = \text{rl}^{*} \,(\!\!(\, \{t\} \,)\!\!)$

$\forall\, f, \text{nrtof} : T \rightarrow \mathbb{F}\, T \mid \text{nrtof} = \text{non\_reflexive}(f)$ •
    dom f = dom nrtof
    $\exists\, \text{rl} : T \leftrightarrow T \mid$ dom rl = dom f •
       $\forall\, t : T \mid t \in$ dom f •
         $f(t) = \text{rl} \,(\!\!(\, \{t\} \,)\!\!)\, \wedge \text{nrtof}(t) = \text{rl}^{+} \,(\!\!(\, \{t\} \,)\!\!)$

The notation
$\rightarrow$
indicates a total function, and
$\leftrightarrow$
a relation.

The symbol $\mathbb{F}$ indicates a finite set of objects.

The image of a set through a function:
$f \,(\!\!(\, x \,)\!\!)$
gives the set of results obtained by applying f to every element of the set x:
$f \,(\!\!(\, \{ a, b, c \} \,)\!\!)\, = \{ f\, a, f\, b, f\, c \}$

The notation
f^{*}
indicates the reflexive transitive closure of the function f, and
f^{+}
indicates the non-reflexive transitive closure.

The first function *reflexive* produces a new function whose result is the set consisting of the initial parameter, the results of the original function, and the results of applying the original function to each element of its result set and to each element of each of these result sets recursively. It is thus analogous to the reflexive transitive closure operation on a function whose domain and range both have the same type.

The second function *non_reflexive* is the analogue of the non-reflexive transitive closure operation. Its result is therefore similar to that described above, but the result set does not include the parameter of the new function.

Objects

We now begin the specification proper by starting on our general model of programming languages. First, any programming language can be considered to consist of a set of objects. The nature of these objects is of no concern, although important details about them will be introduced.

[L_OBJ]

These objects can be classified into a collection of types:

$$OT \stackrel{\frown}{=} \text{active} \mid \text{invoked} \mid \text{module} \mid \text{passive} \mid \text{reference} \\ \mid \text{synchronisation} \mid \text{template}$$

The relationship between these types and the sorts of objects found in programming languages are as follows.

- *Active.* These are items which perform independent activity, for example processes or tasks.
- *Invoked.* These are procedures and functions – they perform activity, but only when invoked from elsewhere.
- *Module.* These are units of encapsulation and abstraction, such as Ada packages. They do nothing themselves, but alter the visibility of the objects they contain.
- *Passive.* These are data objects – variables which contain values but which cannot perform changes themselves (but excluding pointers to other objects).
- *Reference.* These are pointers or addresses – references to other objects.
- *Synchronisation.* These are mechanisms used for synchronisation and/or communication between active objects, for example monitors, semaphores, and ports.
- *Template.* These are type definitions – no actual objects exist in these cases, merely templates for the creation of objects. Constants and similar objects are considered to have type template.

When actual languages are considered the connections between these types and the objects of the language will be made explicit, so tying the language to this model and the accompanying specification. This will also resolve any type ambiguity of particular objects.

Having introduced the building blocks, objects and their types, we can begin to introduce concepts into our general language universe.

L_UNIV1 _____

  objtype : L_OBJ $\rightarrow$ OT

  params,
  visible,
  hidden : L_OBJ $\rightarrow$ F L_OBJ

  templateof : L_OBJ $\nrightarrow$ OT

  ──

  $\forall$ s : L_OBJ | objtype s = template •
   params s = { }
   visible s = { }
   hidden s = { }

  objtype $(\!|$ dom templateof $|\!)$ = { template }
  template $\notin$ rng templateof

──────────────────────────

The notation
$\nrightarrow$
indicates a partial function.

──────────────────────────

Any object has a type, and may have some parameters and contain both hidden and visible objects. The *templateof* function can be applied to any object of type template, returning the type of object to be instantiated from it. We do not allow templates for templates; constants and similar template objects are considered as templates for passive objects. The predicate that template objects have no parameters nor contain parts is not a proposition about languages conforming to this model, but a statement that we do not wish to consider the internal structure of such objects.

These fundamental properties of objects can now be used to place some constraints and to construct some further functions which will be useful later.

L_UNIV2 ⎯⎯⎯⎯⎯⎯⎯⎯⎯⎯⎯⎯⎯⎯⎯⎯⎯⎯⎯⎯⎯⎯⎯⎯⎯⎯⎯⎯⎯⎯⎯⎯⎯⎯⎯
┌
│ L_UNIV1
│
│ contains,
│ in,
│ visin   : L_OBJ $\rightarrow$ $\mathbb{F}$ L_OBJ
│ ⎯⎯⎯⎯⎯⎯⎯⎯⎯⎯⎯⎯⎯⎯⎯⎯⎯⎯⎯⎯⎯⎯⎯⎯⎯⎯⎯⎯⎯⎯⎯⎯⎯
│ $\forall$ o1 : L_OBJ •
│   contains o1 = visible o1 $\cup$ hidden o1
│ $\forall$ o2 : L_OBJ | o2 $\notin$ reflexive(contains) o1 $\wedge$
│   o1 $\notin$ reflexive(contains) o2 •
│   contains o1 $\cap$ contains o2 = { }
│
│ in = reflexive(contains)
│ visin = non_reflexive(visible)
└

These functions allow us to refer to all objects directly or indirectly contained or visible within a particular object (objects are considered to be in themselves, but not to be visible within themselves). The constraint that any object can be contained in only one object hierarchy is placed as any language not satisfying this (such as C++) could otherwise produce programs which satisfy the remainder of this specification but cannot be distributed. Root objects

Some objects are not contained within any other objects, and these will be of special interest to us:

L_UNIV3 ⎯⎯⎯⎯⎯⎯⎯⎯⎯⎯⎯⎯⎯⎯⎯⎯⎯⎯⎯⎯⎯⎯⎯⎯⎯⎯⎯⎯⎯⎯⎯⎯⎯⎯⎯
┌
│ L_UNIV2
│ root_obj : $\mathbb{P}$ L_OBJ
│ ⎯⎯⎯⎯⎯⎯⎯⎯⎯⎯⎯⎯⎯⎯⎯⎯⎯⎯⎯⎯⎯⎯⎯⎯⎯⎯⎯⎯⎯⎯⎯⎯⎯
│ $\forall$ r : L_OBJ •
│   r $\in$ root_obj $\Longleftrightarrow$ r $\notin$ $\cup$ rng contains
└

⎯⎯⎯⎯⎯⎯⎯⎯⎯⎯⎯⎯⎯⎯⎯⎯⎯⎯⎯⎯

Complementing $\mathbb{F}$, the symbol $\mathbb{P}$ indicates a potentially infinite set of objects.

The symbol $\cup$ indicates distributed set union, which has the effect:
$\cup$ { {x}, {y}, {z} } = {x} $\cup$ {y} $\cup$ {z} = { x, y, z }

⎯⎯⎯⎯⎯⎯⎯⎯⎯⎯⎯⎯⎯⎯⎯⎯⎯⎯⎯⎯

These root objects have special properties in many languages – for example, the library units of Ada are root objects.

Program libraries

We can now introduce the concept of a larger structure, the program library. Program libraries consist of collections of root objects, together with dependencies between these objects. A dependency between two objects means that the first in some way needs the second in order to operate. As an example, *dependson* applied to an Ada library unit would yield all those units named directly by it in WITH clauses. Although not all languages will confine such dependencies to be between root objects, such connections between other objects can be mapped onto the dependencies they produce between the enclosing root objects. For our purposes these resulting dependencies between root objects will be sufficient.

L_UNIV4 _____

   L_UNIV3
   prog_libs : $\mathbb{P}$ $\mathbb{F}$ root_obj
   dependson : prog_libs $\rightarrow$ (root_obj $\twoheadrightarrow$ $\mathbb{F}$ root_obj)
   ——————————————————————————————————————

   $\forall$ p : prog_libs •
    $\forall$ a : root_obj | a $\in$ p •
     $\forall$ b : root_obj | b $\in$ reflexive(dependson p) a •
      b $\in$ p

As we are interested only in complete program libraries, we impose the condition that any object depended upon by another object in the library must itself be present in the library.

The last part of the model is to introduce programs, these being some form of executable item:

   [PROGS]

Within our universe there is a set of these programs which are defined, and for each of these we can identify the library from which it is taken, the collection of root objects which are sufficient to extract the entire program, and the collection of root objects which make up the entire program. The way in which *rootsofprog* is provided will be dependent upon the language under consideration, while *elemsofprog* consists of the roots plus all that they depend upon.

```
L_UNIV _____

  L_UNIV4
  defined_progs : P PROGS
  libofprog : PROGS ↦ prog_libs
  rootsofprog : PROGS ↦ F root_obj
  elemsofprog : PROGS ↦ F root_obj
  _____

  ∀ p : PROGS | p ∈ defined_progs •
   ∃ pl : prog_libs •
   pl = libofprog p
   rootsofprog p ⊆ pl
   elemsofprog p = ∪ reflexive( dependson pl ) ⦇ rootsofprog p ⦈
```

10.2.6 The restrictions on distributable programs

Having completed our model of the general language universe we can go on to consider the distributable programs which exist within it. To begin this we introduce virtual node roots. Virtual node roots are the objects from which the virtual nodes of a distributed program can be extracted in the context of the associated program library. The virtual node root defines the interface to the node by means of the objects visible within it. The virtual node consists of the root together with those objects which the root depends upon.

```
DL_UNIV1 _____

  L_UNIV
  vnt : OT
  vnr : P L_OBJ
  _____

  ∀ o: L_OBJ | o ∈ vnr •
   objtype o = vnt
   objtype⦇ visin o ⦈ ⊆ { template, invoked, module }

   ∀ v : L_OBJ | v ∈ visin o ∧ objtype v = invoked •
    ∀ p : L_OBJ | p ∈ non_reflexive(params) v •
    objtype p ∈ { passive, invoked, vnt }
    objtype p = vnt ⇒ p ∈ vnr

   ∀ t : L_OBJ | t ∈ visin o ∧ objtype t = template •
    templateof t ∈ { passive, reference }
```

All virtual node roots are of the same type, which is the unit of encapsulation of the particular language. Each virtual node must present an interface which forces all communication between nodes to be by remote procedure call and which prevents the sharing of memory between nodes.

To prevent shared memory, the only objects which may be visible from outside a virtual node, and so be visible within a virtual node root module, are:

- templates for passive and reference objects (other templates may be for objects which, due to scope rules, would have access to the local state of the node which defines them when instantiated on another node);

- invoked objects (to be called via the RPC mechanism);

- and modules (in languages where these can be nested within other modues and so long as the objects visible within them also conform to these conditions).

Any invoked objects visible from outside a virtual node may be called by the RPC mechanism, so some restrictions must be placed on their parameters to prevent the addressing of non-local memory by means of values passed in. The types of parameters allowed by these restrictions are:

- Passive objects, as their values can be passed and a local copy acted upon;

- Invoked objects, to which calls may be made via the RPC mechanism, so long as their parameters conform in turn to these restrictions;

- Virtual node roots, whose visible parts must form a valid virtual node interface and so can be called by the RPC mechanism.

Sharable root objects

In order to provide flexibility we wish to allow root objects to be included in more than one virtual node if this will not require shared memory or allow non-RPC communications. This means that such a shared object must be capable of being replicated in each node which requires it without violating the semantics of sharing a single copy.

DL_UNIV2 _____

> DL_UNIV1
> replicatable : $\mathbb{P}$ root_obj
>
> _____
>
> $\forall$ o : root_obj •
> o $\in$ replicatable $\iff$
> objtype(in o) $\subseteq$ { template, invoked, module }

The objects which can safely be replicated are those which themselves contain only objects which can safely be replicated, those replicatable objects being:

- Templates, as they serve only as models for the instantiation of other objects;

- Modules, as they are units of encapsulation which affect only visibility and naming;

- Invoked objects, which are assumed to be reentrant, as the replicatability conditions exclude them having access to any state information which persists between calls.

A distributable program is one which consists solely of a collection of valid virtual nodes. For these virtual nodes to be valid each must present a valid RPC interface and any objects shared by more than one node must be suitable for replication on each node requiring them. The way in which the virtual nodes are identified will be dependent upon particular languages for which the model is instantiated. At this stage we assume that some suitable mechanism exists.

DL_UNIV ──

DL_UNIV2
distprogs : $\mathbb{P}$ PROGS
includes : PROGS $\rightarrow\!\!\!\!+$ root_obj $\rightarrow\!\!\!\!+$ $\mathbb{F}$ root_obj

───

distprogs $\subseteq$ defined_progs

$\forall$ p : PROGS •
  p $\in$ distprogs $\iff$
    $\exists$ vn_set : $\mathbb{F}$ root_obj | vn_set $\subseteq$ vnr $\land$
                      vn_set $\subseteq$ elemsofprog p •
      includes p =
        reflexive((dependson libofprog p) $\triangleright$ vn_set)

    rootsofprog p $\subseteq$ vn_set

    $\forall$ v1, v2 : vn_set | v1 $\neq$ v2 •
      $\forall$ o:root_obj | o $\in$ includes p v1 $\land$
                        o $\in$ includes p v2 •
        o $\in$ replicatable

──

───────────────────────────────

The symbol $\triangleright$ indicates range subtraction of a function. Given:
$f : X \longrightarrow Y$ and $y : \mathbb{F} Y$
then
$f \triangleright y$
indicates the function f with all elements of the set y removed from its result space (and all those X which map onto elements of y removed from its domain).

───────────────────────────────

For any distributed program we can identify the collection of virtual node roots, called *vn_set* above, from which the virtual nodes can be derived. The function includes identifies all the root objects required by a given virtual node. These consist of everything which the virtual node root depends upon, with the exclusion of other virtual nodes. The collection of root objects used to extract the entire program must consist only of virtual node roots. This condition ensures that a distributed program consists only of virtual nodes. Finally, any object which is required by more than one virtual node must be capable of being replicated in each virtual node which needs it.

10.2.7 Application of the model to Ada

The application of the general specification to yield distributable Ada programs consists of two parts; first the connection of Ada to the general language model, followed by the addition of Ada-specific details to the specification of distributable programs.

Informally a distributed Ada program consists of a collection of virtual nodes, each of which has a package as its root. This means that each of these virtual node root packages must present a valid RPC interface in its specification. The virtual node roots are extracted from the appropriate program library by means of a 'dummy' main procedure, which also forces the elaboration of each virtual node when program execution begins. This main procedure has the form:

```
WITH vnode1, vnode2,...
procedure main is

     begin
          null;
     end;
```

Note that packages `vnode1`, `vnode2`, etc. can be elaborated in parallel as long as the partial ordering implied by the elaboration is preserved [65] (see Section 10.5 of the Ada Language Reference Manual).

Ada and the general language model

This section gives the correspondence between the Ada language and the general language model developed earlier in this chapter.

The aim is to specify the programs which our approach can distribute rather than to develop a complete model of Ada, so there are many places where the general model omits restrictions which are required in valid Ada. This is not of concern here as distributability under our model implies distributability under the stronger conditions of valid Ada – problems would only occur if our model were to conflict with the restrictions of valid Ada.

The correspondence between Ada program fragments and the object types of our model is as follows:

- *Active.* The objects of this type are tasks, including any records or arrays containing tasks.
- *Invoked.* The objects of this type are Ada subprograms (procedures and functions).
- *Module.* Packages are the only objects having this type.
- *Passive.* The items which have this type are Ada variables which do not contain elements of either an access type or a task type.
- *Reference.* This type corresponds to Ada access types, including records and arrays containing instances of such types.
- *Synchronisation.* This does not have a direct representation in Ada as there

are no objects, as such, which are used to obtain synchronisation. However, they may be considered as entry points in tasks.

- *Template.* This type covers all items where no actual object exists – type declarations, exception declarations, generics and some constants. Constants of task types are considered to be active objects; and those of access types to have the type of the object which they access.

There are several points to note:

- The inclusion of exception declarations in the type template allows for the raising of exceptions between virtual nodes.

- The local variables of an invoked object are considered as part of the object itself, rather than as individual passive objects, as new copies are created with each invocation and they are accessible only from within the invoked object.

- The parameter set of a function is considered to contain any results which that function passes back to its point of call.

- There is a distinction between generics, which are of type template, and instantiations of generics, which have the type of the object for which the generic is a template.

- From the descriptions above a record containing both tasks and access variables has ambiguous type. In such cases the type selected at each point in the specification is that which avoids any restrictions being contravened. For example, if active objects were allowed but references were not then the type of the object would be reference.

- Private types in the visible part of a virtual node root are treated exactly as if they were not hidden.

- Although our approach localises most of the complex features of Ada within virtual nodes, certain uses of the abort statement can require the remote abortion of tasks spawned by remote subprogram invocation.

The connections between Ada and the remainder of the model follow from the classifications given above. The dependson function becomes an abstraction of the WITH clause mechanism, while the selection of the roots of a program is an issue dependent upon particular Ada implementations.

The use of inline pragmas can also cause dependencies between objects in Ada. These are ignored here as they are of no significance to us within virtual nodes and can legally be ignored if they would cause dependencies between nodes. The dependencies between generic instantiations and the generic units which they instantiate are also of no special concern to us as we are interested only in the properties of the final objects, no distinction being made between specifications and bodies.

The restrictions on distributable Ada

The general specification gives a sufficient set of conditions to allow a program to be distributed by our proposed mechanism. As a result, the specification of distributable Ada programs consists of this, together with the propositions that virtual node roots, being packages, are of type module, and that the program is extracted from its library by means of a 'dummy' main procedure:

```
ᴅADA_UNIV _____
  DL_UNIV
  main : ℙ root_obj
  _____

  vnt = module

  ∀ p : PROGS •
    p ∈ distprogs ⟺
      ∃ m : main •
      rootsofprog p = dependson (libofprog p) m
      m = procedure main is
              begin
                null;
              end;
```

Predefined language environment

An Ada program executes in a predefined environment the interface to which is specified by several standard packages. These include the packages: `standard`, `system`, `calendar` and `text_io`. The bodies of these packages will vary from implementation to implementation and for some of them will be provided directly by the compiler inline. We make the assumption that all the packages which make up the standard environment can be replicated. Whilst this may be valid for package standard and package system there is little chance that the `text_io` package can be replicated given our restrictions. In these cases such packages must be rewritten as generics.

10.3 Distributed Debugging

Once a distributed application has been designed and written, almost inevitably it needs to be debugged. Unfortunately there is currently little support available for the debugging of distributed systems. In this section we discuss the design of a debugger for such systems, based upon an approach previously proposed by Harrison [59], and similar to that employed by Curtis and Wittie [39]. Whilst, for the purposes of this discussion, we will concentrate on the the debugging of distributed programs written in Ada, the same basic principles apply to the debugging of distributed programs written in other imperative languages.

We begin by outlining the types of error which can arise in distributed Ada programs, and explaining the derivation of the basic mechanism of the debugger.

10.3.1 Debugging distributed Ada programs

The debugging of Ada programs which consist of multiple tasks has certain similarities to the debugging of single task programs, but there are also important differences. The similarities arise because in a multi-task system it is still possible, to a certain extent, to consider the individual tasks in isolation, and to apply conventional debugging techniques in order to discover various sorts of algorithmic error within those tasks. The differences arise because multi-task programs, whether they are run on a single processor or on multiple processors, are affected by a class of errors which are not applicable to single-task programs; these errors concern the ways in which tasks interact with one another.

Tasks interact in a limited number of well-defined ways, which generally concern the communication between pairs of tasks: in our model of distributed Ada this involves rendezvous and shared variable communication between tasks residing in the same virtual node, and RPC communication between tasks residing in different virtual nodes. Other types of interaction concern task creation, activation, and termination. These interactions are collectively referred to as *Inter-task events (ITEs)*. A summary of all of the types of ITE which we have identified as being of relevance when considering distributed Ada programs can be found in Table 10.1. A formal specification, written in Z [95], of these types of ITE and of the restrictions on their ordering can be found in a previous document by Snowden [92].

In theory it should be possible to detect errors of task interaction simply by observing the ITEs that occur, but in practise the observation of ITEs in real time is not really practicable. One solution to this problem is to monitor the execution of a collection of tasks in real time, and to record in a *trace* the details of the ITEs that occur. The trace can subsequently be examined at leisure.

Whilst examining the contents of an ITE trace is sufficient for determining the existence of an erroneous sequence of ITEs, it is not sufficient for determining the underlying algorithmic error in the individual tasks within the system which has given rise to that sequence. In order to be able to do that, the entries in the ITE trace need to be tied back to the execution of the tasks themselves. This can be achieved by using the trace to drive a *replay* of some or all of the tasks in the original program. During such a replay the user can examine the behaviour of individual tasks at the statement level using the facilities of a conventional symbolic debugger; for example, examining the values of variables, setting breakpoints, and single-stepping execution.

We now proceed to discuss a number of issues relating to the design of a *trace-replay* debugging system for distributed Ada programs, and to suggest a number of ways in which the facilities provided by such a system may be applied. In our discussion we concentrate upon a hardware configuration which consists of a collection of networked target machines with a link to a host machine. We also concentrate on the debugging of tasks in the target machine context; debugging in the virtual node context is broadly similar.

ITE	Description
TASK_CREATED	the task has been created by elaboration or by an allocator
START_ACTIVATION	the task has started its activation
ACTIVATION_COMPLETE	the task has finished its activation
TASK_COMPLETED	the task has completed
TASK_TERMINATED	the task has terminated
ACTIVATE_TASKS	the task is activating dependent tasks
ACTIVATE_TASKS_COMPLETE	the activation of the dependent tasks has finished
WAIT_FOR_DEP_TASKS	the task is waiting for its dependent tasks to terminate
DEP_TASK_TERMINATED	a dependent task has terminated
WAIT_FOR_DEP_TASKS_COMPLETE	all dependented tasks have terminated
DELAY_STATEMENT	the task has executed a delay statement
DELAY_TIMEOUT	the delay on which a task is waiting has expired
ENTRY_CALL_STATEMENT	the task has encountered an entry call statement
CONDITIONAL_ENTRY_CALL	the task has encountered a conditional entry call
TIMED_ENTRY_CALL	the task has encountered a timed entry call
COMMENCE_ENTRY_CALL	the (calling) task has commenced a rendezvous
ENTRY_CALL_COMPLETE	the (calling) task has finished a rendezvous
ACCEPT_STATEMENT	the task has encountered an accept statement
SELECTIVE_WAIT	the task has encounted a selective wait statement
ACCEPT_ENTRY_CALL	the (accepting) task has commenced a rendezvous
ACCEPT_ENTRY_CALL_COMPLETE	the (accepting) task has finished a rendezvous
ENTRY_COUNT	the number of calls queued on an entry has been requested
ABORT_STATEMENT	the task has aborted other tasks
TASK_ABORTED	the task has been aborted
EXCEPTION	an exception has been raised in the task
INTERRUPT	an interrupt has been raised
READ_DEVICE_REGISTER	the task has read from a device register
WRITE_DEVICE_REGISTER	the task has written to a device register
COMMENCE_SV_ACCESS	the task has commenced a shared variable access
SV_ACCESS_COMPLETE	the shared variable access has finished
CALL_RP	the task has called a remote procedure
RPC_RESULT	the task has received the result from a RPC
RPC_RECEIVED	a remote procedure call has been received
RETURN_FROM_RPC	a called remote procedure has finished executing
START_TASK	the task has been scheduled
SUSPEND_TASK	the task has been suspended

Table 10.1 Ada inter-task events

10.3.2 Primary requirements of the trace-replay mechanism

In this section we consider some of the basic requirements which apply to the design of the mechanism of a trace-replay debugging system.

Trace collection

When collecting a trace it is imperative that the action of recording the ITEs in the trace should disturb the behaviour of the monitored user program as little as possible. However, it is inevitable that some disturbance will result, and as a consequence there will always be some bugs which will disappear when trace collection is applied. We can only seek to minimise the likelihood of this by minimising the disturbance caused by the collection of a trace.

One way in which to minimise the disturbance caused by the collection of a trace is to arrange for the ITEs relating to particular tasks to be recorded on the target machines where those tasks are executed. The alternative, to send details of every ITE back to the host, would have a greater effect on the behaviour of the user program, not least because of the extra load which it would place on the communications subsystem. If traces are to be stored on the target machines then we must make the assumption that there is sufficient space available on the target machines for that purpose. However, the space on the target machines is obviously finite, and the trace collection mechanism must take this into account.

Snapshots

If it is wished to be able to replay the user program in such a way that a conventional symbolic debugger can be applied to individual tasks within the program, then it is necessary to precede the collection of the trace with a snapshot of the states of each of the tasks. If space on the target machines permits then the snapshots might be stored there, otherwise they must be up-lined to the host at some appropriate time. Wherever snapshots are stored, the action of recording them is likely to have some effect on the behaviour of the user program irrespective of whether the program is actually suspended whilst the snapshots are taken.

As the user program may be distributed over a number of target machines it is necessary to provide a mechanism for synchronising the snapshots on each of the target machines so that together they represent a consistent starting state for the replay of the tasks of the user program.

Integrating snapshots and trace collection

The simplest implementation of a snapshot-and-trace mechanism involves taking a snapshot of the initial state of the tasks within the user program, and then recording ITEs in a trace for as long as is required. However, this could involve collecting a trace of arbitrary length, which is clearly infeasible given the limited amount of space likely to be available on the target machines. Given that the snapshot-and-trace mechanism is constrained by the space available on the target machines, it is essential to allow a reasonable degree of flexibility over when the snapshots are taken and the collection of the trace commences.

Replay

As far as the replay of a user program is concerned, the main consideration, apart from the way in which the trace is to be used to drive the replay, is the need to provide extra functionality on the target machines to support the facilities of the symbolic debugger; for example, the examination of variables, the setting of breakpoints, and the control of execution.

10.3.3 Monitoring considerations

In this section we consider various issues relating to the collection of traces and snapshots during the monitoring of a user program.

What to trace

We have already stated that a trace is used to record details of the ITEs that occur during the monitoring of the tasks within a program. Not surprisingly, each type of ITE corresponds closely to a particular routine within the Ada run-time kernel, and so the most obvious way to record the occurrence of ITEs is to add code to the appropriate kernel routines to copy the details of each ITE into the trace. The actual details to be recorded depend on the type of the ITE, but typically they include the identity of the task which gave rise to the ITE, the type of the ITE, and the time at which it occurred.

It is not always necessary to record all of the ITEs that arise from the execution of a program, so it may be useful to facilitate the conditional recording of ITEs. The sort of conditions which might be applied can be based upon the attributes of an ITE, such as the task which gave rise to it, and the type of the ITE. One advantage of being selective about which ITEs are recorded is that it reduces the rate at which ITEs are recorded, hence enabling trace collection to span a greater period of time. The disadvantages are that the evaluation of the conditions increases the effect on the behaviour of the user program, and that the resulting trace can not be used to drive a replay (see sections on event level replay and full replay).

Methods of trace collection

There are two possible approaches to collecting a trace; they differ in the ways in which they manage the *trace buffer* (the buffer holding the ITE details which constitute the trace). These approaches are:

- one-off trace collection: recording ITEs only until the trace buffer becomes full;

- cyclic trace collection: recording ITEs in a circular trace buffer. This method continues until the recording is halted for some other reason (see section on terminating trace collection).

Initiating trace collection

The commencement of the collection of traces can be triggered in three ways:

- by the start of execution of the monitored program;

- by the user issuing an explicit command; as this is done on-the-fly its usefulness may be limited;

- by some specified condition becoming satisfied. Just how complex such conditions might be is a matter for debate; in general the more complex a condition is the longer it will take to evaluate, and the more likely it is that its evaluation will affect the behaviour of the user program. This applies particularly to conditions which relate to multiple tasks or to sequences of ITEs.

Terminating trace collection

The termination of the collection of traces can be triggered in three ways:

- by the trace buffer becoming full (this only applies to the one-off method of trace collection).
- by the user issuing an explicit command.
- by some specified condition becoming true. The types of condition permitted here are the same as those which can be used to trigger the commencement of trace collection.

Synchronising the traces

Each target machine maintains its own clock which keeps logical time [74]. Assuming that tasks on different target machines communicate sufficiently frequently to keep the logical clocks reasonably in step, the traces on each of the target machines will appear to cover roughly the same periods of logical time: that is, the traces should exhibit a reasonable overlap. The synchronisation of the commencement and termination of trace collection on each of the target machines requires the ability to request that all target machines start/stop trace collection instantaneously. In the absence of suitable hardware support such synchronisation has to be achieved by the propagation of special 'software signals'. Inevitably this method will allow the target machines, and hence the tasks running on them, to get slightly out of step with one another. As a result, the behaviour of the user program may be affected. Unfortunately this is unavoidable.

What to snapshot

There are several possible approaches to taking snapshots which differ in the amounts of information which are recorded. The simplest approach is to snapshot the entire executable image of the parts of the user program residing on each of the target machines; this includes both code and data. If it can be assumed that the code on each of the target machines is not self-modifying and that it will not be damaged during monitoring because of bugs in the user program, then it is only really necessary to snapshot the *data* areas on each target machine; this will obviously reduce the size of the snapshots.

It is also possible to reduce the size of a snapshot by recording only the details pertaining to specific tasks within the program. This approach is complicated by the presence of shared variables which do not lie in the data areas belonging to any particular task, but which still need to be recorded. For this reason it may be more appropriate to snapshot individual virtual nodes rather than individual tasks.

Under some circumstances it can be sufficient to snapshot only a very limited amount of information pertaining to individual tasks; for example, their run-states, and the queues associated with each of their entries. This minimal information can be used in conjunction with the event level replay mechanism (see section on event level replay).

Methods of snapshotting

There are two possible approaches to taking snapshots which correspond directly to the methods of trace collection:

- take a snapshot and follow it by the collection of a one-off trace;
- repeat a cycle of snapshot and trace, taking a snapshot each time the trace buffer becomes 'full', then continuing with the cyclic filling of the trace buffer.

Initiating and terminating snapshotting

The snapshot and trace mechanism can be controlled in exactly the same ways as were previously described in relation to the trace-only mechanism.

Synchronising snapshots

As the snapshots are to be used as the starting point for the replay of the user program, it is essential that the taking of snapshots on the individual target machines is synchronised so that together the snapshots form a consistent representation of the state of the user program at a given instant. Since snapshots are taken immediately prior to the commencement of the collection of a trace, their synchronisation is a consequence of the mechanism for the synchronisation of trace collection.

Multiple snapshots and traces

A potential drawback of the snapshot-and-trace mechanism is that a target machine may be instructed to cease trace collection when it has only just taken a snapshot, and hence when there is little or no subsequent trace available for use in a replay. For this reason it can be useful to retain at least one previous generation of snapshot and trace which can be called upon if required. This obviously increase the storage requirements for holding the snapshots and the traces.

10.3.4 Trace browsing

One of the simplest approaches to using a trace as a basis for debugging is to browse through the ITEs contained within the trace. A trace browsing tool allows a user to look through the chronologically-ordered entries in an ITE trace, and provides them with the facilities to search for ITEs whose attributes satisfy certain conditions.

As the ITE traces are held in the trace buffers on the individual target machines at the end of trace collection, some method of accessing these traces for browsing is required. This is most easily achieved by up-lining the traces to the host machine and merging them to form a single, combined trace in which all the ITEs from different target machines are ordered by logical time. The trace browser can then be run entirely on the host machine.

Note that whilst snapshots are not required for trace browsing, there is no reason why the trace browser cannot be applied in situations where a snapshot has been collected as well as the trace.

10.3.5 Event level replay

A slight refinement on the simple trace browsing approach is to use the ITEs contained in the combined trace to drive a replay of the behaviour of the tasks within a program at the ITE level. Such a facility, running on the host machine, allows the user to step through the ITEs (either singly, or until an ITE with specified attributes is encountered) and observe such things as the run-states of the tasks, the states of their entry queues, and the values of the parameters of the individual entry calls. Note that the information which drives the event level replay is derived solely from the combined trace; no execution of the code of the user tasks is involved, and so no details of the internal states of the user tasks themselves are available. Note also that if no snapshots were collected along with the trace, the initial run-states of the tasks and the initial states of their entry queues will be unknown.

10.3.6 Full replay

Whilst the trace browser and the event level replay system facilitate varying degrees of examination of the behaviour of tasks at the ITE level, they do not address the problem of examining the code of the user tasks to determine the underlying algorithmic errors. This can be achieved by driving a full replay of the user program from the combined trace. The facilities provided by full replay are similar to those provided by event level replay, but they are extended by the provision of a symbolic debugger which can be applied to the individual tasks within the program.

The most straightforward way to implement full replay is to run the code of the individual tasks on the target machines where they ran during trace collection, and to control the replay from the host machine. To prepare the system for replay it is first necessary to reset the target machines to a consistent state; this can be achieved by reloading the appropriate snapshot details into each machine. Replay is then driven by the contents of the combined ITE trace in such a way that the order in which the ITEs occur during the replay is constrained to be the same as the order in which they occurred during monitoring. In order to achieve this it is necessary to alter the behaviour of the run-time kernel routines associated with particular ITEs so that, for example, a task which would receive an entry call direct from some other task during live running will actually have the details of the appropriate call provided from the combined trace by the host machine. The behaviour of the kernel routines also needs to be modified when replaying to prevent the collection of further traces and snapshots.

Note that, in order for it to be possible to replay a task, all of that task's ITEs must be recorded in the original trace. If only a subset of a task's ITEs are recorded then it is not possible to relate ITEs arising during replay to ITEs from the trace, and hence the detection of trace invalidation (as explained in the section on the mechanism of replay) becomes impossible.

Granularity of replay

It might be considered desirable to depict a number of tasks which ran on different target machines during monitoring as executing truly in parallel during replay, whether the execution be continuous or single-stepped. However, to guarantee accurate parallel replay at the level of the individual statement would require that each target machine enter a timestamped record of the execution of every statement into its trace. There would be a very large overhead in terms of both the time and space required to record this information. It is clearly not practicable to collect such a detailed trace, and hence it is not possible to depict the parallel execution of tasks at the statement level.

Given that only ITEs are recorded in the trace, the granularity of the replay (at least in terms of the apparent relative execution of different tasks) is necessarily at the ITE level. Since any attempt to display parallel execution of tasks at the statement level would be meaningless, careful consideration has to be given to the way in which parallel execution is to be presented to the user. The best approach is probably to use a two-level presentation. The first level provides an overview of system execution in pictorial form, displaying the tasks which are being replayed, and illustrating their run-states and the rendezvous between them. The second level provides one window per task, and in those windows the full details of the individual ITEs are displayed in textual form as they are replayed.

Whilst the execution of a number of tasks may be observed at the ITE level at the same time, it is only meaningful to allow the execution of a single task to be observed at the statement level at any given time. The particular task selected to be observed at the statement level at any given time will be referred to as the *current task,* and is the one to which the facilities of the symbolic debugger may be applied. The selection of the current task may be explicit, or it may come about as a result of the occurrence of a statement level breakpoint or a specified ITE in a task.

Mechanism of replay

When carrying out a full replay, the execution of the tasks is commenced from the states which they were in when the previous snapshot was taken. The replay of the tasks is then driven by the contents of the combined trace in the following way. Initially, the first ITE is taken from the combined trace, and the task which gave rise to that ITE during trace collection is then run until the corresponding ITE occurs. Then the next ITE is taken from the trace, the corresponding task is run, and so on. It should be noted that although the tasks are replayed on the target machines, no actual parallel execution is involved. When a replayed task gets to a point where it would, during monitoring, record an ITE, it is checked to ensure that the ITE would be the same as that which was taken from the trace (and was hence expected to be the next ITE to occur in the replay). When a replayed task is waiting to accept an entry call, the parameters of the call will be supplied from the appropriate ITE in the trace, and not directly from the calling task.

If a statement level breakpoint or specified ITE occurs during the replay of a particular task, the whole replay is halted, that task becomes the current task (if it was not already so), and the facilities of the symbolic debugger can then be applied to that task.

The implementation of statement-level single-stepping by the debugger is complicated by the presence of statements which give rise to ITEs. It has already been stated that the normal execution mechanism for replay always selects the next ITE from the trace and runs the corresponding task. Whilst the user is single-stepping through the statements of a task they might single-step the execution of a statement which gives rise to a particular ITE such that there were other ITEs in other tasks which should have arisen before that one. Although this might not always be significant, in some cases it can change the behaviour of the replayed program in important ways. For example, consider the case of single-stepping through a conditional entry call. It may be that the conditional entry call fails because the called task is apparently not waiting at an accept statement associated with the particular entry. However, it may also be the case that one of the ITEs which should have arisen previously would have signalled the readiness of the called task to accept the entry call, hence implying that the conditional entry call should have succeeded.

There are three possible ways to approach the problem of single-stepping statements which give rise to ITEs:

- to forbid the single-stepping of such statements, at least in those cases where preceding ITEs should have arisen. The consequent need to return to the ITE level in order to arrange for the preceding ITEs to be cleared would almost certainly be an impediment to the debugging process;

- to detect the single-stepping of such statements, and temporarily suspend the single-stepping whilst other tasks are allowed to catch up. Given this approach, it might well prove to be desirable to ignore breakpoints in the other tasks while they are catching up, otherwise the single-stepping could become very complicated from the user's point of view. The disadvantage of this would be that potentially important breakpoints could be ignored;

- to allow the user to single step such statements, but to warn them beforehand that single-stepping a particular statement would cause the trace to be invalidated (see below).

Another issue which needs to be considered concerns what changes, if any, the user should be allowed to make to the tasks and ITEs during replay. It is not immediately obvious whether the user should be allowed to change the values in a task's variables using the symbolic debugger. It is equally uncertain whether the user should be allowed to manipulate the ITEs by, for example, changing the values of particular attributes. In either case there would be a danger that the change which was made would affect the way in which the tasks interacted, thus invalidating the remainder of the ITE trace. However, it is important to realise that the user will normally be investigating a trace which contains an erroneous sequence of ITEs, and that, in order to test their theories about the underlying algorithmic cause of that sequence, they may wish to make changes which are intended to rectify the sequence. This approach, by its very nature, results in the invalidation of the trace. The only alternative approach available to the user when investigating a possible underlying algorithmic cause would be to edit the source, re-compile, re-load, and re-run the program, monitoring its execution again if it still failed to work properly. This would obviously not be a very satisfactory method.

If the user is to be allowed to make alterations to task states and ITEs then it is necessary to allow execution of a program to continue after the trace has been invalidated. Since such execution obviously can not be driven from the trace, the only alternative is to allow 'live' execution of the program to be resumed. It would seem not unreasonable to expect that such live execution could itself be the subject of trace collection for subsequent replay.

The point at which the invalidation of the trace becomes apparent will depend upon the type of alteration which has caused the invalidation. If the alteration was to an ITE then the trace automatically becomes invalidated straight away, but if the alteration was to a task's state then it is not necessarily the case that the trace will be invalidated at all. In the latter case the invalidation of the trace will only become apparent when a subsequent ITE which occurs in the replayed system is found not to match the corresponding ITE from the trace.

The resumption of live running of the tasks following the invalidation of the trace is a simple matter of sending an appropriate start-up message to each of the target machines. However, since the individual tasks are only synchronised at the ITE level (and not at the statement level) during replay, this (taken together with the inevitably non-synchronous start-up of the target machines) may limit the usefulness of the subsequent live running.

Interrupts

An area of the trace-replay mechanism which requires careful consideration is the way in which interrupts are to be handled. In Ada, it is quite straightforward to record ITEs representing an interrupt and the corresponding 'accept' by an interrupt handler, but that alone is not sufficient. It is also necessary to record ITEs representing the accesses to device registers made from within an interrupt handler; particularly so when values are being *read* from the registers.

In order that accesses to device registers may be recorded, they must be easily identifiable. This can be achieved by adopting the approach recommended by Hibbard et al. [60], where device registers are accessed only through the *send_control* and *receive_control* procedures of the package `low_level_io`, and not by associating device registers with variables using address clauses. It can be arranged that the *send_control* and *receive_control* procedures make calls to appropriate routines in the run-time kernel which record ITEs containing the values read from or written to specific device registers.

When replaying a program, further interrupts are disabled, and all interrupt-related ITEs are generated from the trace. Attempted reads from device registers actually pick up the appropriate values from the corresponding ITEs in the trace, whilst attempted writes to device registers have no effect at all.

Whilst it is the case that, during replay, interrupt ITEs will occur in the same order relative to other ITEs as they did during monitoring, it should be emphasised that they will be unlikely to occur at the same point relative to the execution of the individual statements of the tasks within the program. Hence it will not generally be possible to use the trace-replay debugger to find errors whose occurrence is dependent upon the point at which an interrupt arises relative to the execution of individual statements. However, such errors can only be associated with shared variable updates which are considered next. Shared variables

Another area of the trace-replay mechanism which requires careful consideration is the way in which shared variables are to be dealt with. The main difficulty here is in trying to identify those variables in an Ada program which are intended to be shared; this is quite difficult unless a given shared variable also happens to be specified as the argument of a *shared* pragma. In order that shared variable access ITEs can be recorded, it is necessary to arrange for shared variable accesses to be carried out by calls to a routine in the run-time kernel.

We contend that the shared variable is not intended to be the primary means of inter-task communication in Ada, and that where shared variables really are required they should be encapsulated in individual tasks in order to guarantee exclusive access to them. If such an approach can be assumed then the explicit recording of shared variable access ITEs becomes unnecessary. However, if 'free-standing' shared variables are used then we must accept that it will be difficult, or even impossible, to record accesses to them.

10.3.7 Debugging methods

The facilities which have been described so far can be used to implement a number of different methods for the debugging of distributed Ada programs. It is our intention to provide a range of debugging methods which provide varying amounts of information, whilst disturbing the behaviour of the monitored program to different degrees. In general, the more information which a particular method provides, the greater will be the disturbance to the monitored program. The user can try to find a happy medium in any particular case between trying to maximise the amount of useful debugging information which is made available, and disturbing the behaviour of their program to such an extent that the sought bug disappears. It is realised that this strategy relies on the assumption that the particular bug under investigation can be made to manifest itself reasonably frequently. Some of the possible debugging methods are outlined below:

- Single trace collection without snapshot: when execution of the program is suspended, for whatever reason, the trace which has been collected may be browsed or used to drive an event level replay. Whether the trace is collected on a one-off basis or cyclically, this method has the least effect on the behaviour of the monitored program.

- Repeated trace collection without snapshots: when a buffer full of ITEs has been collected, execution of the program is suspended so that the trace may be browsed or used to drive an event level replay. Execution of the program may then be resumed to collect another trace which can itself be browsed or replayed, and so on. The need to suspend the monitored program to allow browsing or event level replay to take place means that this method is more likely to affect the behaviour of the program. Since the effect on the behaviour of the program is exactly the same as it would be if snapshots were also being taken, hence enabling a full replay to be performed, then this method may not be especially useful.

- Single snapshot and trace: the collection of a single snapshot followed by a trace has a fairly minimal effect on program behaviour because execution of the program is only suspended once so that the snapshot may be taken. The resulting snapshot and trace may be used for trace browsing, event level replay, or full replay.

- Single cyclic snapshot and trace (taking a new snapshot every time the ITE trace buffer becomes 'full'): as execution of the program has to be suspended whenever a snapshot is to be taken, the effect of this method on the behaviour of the program increases with the number of cycles of snapshot and trace which take place. When execution of the program is finally suspended, for whatever reason, the most recent snapshot and trace may be used for trace browsing, event level replay, or full replay.

- Repeated snapshot and trace: this involves collecting a snapshot followed by a trace, suspending the execution of the program whilst the trace is used to drive a full replay, resuming the execution of the program to collect another snapshot and trace, and so on. The more often this cycle is repeated, the greater will be its effect on the behaviour of the program. Of course, the traces may also be used for browsing or for event level replay.

10.4 Tool Support for Ada in a Distributed Environment

In order to evaluate our approach to programming and debugging distributed Ada programs we have developed several tools and built an example embedded control program, using the York Ada compiler [50] with a run-time system modified to support distributed operation on stand-alone processor boards. This program drives a model lift system.

10.4.1 The system to be controlled

Our example problem consists of a mechanical model of a lift system [53]. This model stands about a little over a meter high and consists of four lift cars serving six floors. Cars may be called and directed to floors by means of buttons on the floors and in the cars. Movement and positioning is undertaken by means of directional motor control, detectors for every 0.75mm of movement in the car drive cables, and end switches at the extremes of car travel.

The model forms a non-trivial piece of real time hardware with a mixture of polled and interrupt driven operation.

10.4.2 The controlling computer system

The target machines we have been using for our work are standard Motorola M68010 boards (MVME117-3FPA), of which we have five. Each board has a 10MHz 68010 processor, two megabytes of RAM, two serial ports, and two eight bit parallel ports. One of the serial ports on each board is connected, via a simple line driver, to a token-passing broadcast network over which the boards communicate via messages. This network operates at speeds of up to 75K baud, which gives a transmission rate of about 9000 bytes per second once a board gains possession of the token.

Also connected to the network is a sixth board, built in-house and based on a Motorola M68000, which acts as a gateway between the network and a 9600 baud serial line connection to a host machine (Sun workstation).

The network also supports out-of-band message transmission. If a station is already transmitting an in-band message when the request to send an out-of-band message arises, then the out-of-band message will be sent immediately after the in-band one, and before the token is passed on. Otherwise, the out-of-band message is sent next time that the station receives the token, taking precedence over any in-band messages which are waiting to be sent. When a station receives an out-of-band message it is decoded and acted upon immediately, taking precedence over any in-band messages which are waiting to be decoded. The out-of-band message transmission facility is of particular importance to the trace-replay debugging system where it is used to implement the distributed suspend/resume mechanism.

The M68010 boards are interfaced to the lifts by means of the parallel ports. One of the five boards is connected to poll the request buttons on the floors and lift cars, while each of the other four are connected to control the movement and positioning of a single car. The car control consists of outputs for winding motor activation and direction together with an interrupting movement sensor and polled top and bottom switches which provide absolute position information.

10.4.3 The control program

The program is arranged as a central scheduler virtual node reading the request buttons and allocating these requests to four car controller virtual nodes on other boards. Each car controller periodically returns position information to a sixth virtual node which is interrogated by the scheduler to aid sensible request allocation. This arrangement of virtual nodes and their allocation to the five physical processors is shown in Figure 10.1.

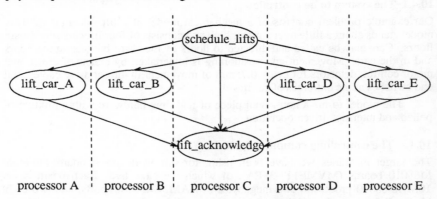

Fig. 10.1 Lift program configuration

Both *schedule_lifts* and *lift_acknowledge* reside on the button-reading processor, while each *lift_car* node is placed on the processor connected to that lift shaft. To give some measure of complexity the approximate program size is:

- Button reading and scheduling node: 2000 lines of Ada.
- Each car control node: 1000 lines of Ada plus about 20 assembler instructions which catch an interrupt that cannot be handled by the current version of the Ada compiler.

There are a total of eighteen tasks in the program, and these contain a mixture of scheduling code and low level operations using records mapped onto hardware devices.

10.4.4 Distribution support

Once a collection of virtual nodes, such as that for the lift control system described above, has been written it must be distributed by allocating virtual nodes to particular processors in the target hardware. This distribution must then be checked for the validity of the virtual node root interfaces it contains, and that any units shared between virtual nodes can be copied in each. Finally, executable code for the chosen distribution must be produced and its execution on the target machines supported.

Implementation of the distribution approach

The single program written by the user as a collection of virtual nodes and then specified as having a particular distribution is transformed into one program per physical processor, these programs communicating via the RPC mechanism. This operation is *transparent* to the application programmer and does not loose any of the consistency checking of the original program. A call from a client in one virtual node to a server in a virtual node located on a different physical processor is carried out by means of the intermediate mechanisms shown here:

Fig. 10.2 RPC implementation technique

The RPC mechanism is provided by the networked processors and run-time system, while the client and server stubs are extra Ada code inserted to interface between the original application program and RPC mechanism.

Client and server stubs

These are produced as transformations of the virtual node root package specification. The client stub replaces the virtual node root body of a remote virtual node. When it is called by the client it packs the call parameters into a record then passes this to the RPC mechanism to carry out the call. When the call returns it unpacks returned values and passes them to the client unless there was a unhandled exception during the call, in which case it re-raises the exception in the client.

The server stub, placed on the processor holding the virtual node, is a template for the server task which is used as the thread of control to execute the incoming call. It unpacks call parameters and passes them to the original server subprogram, then pack the results and passes them to the RPC mechanism to return to the caller. If an unhandled exception occurs during the call execution then this is caught by the server stub and passed back to the client stub for propagation.

The RPC mechanism

A remote procedure call requires the exchange of a pair of messages, the call to carry the identification of the required service and values for *in* parameters, and the reply to return the result and *out* parameter values, or to propagate any unhandled exception raised during execution of the remote call. When the RPC mechanism is called by the client stub it places the call parameter record into the call message, sends this message, and suspends the client task awaiting the arrival of the result message for that call. When the result message arrives the result packet (or exception indication) which it contains is given to the client stub to unpack and return to the original client.

At the server end when the call message arrives the appropriate server stub task is created and given the call record. As this server task is unknown to the user's Ada program there are some optimisations which reduce the overhead normally associated with Ada tasks; for example no server task ever has any entries. When the server stub passes back the result record the RPC mechanism sends the reply message to the caller and the server stub task terminates. A user created task must leave some information when it has terminated as reference may be made to it from elsewhere in the program [111]. Server stub tasks are not known by the original program and so have no such requirement, so there is no permanent memory overhead associated with servicing an RPC request.

The use of dynamically created server stub tasks as threads of control causes parallel execution of RPC requests, so maintaining the Ada semantics for simultaneous subprogram calls from different tasks.

The distribution support tools

These tools run on Sun workstations and check the restrictions required for program distribution, generate additional Ada source code to support distributed operation, and provide for the specification and management of program distribution.

The tools to check that Ada library units conform to the distribution restrictions and generate client and server stubs are based on the University of York Ada compiler [50], and operate on Ada source code, producing source code in the case of the stub generator. This has the advantage that they can be used to support distribution alongside any target compiler for which a suitable run-time environment has been provided.

The specification of actual program distributions is made using a graphical tool based on the Aspect HCI facilities [105, 63]. This tool, shown below displaying the virtual node allocation of the lift control program described earlier, performs management of distributed Ada libraries and coordinates the checking and stub generation tools to ensure that the distribution is valid and required RPC communication support is present.

10.4.5 The trace-replay debugger

The basic form of the various components of the trace-replay debugging system have been described previously. In this section we illustrate the use of these components as they have been implemented in the prototype trace-replay debugger, and point out those facilities which have yet to be implemented.

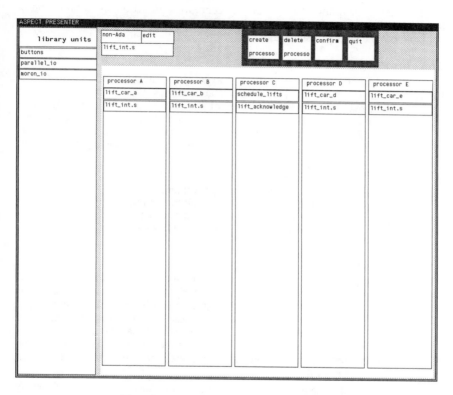

Fig. 10.3 Aspect target configuration tool

System initialisation

When the trace-replay system is invoked, it begins by down-loading and running some bootstrap code on each of the target machines to enable them to decode the various debugger-specific message types. It then down-loads to each machine the appropriate components of the user program; this can be directed either from a system description file or by explicit user command. The user code which is down-loaded must have been linked with the debugging version of the Ada run-time system; this provides the routines and calls necessary for recording events in the trace.

Monitoring

The only monitoring facilities not currently supported by the prototype system are the conditional recording of ITEs, and the conditional initiation and termination of trace collection. Since the prototype system does not support full replay, it also does not facilitate the taking of snapshots.

Trace browsing

The trace browsing component of the prototype system enables the examination of individual entries from the ITE trace. These entries can be stepped through sequentially or searched through for the next ITE which is either of a specified type, or which arose on a specified target machine (processor), or which arose from a specified task. The output is displayed in purely textual form; for example, a typical event recording the occurrence of an entry call statement would be depicted as:

Timestamp:	32
Processor:	A
Task:	car_movement
Event Type:	Entry Call Statement
Called Entry:	car_queue.next_floor
Outcome:	Wait for Rendezvous

Event level replay

The event level replay component of the prototype system provides an overall representation of program status as ITEs from the trace are stepped through either one or more at a time or until an ITE with a specified attribute is encountered (these attributes are the same as those which can be specified in trace browsing). Owing to difficulties in deriving the parameters of an entry call, all that is currently shown is the base address of the parameter area. Note that since there exists no mechanism for taking snapshots, the initial run-states of tasks, and the states of their entry queues, will not be known.

In the current system the event level replay mechanisms uses textual display. For non-trivial concurrent programs the amount of information generated is very large and this can make debugging very cumbersome. Ideally trace-replay debugging should be driven by a graphical interface; an example of a possible display is given in Figure 10.4. The aim of the graphical interface would be to present the large amount of information resulting from tracing and replay in a manageable form. Part of this would be achieved by allowing the user to determine what information is of interest – selecting screen objects would provide more information about those objects, so allowing a customised and dynamic collection of important information to be observed. For example in the display above three tasks executing on processor A have been selected as being of particular interest, causing their state and interactions to be displayed.

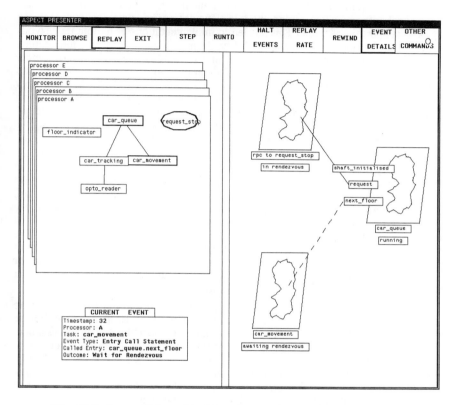

Fig. 10.4 A possible graphical interface to the trace/replay debugger

Full replay

As yet, no attempt has been made to implement the full replay component in the prototype system.

10.5 Issues and Lessons in Supporting Distributed Ada

In this section we consider some of the points that have arisen out of our approach and its prototype support tools.

10.5.1 Model of distribution

The advantages of RPC over distributed rendezvous

Implementing remote rendezvous is difficult as the queue maintenance for conditional entry calls is complex and it is difficult to provide a global synchronised clock to support timed calls. This has led to implementations of remote rendezvous which transfer the timing responsibility from caller to callee, and outlaw problematic issues such as the *CALLABLE* and *TERMINATED* attributes of remote entries and abortion of remote tasks [7]. In comparison a remote subprogram call requires only a message to pass the invocation and parameters followed by a reply to carry back results or to propagate any unhandled exception (remote exception propagation is not a problem if exception declarations are mapped onto internal names which are global and unique within the program).

Termination

Task termination in Ada can be considered in two parts [65]: one is that the termination of a task is dependent on the state of both its children and sibling tasks in the same library unit; the other the termination of library tasks (those that are directly declared in library packages). As the unit of distribution is based on library packages the first task termination mechanism is local to each processor – no exchange of messages through a distributed task hierarchy is required. The conditions for the termination of library tasks, and so the entire program, are not defined by the LRM. We implement the semantics which seem most suitable for distributed systems, that no library task is allowed to terminated until all wish to, at which point the whole program may terminate.

This is implemented based on tasks which wish to terminate 'pretending' to do so and reactivating if they are called at a later time. Each processor in the distributed system maintains a count of the number of currently active processors in the system, initially the number of processors in the system. When the number of non-terminated tasks on a processor reaches zero it sends a message to all other processors to indicate this, and each decrements its active processor count. When all processors have no active tasks this count reaches zero and all processors can terminate. If a processor with no active tasks receives an RPC request then any required tasks can be reactivated and a message sent to the other processors instructing them to increment their counts of active processors.

Elaboration

The Ada language reference manual [71] states in Section 10.5 that elaboration of a program must conform to a partial ordering in which no unit is elaborated until all units which it names in *WITH* clauses have elaborated. This ordering is to try to ensure that no object is used before it has been elaborated.

This ordering can be achieved in a distributed system with no global notion of time by having the compiler determine an elaboration order and then passing checkpoint messages around during elaboration to ensure that it is adhered to, but this involves a complex mechanism and run-time overhead [65].

We instead propose an approach made possible by the restricted forms of interaction between virtual nodes, and which avoids the overheads mentioned above. Distributed elaboration can be carried out by allowing the transformed programs placed on each physical processor to elaborate in parallel, each according to the normal ordering, but deferring execution of any RPC requests that arrive for not yet elaborated subprograms until such time as the subprogram has elaborated. Programs which are illegal as they have no valid elaboration order are detected when deadlock occurs. This technique uses the run-time system to determine partial elaboration order and allows as much of the elaboration as possible to proceed in parallel.

This elaboration mechanism can be seen to conform to the LRM constraints as follows. We consider two virtual nodes v1 and v2 elaborating on different processors and so each having local notions of time t1 and t2. Node v1 makes a remote procedure call to node v2 before v2 has completed elaboration. At this point the clock t1 is ahead of t2, as v2 should have elaborated before being called by v1, so we stall execution of the RPC until t2 has caught up with t1, i.e. until v2 has completed elaboration.

10.5.2 The trace-replay debugger

Recording inter-task events

By and large, the recording of ITEs has proved to be fairly straightforward. The points at which most types of ITE needed to be recorded within the Ada run-time system were reasonably obvious, with only the *task completed* and *task terminated* types requiring special attention – each needing to be recorded in five separate places. The main problem has been with the derivation of particular pieces of information which are required to be recorded for some of the types of ITE; specifically, the parameters of entry calls and remote procedure calls. For the latter of these it has been possible to adopt a fairly naive (and rather inelegant) solution largely because the RPC code is automatically generated by the distribution tools, and so it is quite straightforward to generate extra information for the benefit of the mechanism which records the associated ITEs. In the case of the parameters to entry calls, changes to the mechanism of the compiler would be required, and it would still be difficult always to display the values in a meaningful format. This is a problem which requires further careful consideration.

We should point out that these experiences derive mainly from working with the York Ada run-time system, but some preliminary work which was carried out with another run-time system would seem to indicate their generality.

Separation of debugger functionality

Throughout the design and implementation of the trace-replay debugging system, great care has been taken to confine the functionality of the debugger to within the trace-replay system bootstrap and the debugging version of the Ada run-time system. The major reason for doing this has been to avoid imposing any sort of overhead on the execution of programs when they are not being debugged. However, in two cases it has not been possible to maintain this strict separation: the distributed suspension mechanism, and the distributed clock synchronisation mechanism.

The mechanism for the suspension and resumption of user tasks executing on the distributed target machines required the introduction of two separate sets of message buffers (both receive and transmit) in the the network software running on each machine. This is necessary in order to enable any in-band messages waiting to be transmitted or decoded to be held over when an out-of-band suspend message is received, until execution is resumed again. The penalty which this imposes when not debugging is simply the extra space required for the extra sets of buffers.

In order to implement the distributed clock synchronisation mechanism it was necessary to add a timestamp field to the remote procedure call and result messages. This field is redundant when not debugging, and its presence will obviously slow down the transmission of RPC-related messages slightly.

10.6 Performance

This section presents some performance measurements of our prototype implementation. During the measurements the network serial lines were run at 75Kbaud, and all times are given in milliseconds (ms). Because our system is stand-alone, and was doing no other processing, the timings proved to be repeatable and are accurate to plus or minus one in the last digit given.

The figures are not intended to be exhaustive, and are for a prototype implementation, but should at least give a lower bound to the possible performance of our approach.

10.6.1 Model of distribution

Local and remote procedure calls
The table presents a comparison of execution times for local and remote calls to a parameterless null procedure in systems with different numbers of networked processors. In all cases the systems were otherwise idle.

Processors	Local(ms)	Remote(ms)	Network overhead(%)
1	0.050	n/a	0
2	0.087	11.6	43
3	0.071	14.7	30
4	0.064	16.8	22

These figures illustrate that there is a significant overhead associated with the use of our interrupt-driven network. As one would expect, the cost of a remote procedure call is much greater than that of a local procedure call. This extra cost consists both of communication overheads and the processing overheads associated with remote execution. It is useful to consider how the RPC time for a two processor system is split between communication and processing. A parameterless remote call requires the exchange of 30 bytes of data in two messages, taking about 3.3ms of transmission time with the network running at 75Kbaud. In addition to this the communications overhead involves the latency before each board receives the token in order to transmit the call and result messages. This latency is difficult to measure exactly, but the total for both call and reply lies in the range 0ms to 3.3ms, and must be at the upper end of this range as the increases in RPC time for three and four processors are due to the additional latency when the token has further to travel. This leads to the RPC processing overhead being in the range 5ms to 8.3ms, with a likely figure being about 5.5ms.

All further figures are taken in a two processor system in order to allow valid comparison.

10.6.2 Parameter passing overheads

The following table shows the effects of passing 256 bytes of *in* mode parameters to both local and remote procedures with null bodies, using a two processor system in all cases:

Parameter	Local(ms)	Remote(ms)
none	0.087	11.6
256 byte array	0.091	43.5
64 (4 byte) integers	0.362	43.5

The additional transmission time for the 256 bytes of parameter in each remote case is about 28.5ms. This suggests that there is a small additional overhead for parameter packing and unpacking, but that communication of parameters is the major cost.

The distributed termination mechanism

The distributed termination mechanism described earlier introduces an overhead when a processor is willing to terminate or revokes its willingness to terminate, as a message is broadcast in each case. The figures compare null RPC time with and without a 'will terminate' / 'will not terminate' message pair associated with each call.

With termination(ms)	Without termination(ms)	Termination overhead(ms)
13.4	11.6	1.8

The overhead for our distributed termination mechanism is small, especially as it is only invoked when no tasks are executing on a processor. This contrasts with the complex protocols required to determine termination conditions if task hierarchies are distributed.

10.6.3 The remote exception mechanism

The figures here compare remote and local calls with and without exception raising:

	Local(ms)	Remote(ms)
No handler/No exception raised	0.087	11.6
Handler present/No exception raised	0.112	11.6
Handler present/Exception raised	0.441	11.6

The local timings indicate that there is a run-time overhead associated with the Ada exception mechanism, some overhead being present even when the exception handler is not invoked. There is no extra overhead in the remote case as the exception handlers are always present in the stubs, and because result packing and unpacking are not performed by the server and client when a exception is raised. Although this means that the cost of an unused exception handler is always paid in remote procedure calls this 0.025ms is not significant in comparison to the other overheads.

10.6.4 Comparison with Ada tasking operations

The measurements so far have compared local and remote procedure calls, but the implementation of the RPC mechanism is much closer to that of Ada tasking operations. It may therefore give a better indication of the effect of RPCs on program performance if we compare with tasking operations.

Operation	Time(ms)
Null RPC	11.6
Local Null Rendezvous	1.8
RPC Containing Null Rendezvous	13.3
Local Null Task Execution	7.6
Local Null Task Within Procedure	22.3

The time given for execution of a null task is that for one element of an array of null tasks, this being a comparable operation to an RPC server task. While the null RPC time is greater than that for null task creation the proportion of the RPC time spent executing the call (as discussed above) is less, showing that our optimisations for RPC server tasks are worthwhile. As would be expected the cost of an RPC which makes a null rendezvous is very close to that of both a null RPC and a null rendezvous. The high cost of a call to a procedure containing a nested null task is due to the several context switches required to run both task and procedure, and this time illustrates that the cost of remote procedure calls is within the range of that of Ada tasking operations.

10.6.5 Comparison with other RPC mechanisms

Some perspective may be placed on our performance figures if they are compared with other RPC mechanisms. As we have no figures for other distributed embedded Ada implementations the comparative results presented in the following table are both taken from RPC mechanisms operating between networked workstations. The Cedar RPC [13] mechanism runs on very fast Dorado workstations connected by an Ethernet which provides very low cost communication. Hamilton's CLU [58] mechanism uses Motorola 68000 processors but communication is by means of a Cambridge Ring with dedicated communication processors. In each case the fastest time for minimal calls is given, along with the time taken just to communicate the data involved.

Mechanism	Time For Null Call(ms)	Communication Overhead(ms)
Cedar	1.1	0.13
CLU	6.7	0.83
Ada RPC	11.6	6.1

It is clear that like is not being compared with like due both to major differences in processor and communication speed and to differences in the intended scope of the mechanisms. However, the figures do indicate that our implementation has similar processing cost to other RPC mechanisms, considering the high speed of Xerox

Dorado workstations (between five and ten times that of our M68010 processors). They also illustrate the disproportionate cost of our simple network, this being so high as to mask variations in processing time in our performance measurements.

10.6.6 The trace-replay debugger

The most obvious measurement of the performance of the trace-replay debugging system might be that which seeks to quantify the efficacy of the debugger when applied to real-world situations. However, determining such measurements objectively is notoriously difficult, and making meaningful comparisons with other approaches is harder still. Since we have, as yet, relatively little experience with using the prototype trace-replay debugger, we do not feel that it would be appropriate for us to attempt to quantify such aspects of debugger performance at this stage. Instead we shall concentrate on the effects which the application of the debugger has upon the monitored user program.

The first point to note here is that programs which are to be debugged have to be linked with a special debugging version of the Ada run-time system. Programs which are not being debugged can be linked with the ordinary, non-debugging, version of the run-time system, and hence incur no run-time overheads.

The major run-time overhead incurred when debugging is that which arises from the recording of ITEs in the trace. We have carried out a number of experiments to determine the approximate size of this overhead (which obviously varies from program to program), and have found that the execution of the user program is typically slowed down by a factor of between two and two-and-a-half. However, in pathological cases where the program does little except generate a large number of complicated ITEs (for example, when there are two tasks in tight loops, one repeatedly making an entry call which the other accepts, and where there are no statements inside the body of the **accept** statement), slow-downs by a factor of around six have been observed. It should be emphasised that no attempt has been made in the implementation of the prototype to optimise the mechanism for recording ITEs, so these figures can doubtless be improved upon. On the other hand, the prototype does not yet support on-the-fly ITE recognition (for example, for triggering the commencement of trace collection), a facility which will tend to increase the run-time overhead.

Another aspect of the performance of the trace-replay debugger is the extent to which the suspension and resumption of the execution of the user program's tasks on the target machines alters the relative execution of those tasks. This is a figure which is rather difficult to determine experimentally, but which can be determined more easily by theoretical means.

Firstly we consider the suspension of execution. If the request to suspend originates from the host, it is sent out onto the network as a broadcast out-of-band message which will be received, decoded, and acted on by all of the target machines essentially simultaneously. If the request originates from one of the target machines it is also sent out onto the network as a broadcast out-of-band message. In this case all of the other machines will be halted essentially simultaneously, but the originating machine has effectively been suspended earlier. The delay between suspension on the originating machine and suspension on all the other machines is the sum of the times taken to set up the transmission of the request plus the time it takes to transmit the request on the network. The former value can be determined from an instruction count, and for our target machines can be expected to take around 0.2 milliseconds. The latter value comprises the delay waiting for the token to arrive, and the time taken to transmit the suspend message. The delay waiting for the token could be zero at one extreme, and at the other extreme it could be the time it would take for all the other stations on the network to transmit a maximum length message (currently 512 bytes) before passing on the token. The maximum value for this delay would be around 270 milliseconds. The time taken to transmit the suspend message itself is around 0.63 milliseconds.

The resumption of execution of the user program's tasks on the target machines is currently only requested by the host machine. The use of a broadcast message ensures that all the target machines resume execution essentially simultaneously. The chief exception to this is for the particular target machine (if any) which originated the previous suspend message; it will be in a slightly different state to the other target machines, and its resumption can be expected to take a few microseconds longer than the others.

There is one further way in which the trace-replay debugger can affect the behaviour of the user program; that is by the space it takes up on the target machine. Taking into account the trace-replay system bootstrap and the extra size of the debugging run-time system this amounts to approximately 9K bytes, of which 2K bytes is for the trace itself.

10.7 Integration into Aspect

Although some of the tools we have built use the Aspect HCI facilities, as yet we have not integrated them in the IB. This is because the tools and the IB have been developed in parallel. However, if integration was carried out, the tools would operate on database objects rather than Unix files, and the rich facilities of the database would be used to record inter-object dependencies and version information, rather than the variety of map and library files currently employed.

10.8 Concluding Remarks

10.8.1 Model of distribution

We have shown that although many languages have no direct support for programming distributed systems they can be applied to this application domain if restrictions are imposed on their use. By adopting a standard approach of designing programs as virtual nodes communicating via remote procedure call we are able to specify these restriction in a language independent fashion.

Although we cannot distribute all Ada programs, our choice of language restrictions (which did not cause any problems in our test implementation) has allowed us to use Ada in distributed embedded systems at reasonable cost. However, the performance measurements clearly indicate that a fast communication system would be necessary in any high speed application. Even given the use of a fast communication mechanism, the cost of remote procedure calls confirms our argument that pre-partitioning should be used in the design of distributed systems as it makes such communication explicit and therefore the programmer is aware of where delays will arise. As the processing overhead for remote procedure calls has been shown to be comparable to that of Ada tasking operations then this overhead should be acceptable within Ada programs. However, the high actual cost of all of these mechanisms must raise questions as to Ada's suitability for use in time critical applications.

10.8.2 The trace-replay debugger

We have set out the case for adopting the trace-replay approach as a basis for the debugging of distributed Ada programs, and have presented a range of debugging methods which can be built upon this approach. These methods range from the simple browsing of a trace to the full replay of the user program on the target machines. Given this range of methods, the user is able to select, for debugging a given program, the particular method which provides the maximum amount of debugging assistance possible without significantly disturbing the behaviour of the program.

We have discussed a number of issues, both general and specific, relating to the design and implementation of a trace-replay debugging system, and we have identified thirty-six types of ITE which would need to be recorded when applying such a system to distributed programs written in Ada. Our experiences with implementing a prototype version of the trace-replay debugging system have served to demonstrate the feasibility of collecting and using traces of ITEs, and have also highlighted some of the difficulties, particularly with the recording of parameters to entry calls.

Whilst we have concentrated on the debugging of distributed programs written in Ada, much of what we have said is equally applicable to distributed programs written in other imperative languages; the main area of language dependence being the types of ITE (or more generally, IPE) which are applicable.

Chapter 11

A Comparison of Aspect with Other IPSEs

P. Hitchcock

11.1 Introduction

Aspect falls into a family of IPSEs whose architecture is loosely based on that described in the Stoneman report [29]. That is to say, it provides a tool interface which is based around a central database management system. In itself, it is not an IPSE, but rather a framework which needs to be populated with tools before it is usable. In this chapter we have chosen to compare Aspect with three other IPSEs which have followed this approach. They are widely known and have aims similar to those of Aspect. They are PCTE (the Portable Common Tool Environment funded by the European Commission under the Esprit programme), CAIS (the Common Ada Interface Specification funded by the US Department of Defense) and ATIS (the Atherton Tools Integration Service). In addition, the next chapter compares Aspect with the other Alvey-funded IPSE projects, Eclipse and IPSE 2.5.

11.2 Aspect

Figure 11.1 gives a summary of Aspect functionality which is convenient for the purposes of this comparison.

The lowest layer gives the base operating system. This is extended by providing an object management, or database system, together with a mechanism for enforcing rules stated about the values of data. Above this there is a superstructure which provides basic operations for configuration management,

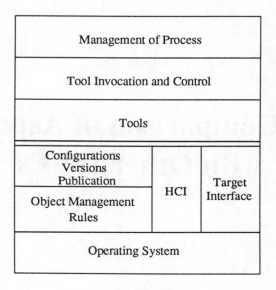

Fig. 11.1 Aspect functionality

version control and publication. This defines part of the public tool interface. Other operations at this interface include the human computer interface component and an interface through to target machines other than the host. Tools are then written to operate within this public tool interface. The next layer of function provides a language within which to invoke these tools and to combine them together into more powerful constructs. Finally, the uppermost layer provides a way of managing the overall process and of bringing together the product, the plan and the personnel carrying it out by providing a process modelling capability.

11.3 PCTE

PCTE, the Portable Common Tool Environment, is the result of an Esprit-funded project.

Esprit is a ten year (1983-1992) program of the European Communities which funds collaborative projects in Information Technology. PCTE was worked on from October 1983 until April 1988 by an industrial consortium with Bull as the prime contractor and GEC, ICL, Nixdorf, Olivetti and Siemens as partners. This resulted in the publication of the PCTE functional specifications as a set of operations written as C functions [27]. They were later specified as an equivalent set of Ada bindings. These specify a public tool interface. Partial prototype implementations were carried out, and a full version of the system, known as Emeraude [30] was separately developed by Bull. In addition there is another Esprit project known as PACT, the PCTE Added Common Tools [36]. A major objective of PCTE was that the definition of the public tool interface should be in the public domain and that it should not be tied to any particular hardware implementation. This explains its separate exploitation as a commercial product, but does not rule out exploitation by others on different hardware platforms.

The PCTE functional specifications provide a number of basic mechanisms, user interface facilities, and a distribution mechanism.

The basic mechanisms are divided into five categories:

- *Execution mechanisms.* These define how the execution of a program can be started or terminated, how parameters are passed and how a program relates to the environment in which it executes.

- *Communication mechanisms.* These deal with the way in which file type objects are accessed and correspond closely to the input-output mechanisms of Unix.

- *Interprocess communication.* PCTE provides a message passing facility and the possibility to share memory segments between users in addition to the pipes and signals of Unix.

- *The object management system (OMS).* The PCTE architecture is centred around the object management system. The OMS data model is based on the entity-relationship model of Chen [32].

  Object instances are entities which have a set of attribute values, a 'contents' which is a repository for unstructured data implementing a Unix file, and a number of relationships to other object instances. Access to objects is by navigation, that is to say, by starting at a root object and following relationships between other objects until the desired object is reached.

  The syntax for doing this is compatible with a Unix path name. Object types and their relationships are defined by in a schema definition set (SDS). A view of the object base is given by a working schema which can be defined in terms of information from a number of SDSs. The intent of the OMS is that tools will mainly work on the 'contents' of an entity. The OMS should be seen as a sophisticated directory to these files. The OMS also tries to avoid any centralised database administrator who is responsible for schema definition and so on. The user is able to modify the system to his or her own needs without this centralised control.

  - Activities. These correspond to the database concept of a transaction. They are atomic and serialisable in a multi-user system. It is also possible to nest activities. This provides support for the construction of robust tools.

  - Distribution. PCTE has been designed to support a distributed architecture of individual workstations connected by a local area network. It supports the distribution of processes and data between nodes in the network.

- *User interface.* This provides for a standard way of managing the user interface, albeit at a fairly low level.

The PACT project is building on top of these primitives to provide a more sophisticated dialogue management facility. The Emeraude implementation of PCTE offers a standard virtual terminal which can act in a number of modes depending on the tool that is using it. These include a mode which acts as a normal alphanumeric terminal, and a mode which allows for the display of graphic or multi-font text zones.

11.3.1 Comparison with Aspect

Direct comparisons are always rather difficult and prone to misinterpretation, particularly in this case where we are comparing a commercial product with an experimental prototype. However, such a comparison can be useful both in showing the way in which PCTE could grow and by showing alternative ways of achieving the same objectives; always important when standards are being considered.

Overall the intent of the two systems is very similar and they are broadly following the same architecture. As would be expected, the functionality of PCTE is somewhat less than that of Aspect. Referring back to Figure 11.1, PCTE provides object management and a more limited human-computer interface. Configuration, versions and publication will be provided by the PACT project as will sets of useful tools. There does not seem to be any work which will deal with the process modelling aspects of an IPSE.

We will look in more detail at a comparison of the central OMS which does exist in common between the two systems. A detailed study of this can be found in [61].

The anticipated usage of the PCTE OMS is rather different from that of the Aspect information base. Essentially the difference is one of granularity. In PCTE, the OMS acts as a sophisticated index. It is used to gain access to entity instances, whose 'contents' are analogous to files, and which are the basic things that will be handled by tools. Furthermore, these objects are reached by navigating along a path from a root node by a mechanism which is compatible with Unix path names. This should make it very easy for PCTE to make use of existing Unix tools. Aspect, on the other hand, would expect tools to use the database to a finer granularity. For example, the dependencies of modules on each other would be held as a number of tuples in a relation rather than a sequential file to be further decomposed by a tool.

Both Aspect and PCTE use a modelling formalism based on the Entity-Relationship model [32]. However, they differ in the data definition and data manipulation languages that are used to represent the model. PCTE has chosen a network representation and Aspect a relational one. The advantage of the network approach to PCTE was the close correspondence it has with Unix pathnames. There are many disadvantages. Date [41] identifies several criteria for a data model. These are:

- *The number of basic constructs should be small.* In Aspect entities and relationships are both represented by relations. In PCTE, the constructs used are different.

- *Distinct concepts should be clearly separated.* Both PCTE and Aspect separate entities from relationships. Aspect has the concept of object identity and deals with naming as a separate construct whereas in PCTE there are no absolute names for objects, rather the issue is confused with access paths. This severely limits data independence.

- *Symmetry should be preserved.* The links of PCTE are intrinsically asymmetric and are dealt with in a very different way if they are one links as opposed to many links. The evolution of the database is highly likely and will among other things be caused by the need to change a one link into a many link. This will require non-trivial changes to tools that are using the data structures. The relational view used by Aspect is completely symmetric and, because of the high level operators, such changes of a one link to a many link will often need no changes to the associated code.

- *High level operators should be available.* The data manipulation language of PCTE is navigational and object-at-a-time. The Aspect language is relational and has operators at the set level as well as at the tuple level. This allows for great economy in programming [62] The high level operators also provide a well defined query language which is also used in Aspect to define database constraints, the pre- and post-conditions on activities and contributed towards a sound view mechanism to support data independence.

- *The model should have a sound theoretical base.* The relational model has its foundation in mathematical set theory and has a considerable body of associated theoretical work, whereas the network model of PCTE has been formally defined after its implementation.

To summarise: PCTE is available as a commercial product called Emeraude. It provides a lower level of function than Aspect, relying on other projects to provide some of the things that Aspect has. The object management system relies on a network model and so is somewhat dated from a database technology point of view. There is strong political pressure for PCTE to become adopted within Europe as a standard IPSE framework. This seems to be somewhat premature given how little experience there actually is in using IPSEs, and to some extent is only solving half of the problem. For tools to share data they must agree first on the data structures to be shared and only then on their implementation.

11.4 Common APSE Interface Set

Based on the Stoneman report [29], the US Department of Defense recognised the need for a common interface for tools that would form part of an Ada Programming Support Environment (APSE). This would allow for the transfer of tools and data between different APSEs.

Again the proposed architecture is very similar to that of Aspect, and is centred around a database system. The database used is also an implementation of the Entity-Relationship model known as the CAIS node model [81]. There are three predefined node types:

1. A structural node which acts like a directory.

2.   A file node to represent Ada files.

3.   A process node to represent the execution of an Ada program.

These nodes are connected by uni-directional links (known to CAIS as relationships). When a new node instance is created it must be linked by a primary relationship to an existing node. This gives a unique path to any node which is given by following the primary relationships from the root node in a similar way to PCTE or the Unix directory system. Secondary relationships can also be defined between any two existing nodes.

Nodes and relationships can themselves have attributes which may be user defined. Every node and relationship instance has attributes which record the creation date and the creator's identifier and, in addition, file nodes have a contents attribute which can contain an Ada file.

Process nodes have attributes recording start-time, finish-time and resource usage etc. and are linked by primary relationships to the process nodes that invoked them. In addition, there are secondary relationships linking to the current user, current job etc. for that process.

This data model can be seen as a simpler form of that used by PCTE. There is no concept of a schema which defines a pattern for possible instances. Instead relationships are created as they are needed.

CAIS has been revised to become CAIS-A and the lack of a schema has been remedied by the introduction of a typing mechanism to the node model. This mechanism constrains instances of a type in the following ways: for nodes it defines the allowable relationships and attributes including contents; for relationships it defines the source and target node types, the attributes and degree of the relationship; and for attributes the type definition defines the value set and default initial value.

In addition, CAIS-A introduces the concept of views which allow for a structure to be renamed or to omit some object instances. This gives a subset view. In addition, CAIS-A introduces a simple form of nested transactions.

11.4.1 CAIS, PCTE and Aspect

The CAIS data model is very similar to that of PCTE, and hence most of what was said in the previous section applies here also. PCTE is being enhanced to become PCTE+. In particular, PCTE+ extends PCTE by improving the security mechanism (a strong feature of CAIS) and by treating processes as objects in a similar way to CAIS. Thus, PCTE+ and CAIS-A are coming closer together in function. However, they still have the network model of data and the lack of any naming scheme for objects which is independent of the access path to them.

Neither has yet caught up with current database technology.

11.5 ATIS

ATIS, the Atherton Tools Integration Service, provides a somewhat different approach to that adopted by CAIS or PCTE. It adopts an object-oriented design to the shared structure used for tool integration [103].

The central component of ATIS is a predefined type hierarchy shown in Figure 11.2. This forms the basis for a rich structure. Object instances are created in terms of the type structure.

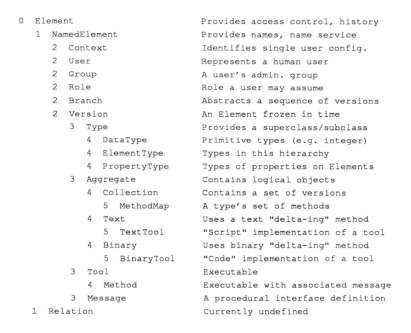

```
0  Element                   Provides access control, history
   1  NamedElement           Provides names, name service
      2  Context             Identifies single user config.
      2  User                Represents a human user
      2  Group               A user's admin. group
      2  Role                Role a user may assume
      2  Branch              Abstracts a sequence of versions
      2  Version             An Element frozen in time
         3  Type             Provides a superclass/subclass
            4  DataType      Primitive types (e.g. integer)
            4  ElementType   Types in this hierarchy
            4  PropertyType  Types of properties on Elements
         3  Aggregate        Contains logical objects
            4  Collection    Contains a set of versions
               5  MethodMap  A type's set of methods
            4  Text          Uses a text "delta-ing" method
               5  TextTool   "Script" implementation of a tool
            4  Binary        Uses binary "delta-ing" method
               5  BinaryTool "Code" implementation of a tool
         3  Tool             Executable
            4  Method        Executable with associated message
         3  Message          A procedural interface definition
   1  Relation               Currently undefined
```

Fig. 11.2 The predefined ATIS type hierarchy

They have methods or operations associated with them, which may be inherited. In addition the object instances have properties, or attributes. These can include references to other object instances, imposing a navigational or network view of data, as is the case with all object-oriented database management systems. The view that will be seen by tools is thus a schema of object types and their associated methods. The tools are shielded from the lower level implementation structures. This concept effectively finesses any discussion about the implementation level by concentrating on the actual objects that are to be shared. This is the appropriate level for standardisation. The higher level shared objects are defined and the details of the lower level facilities that might be used for implementation, e.g. CAIS or PCTE, are not standardised. They are just different implementation vehicles. Atherton themselves have an implementation called the

Software BackPlane. ATIS is a generalisation of the Backplane.

The type structure illustrated in Figure 11.2 gives a good impression of the level of functionality provided by ATIS. The schema that a particular user sees is given by an instance of the type *ElementType*. Its properties give a list of all the types and methods that are available for this view. These types can be given user defined names and can be used in an analogous way to, for example, the path name scheme of Unix or VMS. ATIS provides a generic structure within which a naming scheme can be defined. Detailed implementation could turn this into, say, a Unix or a VMS scheme.

Versioning is handled via a network structure. Components are represented by a Branch. Branches contain version instances, which can themselves be branches. The properties on Branch and Version enable this network to be traversed and the methods allow for the creation and maintenance of this network, and for the checking in and out of versions that are going to be worked on.

A Configuration Manager manages configurations of versions, where a configuration is defined to be a set of versions which is used in a particular build of the system. The build can be controlled from a design hierarchy which is identified by a particular context for a particular user's role.

11.5.1 ATIS and Aspect

ATIS and Aspect have a lot in common. The level of functionality provided is very similar. Both contain mechanisms for configuration management, version control and publication, as well as for transaction management. At the level of controlling the software process, Aspect is probably more advanced, but we must distinguish between what is achievable in a prototype and the need for some kind of consensus before something can be included in a proposed standard. There is general consensus about configuration management etc. throughout the industry, the same is not true about process modelling.

ATIS goes further than Aspect in some respects. Aspect was intended to be an IPSE kit and to provide the basic functions so that any kind of, say, a version manager could be built. ATIS defines the structures for a particular kind of version manager. This is the correct approach for a standard if tool interworking is to be achieved. Standardising at a lower level is not sufficient.

The other key difference is in the database system used. Aspect used a relational database system and was able to build on the query language that this provided to give a rules mechanism which, in turn, became an essential part of the process modelling mechanism. ATIS uses an object-oriented database system. Object-oriented systems have advantages of integrating methods with objects in a clean and concise way, but bring along with them the disadvantage that the data access is navigational with the ramifications that this has with respect to data independence. This is ameliorated somewhat by the close binding of the methods to the data structures. If the data structures are changed, methods can be changed to compensate, and so the tools that use these methods may not need to be changed very much. The other disadvantage that object-oriented database management systems bring is the lack of a high level query language and so the use of this for a rule mechanism and for process modelling. Combining query languages with object-oriented systems is an area of current database research. The Aspect view mechanism extended the traditional database concept of views by including operations and rules as part of a view. This can give similar advantages to that of an object-oriented database.

11.6 Summary

Aspect has shown that it is possible to define a generic superstructure for an IPSE which deals with views, rules, versions, configurations, publication and process modelling. As such it was somewhat ahead of the other IPSEs that we have compared it with, although there is a world of difference between prototyping ideas and defining standards. We believe that such a superstructure is the direction in which standards must move. This is the position being adopted by ATIS. PCTE and CAIS are working at a much lower level which we believe is not appropriate.

It is interesting to note that in the area of commercial data processing there is a draft ISO standard for an Information Resource Dictionary System [1]. This will provide the central database resource for the many Computer-Aided Software Engineering (CASE) tools that are available. It has been defined in terms of the relational language SQL, which is itself an ISO standard.

Chapter 12

Summary and Conclusions

A.W. Brown and R.J. Stroud

12.1 Introduction

Current work in IPSEs is very much in the research and experimental stages. While there is a great deal of activity in the general area of IPSE technology, very few successful commercial systems have been developed. Hence, it is vital to analyse the work that is carried out on any IPSE project as if it were a scientific experiment, asking ''what were the experiences gained from carrying out this work?'', and ''how can we make a better attempt the next time?''.

In this final chapter, we review the achievements of the Aspect project in the context of the Alvey programme which funded the research, and in the light of the original aims of the Aspect project – to undertake research into the facilities required for the construction of a second generation IPSE [12].

12.2 Aspect and the Alvey Programme

The Alvey programme which funded the Aspect project, also funded two other IPSE development projects, namely Eclipse [17] and IPSE 2.5 [93]. In this section we will describe these IPSE projects and draw some comparisons between them and Aspect.

Like Aspect, Eclipse was a second generation IPSE based on database technology. The two projects therefore have much in common and comparisons between them are interesting and useful. Comparisons between IPSE 2.5 and

Aspect are more difficult because IPSE 2.5 had more ambitious goals than Aspect; as its name would suggest, IPSE 2.5 was intended to be an evolutionary step towards the ultimate goal of the Alvey IPSE programme, the third generation IPSE or Information Systems Factory (ISF), and the project investigated IPSE technology somewhere between databases and knowledge bases (the characterisations of second and third generation IPSEs in the Alvey classification). It is also difficult to draw comparisons between Aspect and IPSE 2.5 because the IPSE 2.5 project has only just finished and thus not much has appeared about it in the literature. Nevertheless, we will attempt to demonstrate that Aspect and IPSE 2.5 tackled some of the same problems although they used very different technology to address them.

12.2.1 Eclipse

The objective of the Eclipse project was to build a second generation IPSE based on database technology and to populate it with tools to support several software development methods and Ada programming. In particular, the project was interested in developing an IPSE kernel and demonstrating how the facilities provided by such a kernel could enable integrated tool sets to be built. Eclipse was successful in achieving these goals and produced an IPSE kernel in the form of a tool builder's kit together with three tool sets built using this kit, namely tools to support LSDM (a requirements analysis and system design method similar to SSADM [5]), MASCOT 3 [9] and Ada programming. The MASCOT tool set could produce Ada package specifications from a detailed physical system design but otherwise the tool sets were not integrated with each other.

The Eclipse tool builder's kit is built on top of PCTE although a Unix implementation also exists. It supports the construction of integrated tool sets through the provision of common database and user interface facilities. It also includes a number of meta-tools that can easily be customised to produce a family of related tools. For example, the Eclipse design editor makes it relatively straightforward to construct graphical editors for typical software engineering design notations. Several tools in the various Eclipse tool sets mentioned above (in particular, editors for the LSDM and MASCOT design notations) were built by customising this generic meta-tool.

Since the end of the Eclipse project, the Eclipse tool builder's kit has been further developed and used on other research projects (in particular, the ESPRIT 2 project MACS which is concerned with software maintenance and the RACE project ARISE which is concerned with defining an IPSE for telecommunications software development). The tool builder's kit is now marketed as a commercial product together with a HOOD [2] toolset built using it.

Before discussing the facilities provided by the Eclipse tool builder's kit in detail and drawing comparisons with Aspect, it is important to note an important difference in the philosophy of the two projects. Broadly speaking, the focus of the Eclipse project was on building a commercial prototype IPSE based on current technology, whereas Aspect was more research oriented and concerned with exploring advanced IPSE technology. That is not to say that the Eclipse project did not have elements of research nor that Aspect did not have a commercial thread. However, it is important to highlight that the projects had a different emphasis. As a result, the

Eclipse project concentrated more on building end-user tool sets and adopted some pragmatic solutions to integration problems whilst Aspect explored the idea of a customisable IPSE kit and the use of innovative database and user interface technologies. However, the purpose of this detailed critique and comparison is not to prove that one IPSE is better than the other (because neither is better in any absolute sense) but rather to shed light on the various design trade-offs and issues involved in building an IPSE.

The Eclipse database

The Eclipse database facilities are unusual in that they are based on an amalgam of two underlying database technologies – the PCTE object store [54] and a language for describing abstract data structures called IDL [110]. These are unified by the use of a functional data model in which attributes are represented by functions of entities, and relationships are represented by entity valued functions.

The Eclipse database effectively exists in two tiers. The first tier is implemented by PCTE and supports relationships between file-sized entities with unstructured contents. In fact it is not clear from the PCTE specification what granularity entities are supposed to be (not all entities have contents for example), but current implementations of PCTE are based on Unix, and the PCTE object store is effectively an extension of the Unix file system that allows files to be typed and to have attributes and arbitrary relationships with each other. However, PCTE does not address the problem of modelling the contents of files (a serious problem for tool integration if tools need to share common data structures), except in the sense that PCTE's equivalent of files, namely objects, are typed with the type of an object determining its attributes and relationships but not the structure of its contents. Thus, tools that share the same data can be written to access the same type of object but how they interpret the contents of that object is left up to the individual tool writers.

Eclipse overcomes this limitation of the PCTE data model by introducing a second tier of data in which PCTE object contents are modelled using an extension of IDL for Eclipse called IDLE. Such fine structured objects themselves contain IDLE objects, relationships and attributes. Relationships are allowed to exist between first and second tier objects and PCTE mechanisms are used to guarantee the referential integrity of these relationships by ensuring that a relationship exists at the first tier for every relationship at the second tier spanning two or more first tier objects. (Without such an abstraction of the second tier relationships at the first tier, PCTE might allow an entire first tier object to be deleted even though another object contained a reference to it or its contents at the second tier.)

The Eclipse two-tier data model is a pragmatic attempt to tackle the problem of storing both fine and coarse grained data items without incurring a high performance penalty. Despite the successful unification of two different database technologies beneath a common abstract database interface based on the functional data model, the two tiers of data are an additional complication for the tool builder. Differences in the underlying data models do show through – although the abstract interface to the PCTE object store provided by the Eclipse database interface is a considerable improvement on the native PCTE interface, the IDLE data model is much richer and more efficient at making arbitrary queries since it is implemented using indexes rather than linear searches of Unix-like directories. Thus, many of the more interesting and useful facilities of the Eclipse data model are only supported at the second tier. One solution for the tool builder is to simply abandon the first tier altogether which is effectively what the Unix implementation of the Eclipse tool builder's kit does.

It is interesting to compare the Eclipse functional data model with the extended relational model on which the Aspect IBE is based. The ability to perform functional composition in a query (i.e. query attributes of attributes) is similar to the relational *join* operator except that all but the last function in such a query must be entity valued (i.e. represent a relationship). Similarly, the use of virtual attributes to perform pattern matching in queries is equivalent to the relational *select* operator. However, the functional data model provides no equivalent of the relational *project* operation because it is not possible to view an entity as a tuple of attribute values without making multiple queries to evaluate each attribute in turn. Ultimately, the relational model is more orthogonal than the functional model and therefore allows more elaborate queries to be built up. It would be much harder to define an effective view mechanism for the functional data model because of its lack of orthogonality but such a view mechanism is essential because the navigational style of query provided by the functional model makes programs very susceptible to changes in the underlying data structures [61].

The two tiers provided by the Eclipse data model also provide an interesting point of comparison with Aspect. Although Aspect uses entities at a finer grain than PCTE objects, the RM/T implementation still provides a loophole in the form of file entities which represent arbitrary amounts of unstructured data. Such file objects are essential for software engineering databases, both to support existing tools and because there is a clear need to represent large objects such as program source code or documentation as atomic entities in such databases. However, because Aspect provides no facilities for modelling the contents of file entities (in other words, because the Aspect data model is not recursive), in this sense, Aspect is no better than PCTE in that it only supports first tier objects. Furthermore, any performance advantage that Aspect might have over PCTE by virtue of being based on a proper database rather than an extended file system is lost by the inefficient layered implementation of RM/T as one database on top of another (which is appropriate for a research prototype because it clarifies the semantics of RM/T but is not a viable implementation technique for a serious commercial product). However, although the Eclipse two-tier data model does address the granularity issue by allowing an object to be viewed as atomic at one level and structured at another level, it is not clear that this is the only solution to the problem. What seems to be required is some form of abstraction mechanism that allows complex objects to be treated atomically. However, this should operate uniformly across all levels of the data and there should be no performance advantage of one level over another. The Eclipse approach is a pragmatic step towards achieving this rather idealistic goal. Whilst the relational model is undoubtedly weak at handling complex objects, its orthogonality makes it possible to define view mechanisms that build abstractions of the data and go some way towards implementing complex objects [21] – the problem is achieving good performance despite the multiple levels of indirection that a nested view places between the application using the view and the database.

Another difference between the Eclipse database and the Aspect database is the use of a data definition language by Eclipse. This is required by the underlying database technologies of Eclipse: PCTE requires a schema and IDLE requires a description of the abstract data types it is being used to model. However, the result is a rather static approach to data definition which is not amenable to change. Although PCTE provides elaborate facilities for extending schemas, these are masked by the Eclipse database interface. This would be an advantage because the PCTE facilities are overly complex and almost unusable except that there is no equivalent functionality provided by Eclipse. Unfortunately, with current implementations of PCTE, the alternative approach of deleting and recompiling a schema causes objects defined by the original schema to become permanently inaccessible, a real trap for the unwary. The consequences of changing an IDLE schema in this way are not clear. Although Eclipse allows IDLE schemas to be further refined by a kind of sub-typing mechanism, it does not make any provision for updating the contents of a fine structured object created using an old version of a schema. PCTE provides facilities for combining schema definitions into a working set but these are not adequate for defining views because definitions imported from one schema into another are resolved dynamically at run-time rather than statically at schema compilation time, requiring all schemas to be present in the working set at run-time. Eclipse provides no equivalent of the PCTE schema working set at the second tier because the IDLE schema for a fine structured object is accessed implicitly via the type of the object at the first tier rather than explicitly through a notion of current working schema. Thus, an important aspect of the Eclipse database system, namely the facilities it provides for defining new types of entity, relationship and attribute and determining the scope of these definitions at run-time, do not form part of the Eclipse database interface but are supported by external tools and mechanisms. This presents a serious barrier to flexible and extensible use of the database. In contrast, RM/T allows new entity types to be defined dynamically and requires no pre-defined schema. Views may be used to delimit the scope of type definitions. Both databases store catalog information self-referentially in the database itself (thus, an Eclipse schema can be accessed as a fine structured object) but there are some subtle differences between the representation of first and second tier schemas in Eclipse and not all the PCTE schemas used at the first tier have been made available in the Eclipse database, making it impossible to access all first tier type information without delving into PCTE structures, not something to be undertaken lightly by the fainthearted! (In fairness to PCTE, it should be stated that the whole area of schema representation and access has been revisited in PCTE+ where schemas are stored self-referentially as part of the object store. This should reduce some of the complexity of the existing PCTE mechanisms for handling schemas.)

One final difference between the Eclipse and Aspect databases which is worth discussing here is their approach to distribution. This is a very difficult area but it is also a very important consideration in the design of an IPSE which may well be used by many people across many computers within a single organisation, let alone between multiple organisations on a collaborative project. Although the Eclipse project originally intended to do work on distribution, the decision to adopt PCTE as a basis for implementation meant that it was possible to rely on the transparent distribution facilities provided by the PCTE object store at the first tier. Aspect also relied on a transparent distribution mechanism in implementing its solution to the distribution problem, namely the Newcastle Connection. However, this was applied at a different level of abstraction because it was recognised that users require some model to work with in which distribution is not transparent. This was achieved in Aspect by extending the domain based concurrency control mechanisms provided by the IBS to allow publication of objects between domains on different machines.

Unlike Aspect, Eclipse does not provide any equivalent of the IBS. Thus, there are no rules, views, activities, users or roles and Eclipse provides no process modelling facilities. A conscious decision was taken by the Eclipse project not to address project management issues and the Eclipse tool builder's kit does not provide any mechanisms to support integration by control. However, one area of the Aspect IBS in which comparisons with Eclipse are possible is the version control facilities provided by each IPSE. Eclipse provides rudimentary support for versions at the first tier in the form of a special entity type called an item. Versions of an item are attached to it by a linktype known to the Eclipse database which is therefore able to retrieve the latest version of an item automatically. There is also a notion of a configuration which delimits the set of versions of items (but not the set of items) currently in scope. New versions are created as part of a particular configuration but may subsequently be published read-only to other configurations. In this respect, Eclipse's configurations are similar to Aspect's domains, even to the extent of using the same two-way handshake for publication (publish, acquire, release, withdraw). However, one of the difficulties with the Eclipse model of versioning is that it only operates at the first tier of data. This makes it awkward to handle versioning at the second tier between individual items of a complex structured document, especially if such documents are heavily cross-referenced. Both the MASCOT and LSDM tool sets had problems in this area. Another difficulty is that the publish operation for versions should really operate transitively to publish all the parts compromising a particular sub-system. Aspect attempted to address some of these issues by providing support for configurations as graphs of versions and generalising the notion of publication. However, these are difficult problems and perhaps for this reason the original Eclipse versioning mechanisms no longer form part of the Eclipse tool builder's kit but are instead being replaced by a proper change management system as part of the development of Eclipse within other research projects. Similarly, a process modelling and management system is being added to Eclipse to address its lack of support for project management facilities.

The Eclipse user interface

The Eclipse database supports the integration of tools by data. The other way in which Eclipse supports the integration of tools is through the provision of a common set of user interface facilities. This is made up of several sub-systems: a message logging facility, an integrated help facility and an applications interface which supports a house style and thus ensures that all tools written to use it share a common "look and feel". Aspect has no equivalent of the Eclipse message system or help system because it had a different philosophy towards support for HCI. Such facilities could easily be implemented using the Aspect database and HCI facilities but the project chose to expend its effort in other directions because of its different focus. Nevertheless, it is still possible to draw interesting comparisons between the Eclipse applications interface and Aspect's equivalent facilities, Presenter and Doubleview.

Before doing so however, it is interesting to note in passing that whereas the Eclipse help system uses the Eclipse database system to store its help information, the Eclipse message system is unable to store its message texts in the same way because the database system uses the message system to log errors causing a potential circularity. This sort of dependency between the elements of a complex but powerful tool builder's kit arises because of the inevitable temptation faced by the designer of the kit to use the facilities he is building in their own construction. With care, this can lead to a better tool builder's kit that is more uniform because it uses the facilities it provides and not some other mechanism to implement functionality such as message logging and data storage. However, there is a danger that the dependencies will get out of hand, making it impossible to build tools that use only part of the tool kit without having to include the rest of the tool kit. Such a dependency exists in the Eclipse tool builder's kit – the database interface uses the message interface which in turn will use the applications interface to log messages if care is not taken to break the chain of dependencies.

The Eclipse applications interface supports a house style based on a control panel metaphor. Every Eclipse tool is driven by a control panel that contains various signs and indicators describing the state of the tool, together with various buttons and menus to invoke the functions provided by the tool. The use of a small set of interaction objects in this way imposes a uniform user interface across all tools built using the Eclipse tool builder's kit – they all look the same and are used in the same sort of way, even if they perform different functions.

This commonality is further enhanced by the provision of meta-tools that support an abstraction of some generic function but can be specialised to realise customised implementations of that function which differ in form but not in substance. An example of such a tool is the Eclipse design editor which supports the creation of diagrams drawn using the kind of graphical notation often used by software engineering design methods. This can be customised to produce a whole family of editors supporting different graphical notations but all sharing the same basic user interface. For example, it has been estimated that the software design methods LSDM, MASCOT 3 and JSD between them require editors for over twenty different diagram types, all of which could be built by a simple customisation of the Eclipse design editor.

The generic design editor works in terms of an abstract model of diagrams represented as directed graphs containing typed arcs and nodes. The representation of this graph structure as an Eclipse database fine structured object is also defined, making design diagrams persistent objects and allowing integration with other tools. Customising the design editor to support a particular design notation involves specifying the various types of arcs and nodes used by that notation, describing their physical appearance on the screen and their rules of combination (i.e. which kinds of node can be connected together with which kind of arc), and describing any additional method-specific attributes or relationships required in the database representation of the diagram. It is also possible to define method-specific operations as part of the customisation process that are invoked on the diagram in the same way as the generic operators provided by the design editor to create and delete arcs and nodes. Special languages are used for this purpose to describe the semantics of the design notation, its representation in the database and the user interface to the design editor.

The process of customising the design editor may be thought of in object-oriented terms as that of defining a sub-class of an abstract design editor super-class, inheriting and modifying the behaviour of this super-class as appropriate. However, in practice the Eclipse design editor is not as flexible or as customisable as this might suggest (although this is more a limitation of its implementation than a conceptual difficulty). Aspect provides no equivalent tool and consequently it would be an interesting exercise to re-implement the Eclipse design editor using the Aspect technology of Presenter, Doubleview and the RM/T IBE.

The Eclipse applications interface is implemented using a special language called FDL which describes the layout of the tool in terms of its control panel and the various interaction objects this panel contains. Operations to be performed when certain user induced events occur (e.g. an item is selected from a menu or a button is pressed) are specified in this language and are invoked as functions defined by the tool associated with the FDL. The Eclipse applications interface provides operations which the tool writer uses to load and then interpret the FDL. Callbacks are used by the applications interface to invoke tool functions in response to FDL events with the mapping between operation names in the FDL and tool functions being determined by a mapping table specified by the tool writer. Thus, tools are effectively event driven.

The advantages of separating user interface functionality from tool functionality are well understood [24]. FDL provides a mechanism for achieving this separation and allows cosmetic changes to be made to the user interface of a tool without altering the tool's code in any way. This mechanism is used to support part of the design editor customisation process. Aspect provides a similar separation with Doubleview and Presenter – Aspect tools can load and interpret Presenter structures that have been prepared in advance using Doubleview. Doubleview does not provide a linguistic interface for editing and describing Presenter structures in the same way that FDL describes Eclipse tool interfaces and this has both advantages and disadvantages. One of the advantages of the Doubleview approach is that the tool builder can edit the user interface graphically and does not have to learn a strange new language. On the other hand, FDL allows things to be specified more precisely and in particular provides an elegant mechanism for binding user interface events to operations in the tool – the Presenter programmer must effectively write his or her own event handling loop and map events in Presenter regions to tool operations. Another difference is that Presenter can be used either statically or dynamically whereas FDL can only be used statically. The recursive nature of Presenter and in particular the ability to paste an entire Presenter structure into another structure and interpret its behaviour dynamically is what makes it possible to write a tool like Doubleview. It would be much harder to write an equivalent tool for Eclipse that allowed FDL structures to be edited graphically because the Eclipse application programmer does not have access to the FDL structures at run-time. (Some attempts at producing such a tool were made during the Eclipse project but they did not form part of the eventual tool builder's kit and were presumably just research prototypes.)

But there is a more fundamental difference between the user interface philosophies of Aspect and Eclipse. Aspect deliberately imposes no house style on applications, preferring the "mechanism not policy" philosophy of the X window system [76]. However, Presenter goes beyond X in trying to break away from the world of nested windows. Although Presenter supports the concept of building up interfaces recursively as trees of regions, it does not impose the restriction that child regions must be physically contained by their parent regions. Thus, a user interface built using Presenter can look radically different from an interface built using more conventional technology such as X or the Sun windowing system on which the Eclipse implementation of FDL is based. Furthermore, Presenter tries to free the application programmer from many of the details of user interface programming by allowing behaviour as well as appearance to be specified in Presenter structures. This "mechanism not policy" philosophy results in Presenter providing not a fixed set of interaction objects based on a single interaction metaphor such as the Eclipse control panel but rather an extensible set of primitives that can be used to implement a variety of user interface metaphors (and in particular, some unusual and novel interfaces). Again, this is a consequence of the Aspect project's emphasis on exploring new technology in contrast to the Eclipse philosophy of making the best use of available technology.

The importance of providing extensible user interfaces is demonstrated by examining some of the limitations of the Eclipse applications interface. Presenter is an enabling technology making it possible to build tools like Doubleview whilst FDL and in particular its implementation are constraining because of their lack of extensibility, both in the inability to create FDL structures dynamically and in the inability to create new kinds of FDL interaction objects. Although FDL provides good support for the control panel metaphor, it is much weaker at providing support for other kinds of interaction panel such as text panels or graphics panels.

For example, the graphical editing facilities of the Eclipse design editor could not be implemented using the Eclipse applications interface or FDL because FDL provides no support for graphics panels. Instead, they had to be implemented by the underlying (and now obsolete) Sun window system, creating a barrier to portability. The only support for graphical interfaces (as opposed to constrained control panel interfaces) that the Eclipse tool builder's kit provides is through the design editor. Thus, any application which requires a graphical interface that in some way fits the design editor's paradigm of editing a graphical diagram can be built as a customisation of the design editor but otherwise the tool builder is on their own. Needless to say, constraining graphical interfaces to fit the design editor's paradigm is unnatural, awkward and in some cases not even possible. However, applications that implement their own graphical user interface will fall outside the Eclipse house style and will not have a consistent "look and feel" because the Eclipse tool builder's kit provides no re-usable functionality or integrating mechanisms in this area.

An implementation of the Eclipse user interface on top of the X window system that supported a richer set of interaction objects would go a long way to solving these difficulties but would still not be extensible in the same way as Presenter due to the constraining influence of FDL. It would be necessary to replace FDL with an extensible object-oriented user interface specification language to achieve this (in much the same way that the Eclipse design editor is customisable by means of extensible specification languages). Providing extensibility through customisable meta-tools is not the answer (although it is a powerful technique) because it requires applications to be made to fit the paradigm supported by the meta-tool and no meta-tool can support every possible paradigm naturally.

The Eclipse tool sets

Eclipse provides a number of tool sets to support different parts of the software development life cycle. In contrast, Aspect is relatively weak in this area because it has preferred to concentrate on the research issues involved in building a generic IPSE kit rather than the tool sets required by the end-user of an IPSE. In particular, Eclipse provides the LSDM and MASCOT 3 tool sets for which Aspect has no analogue (although Perspective, a commercial IPSE marketed by one of the Aspect project members which influenced and was in turn influenced by Aspect, includes a MASCOT toolset). Equally, Eclipse has no tool corresponding to Doubleview (although some attempts were made to build such a tool). However, both projects provide support for Ada programming and it is interesting to compare the facilities they provide in this area.

The Eclipse Ada support takes the form of a specialised tool built using the Eclipse applications interface which provides a control panel that allows the user to invoke the functions of an Ada cross-development system. In addition to this, a program library tool was built that captured the dependencies between Ada source modules and package specifications in the Eclipse database and provided configuration management facilities. In contrast, the Aspect target facilities were less well integrated with the Aspect IPSE because they made no use of the Aspect IB, something which caused problems when an attempt was made to integrate the Aspect target facilities with the version control and configuration management facilities provided by the Aspect IBS for the demonstration IPSE. However, the Aspect Ada development facilities were more sophisticated than those provided by Eclipse in that they supported the development of distributed Ada programs and provided tools for dividing up Ada executables between the nodes of a distributed system. They also included a symbolic debugger for distributed Ada programs. Some attempts were made to use the Aspect HCI facilities of Presenter and Doubleview to provide graphical interfaces to these tools, as seen in the Aspect demonstration.

Summary

Although Eclipse and Aspect had similar goals, their emphasis was different and the results achieved by each project are therefore very different. In this comparison, we have tried to show the strengths and weaknesses of each approach and thus illustrate the trade-offs involved in building an effective IPSE. In particular, we note that in the database area, Eclipse has attempted to solve the granularity problem through the mechanism of the two-tier database whilst Aspect has concentrated on building the abstractions of the IBS on top of the extended relational model RM/T to support process modelling. Similarly, in the user interface area, Eclipse has adopted a particular house style and provided some useful meta-tools whilst Aspect has preferred to explore the issues of extensible user interfaces. An interesting difference between the two IPSEs which applies to both the database and user interface facilities provided is the use of specialised languages by Eclipse to configure these facilities statically as opposed to Aspect's use of extensible interfaces that can be configured dynamically at run-time.

12.2.2 IPSE 2.5

It is much harder to draw comparisons between IPSE 2.5 and Aspect than it is to draw comparisons between Eclipse and Aspect because IPSE 2.5 belongs to a different generation of IPSE technology. However, there is one interesting similarity that can be drawn between IPSE 2.5 and Aspect which illustrates that both projects have addressed the same problem but with very different underlying mechanisms and technologies.

The IPSE 2.5 project had two main goals: to raise the level of integration within IPSEs beyond the simple "store+tools" model of Stoneman by supporting process modelling, and to provide effective support for the use of formal methods. The Aspect project's use of the formal specification language Z to specify the Aspect PTI was a major achievement of the project but would have benefited greatly from tool support. However, it is the process modelling facilities of IPSE 2.5 that we will discuss here.

Unlike conventional second generation IPSEs which are integrated about a central database (the "store+tools" model that IPSE 2.5 wished to improve upon), the central integrating concept of the IPSE 2.5 project is a Process Modelling Language (PML) which is used to describe some specific development process. The resultant PML program is executed by the Process Control Engine (PCE). The PCE is a computer system which provides appropriate working environments for its users − the people involved in the development process. In this respect, many similarities can be drawn between the IPSE 2.5 notion of a PCE and the Aspect notion of an IBS built on top of a relational database. Both provide support for process modelling by controlling the interactions between people, tools and information. However, the technology used for IPSE 2.5 is capable of much more than the Aspect technology because it is based on an object oriented persistent programming language rather than a relational database.

For example, the IPSE 2.5 project's approach to configuration management (or the management of change as the project prefers to call it) is based on the notion that change can occur at three levels: change to a process model, change to a process and change to a process product. This is very similar to the concepts Aspect attempted to capture in the IBS with its notion of an activity model integrated with a product model and coupled with an organisational model.

In conclusion, although IPSE 2.5 is more advanced than Aspect in its capabilities, it is encouraging to reflect on the fact that Aspect was moving in the right direction and was able to get a long way using its more primitive technology.

12.3 Achievements of the Aspect Project

In summarising the achievements of Aspect, we note that the main aim of the Aspect project throughout its lifetime has been to attain a better understanding of IPSE technology. To achieve this aim, significant progress has been made in many of the technological areas which are embodied in an IPSE. Here we briefly review the achievements in each of the main research areas studied by the Aspect project.

12.3.1 Information Base Engine

The use of an extended relational model as the IBE for Aspect was a novel and exciting step when the project began in 1984. Although outline descriptions of Codd's extended relational model RM/T had been available for a number of years, there had been very few attempts to implement it (in fact, only two that we were aware of).

In attempting to implement RM/T, we found a number of important omissions and inconsistencies in the existing descriptions, which we resolved by formally specifying the model in Z. The resulting implementation allowed us to experiment with the use of a semantic data model for the support of software development, showing that RM/T does indeed provide many of the necessary semantic capabilities needed to support a software engineering database.

In addition, to make use of the RM/T data model, we devised a new notation for representing RM/T schema, and a number of interactive graphical tools for querying and manipulating an RM/T database.

12.3.2 Information Base Superstructure

In the data storage component of an IPSE, the use of a relational database system for data control was shown to have limitations. The Aspect approach of building higher level services on top of this basis, first with a semantic data model RM/T, and then with facilities specific to software engineering, was particularly innovative. The experience gained in using this approach has agreed closely with results from other projects that took a similar approach.

The different services provided by the IBS have each made their own contribution to the overall achievements of the Aspect project. However, it is the integration of the IBS facilities through the Aspect process model which is perhaps the most significant contribution that has been made. The importance of this work is further highlighted in Section 12.3.5.

12.3.3 Human-Computer Interface

For user-interface services to an IPSE the principle of surface interaction, as embodied in the Aspect Presenter, provided an efficient flexible framework for experimenting with user interface design for IPSE users. The work carried out on the Aspect project provides one of the few insights into the area of user interface design for interactive database applications, recognised as an important, but neglected research area [82].

In fact, the Aspect Presenter, and its associated interactive tool Doubleview, have been recognised as a much more general purpose facility for user interface generation and management. Copies of the Presenter and Doubleview software are being used in a number of academic institution for Computer-Aided Software Engineering (CASE) tool development.

12.3.4 Programming and debugging distributed target systems

Host/target software development is an important area of IPSE support. The Aspect project defined a model of host/target interaction which has proved particularly useful for distributed debugging of Ada programs.

The main achievement of the targets work has been the development of a language-independent approach to designing and debugging distributed target systems. In particular, a simple general model of imperative programming languages was developed, and the restrictions that must be placed on this model for its use in a distributed environment were formally specified. The language-independent nature of this specification means that it gives a *single* formal description of how imperative programs can be distributed without recourse to individual language details.

The model has been successfully applied to several languages, in particular to the Ada language. To test its efficacy further, a tool set which enforces the model's restrictions on programs written in Ada was then developed. This tool set was used to design, implement and test a distributed Ada program which controls the operation of a distributed lift system – the lift is controlled by multiple M68010 computer systems connected by a local-area network.

It is clear that some of the principal benefits of IPSEs will come from their use for the development of large, real-time, distributed applications (e.g. fly-by-wire aircraft, process control, and so on). The Aspect project is one of the few IPSE projects to invest significant time in this area.

12.3.5 Integration of IPSE services

While progress has been made in all of these technical areas, perhaps the most significant contribution has been in Aspect's attempts to examine the *integration* of these services within a single system, based around a model of the software development process itself. There are many issues which could be discussed as achievements of the Aspect project in this area, but perhaps the most interesting are in relation to the work on software process modelling, and to the development of object-oriented databases.

In particular, early in the project Aspect developed the notion of tasks, or activities, as being a key concept in the integration of IPSE services. The activity model embodied the concept that a high-level definition of the development process is required as a focal point for users, tools, documents, and so on. It is interesting to note that the field of software process modelling which has emerged over the past five years as a key area of software engineering is largely based on a similar notion of activity modelling [107]. We believe that the Aspect project brings a great wealth of experience to this area, and has provided a useful and significant insight into the major issues.

With regard to object-oriented databases (OODBs), the recognition within the project of the need for extended database semantics greatly influenced the architectural design of the Aspect IPSE. New database functionality was added as a key component of the data services required for a software engineering database. With hindsight it is clear that the Aspect Information Base has in fact been taking an evolutionary step towards an OODB – using system generated surrogates as unique object identifiers, providing a type hierarchy with inheritance, and attaching operators to types through the notion of an abstract environment [23].

With the confusion that is surrounding this new area of OODBs, the work of the Aspect project is very important in tracing the evolution from relational databases to object-oriented databases. A number of papers published by the project have explored the important link that Aspect provides in this work [23, 20].

12.4 Summary

The main aim of the Aspect project was to examine the technology necessary for the development of second generation IPSEs. Aspect has made significant progress in this by examining several areas of IPSE technology in isolation, and has made a particular contribution in relation to the integration of those technologies within a single system.

In a wider context, perhaps the single most important aim of the Alvey programme was to promote the importance of software engineering as a discipline, and to train a new generation of researchers in its basic techniques. In this aim the Alvey programme has been particularly successful. The researchers who took part in the Aspect project have investigated many of the issues which will be of prime importance to software engineering over the next decade. This book has been a chance to share some of the many insights we have gained through this work.

References

1. "Information Resource Dictionary System (IRDS)", ISO/IEC JTC1/SC 21/WG3 N752 (January 1989).

2. European Space Agency, *HOOD Manual (Issue 2.2)*, April 1988.

3. M. Agnew and J. R. Ward, "The DB++ Relational Database Management System", *European UNIX Systems User Group Autumn Conference*, pp. 1-15 (April 1986).

4. G.R. Andrews and F. Schneider, "Concepts and Notations for Concurrent Programming", *ACM Computing Surveys* **15**(1), pp. 3-44 (March 1983).

5. C. Ashworth and M. Goodland, *SSADM: A Practical Approach*, McGraw-Hill (1990).

6. M.M. Astrahan et al., "System R: Relational Approach to Database Management", *ACM TODS* **1**(2) (June 1976).

7. C. Atkinson, T. Moreton and A. Natali, *Ada for Distributed Systems*, Ada Companion Series, Cambridge University Press (1988).

8. F. Bancilhon, "Supporting View Updates in Relational Databases", in *Database Architectures*, ed. Bracci, North Holland (1979).

9. G. Bate, "Mascot3 : An Informal Introductory Tutorial", *Software Engineering Journal* **1**(3), pp. 95-102 (May 1986).

10. BCS, "Data Dictionary Systems Working Party Interim Report", *ACM SIGMOD Record* **9**(4) (1977).

11. I.D. Benest, "A Review of Computer Graphics Publications", *Computers and Graphics* **4**, pp. 95-136 (1979).

12. I.D. Benest and Others, "Joint Final Report to the SERC on the Fourth Year of the Alvey Aspect Project", *Internal Report* (June 1989).

13. A.D. Birrell and B.J. Nelson, "Implementing Remote Procedure Calls", *ACM Transactions on Computer Systems* **2**(1), pp. 39-59 (1984).

14. B.W. Boehm, *Software Engineering Economics*, Prentice-Hall (1981).

15. G. Booch, *Software Engineering with Ada*, Benjamin/Cummings Pub. Co.

(1983).

16. A. Borning, "The Programming Language Aspects of ThingLab, a Constraint- Oriented Simulation Laboratory", *ACM Transactions on Programming Languages and Systems* 3(4), pp. 353-387 (October 1981).

17. M.F. Bott (Ed.), *ECLIPSE: An Integrated Project Support Environment*, IEE Books (1989).

18. F.P. Brooks, *The Mythical Man-Month*, Addison-Wesley (1975).

19. A.W. Brown, "Integrated Project Support Environments", *Information and Management* 15, pp. 125-134 (1988).

20. A.W. Brown, "An Object-Based Interface to an IPSE Database", pp. 5-20 in *Proceedings of 6th British National Conference on Databases (BNCOD6)*, ed. W.A. Gray, Cambridge University Press (11th-13th July 1988).

21. A.W. Brown, "Database Support for Complex Objects", YCS.113, Department of Computer Science, University of York (January 1989).

22. A.W. Brown, *Database Support for Software Engineering*, Kogan Page Ltd (1989).

23. A.W. Brown, "From Semantic Data Models to Object-Orientation in Design Databases", *Information and Software Technology Journal* 31(1), pp. 39-46, Butterworth (January 1989).

24. A.W. Brown, R.K. Took and W.G. Daly, "Design and Construction of Graphical User Interfaces using Surface Interaction", in *Proceedings of the 8th British National Conference on Databases (BNCOD-8)*, ed. A.W. Brown and P. Hitchcock, Pitman Publishing Ltd (9th-11th July 1990).

25. D. Brownbridge, L. Marshall and B. Randell, "Newcastle Connection, or UNIXes of the World Unite!", *Software Practice and Experience* 12, pp. 1147-1162 (December 1982).

26. H. Brown, "Support Software for Large Systems", *NATO Conference on Software Engineering Techniques* (1969).

27. Bull, ICL, Nixdorf, Olivetti and Siemens, *PCTE: A Basis for a Portable Common Tool Environment - C Functional Specification*, 1985.

28. A. Burns, A.M. Lister and A.J. Wellings, "A Review of Ada Tasking", in *Lecture Notes in Computer Science, Volume 262*, Springer-Verlag (1987).

29. J.N. Buxton, *Requirements for APSE - STONEMAN*, US Department of Defence (February 1980).

30. I. Campbell, "Emeraude - A Portable Common Tool Environment", *Information and Software Technology* 30(4) (May 1988).

31. S. Ceri and G. Pelagatti, *Distributed Databases Principles and Systems*, McGraw Hill (1985).

32. P.P. Chen, "The Entity-Relationship Model - Toward a Unified View of Data", *ACM Transactions on Database Systems* 1(1), pp. 9-36 (March 1976).

33. G. Cockton, "A New Model for Separable Interactive Systems", pp. 1033-1038 in *Human-Computer Interaction - INTERACT '87 (Participants' Edition)*, ed. H. -J. Bullinger and B. Shackel, North-Holland (1987).

34. E. F. Codd, "A Relational Model of Data for Large Shared Data Banks", *Communications of ACM* **13**(6), pp. 377-387 (June 1970).

35. E. F. Codd, "Extending the Database Relational Model to Capture More Meaning", *ACM Transactions on Database Systems* **4**(4), pp. 397-434 (December 1979).

36. PACT Consortium, *PACT, the PCTE Added Common Tool Environment*, Louveciennes, France, 1989.

37. R. P. Cook, "*MOD - A Language for Distributed Programming", *Proceedings of the 1st International Conference on Distributed Computing Systems*, Huntsville, Alabama, pp. 233-241 (October 1979).

38. D. Cornhill, "A Survivable Distributed Computing System for Embedded Application Programs Written in Ada", *Ada Letters* **3**(3), pp. 79-86 (November/December 1983).

39. R. Curtis and L. Wittie, "BugNet: A Debugging System for Parallel Programming Environments", pp. 394-399 in *Proc. IEEE Third International Conference on Distributed Computing Systems* (October 1982).

40. C.J. Date, *An Introduction to Database Systems - Volume II*, Addison-Wesley (1983).

41. C.J. Date, *An Introduction to Database Systems - Volume I*, Addison-Wesley (1986).

42. T. DeMarco, *Controlling Software Projects*, Yourdon Press (1982).

43. B. R. Dillistone, "VCMF - A Version and Configuration Modelling Formalism", pp. 145-163 in *Proceedings of Software Engineering 86*, ed. D. Barnes and P.Brown, Peter Peregrinus Ltd, Southampton (September 1986).

44. A.N. Earl and R.P. Whittington, "Capturing the Semantics of an IPSE Database - Problems, Solutions and an Example", *Data Processing* **27**(9), Butterworth (November 1985).

45. A.N. Earl, R.P. Whittington, P. Hitchcock and J.A. Hall, "Specifying a Semantic Model for use in an Integrated Project Support Environment", pp. 202-219 in *Software Engineering Environments*, ed. I. Sommerville, Peter Peregrinus (1986).

46. G. Enderle, K. Kansy and G. Pfaff, *Computer Graphics Programming*, Springer-Verlag (1984).

47. D. Englebart, "Design Considerations for Knowledge Workshop Terminals", *AFIPS* **42**, pp. 221-227 (1973).

48. V. B. Erickson and J. F. Pellegrin, "Build - A Software Construction Tool", *Bell Systems Technical Journal* (1984).

49. S. I. Feldman, "Make - A program for Maintaining Computer Programs", *Software Practice and Experience* **9**, pp. 255-265 (April 1979).

50. J.R. Firth, C.H. Forsyth, L. Tsao, K.S. Walker and I.C. Wand, "York Ada Workbench Compiler Release 2 User Guide", YCS.87, Department of Computer Science, University of York (March 1987).

51. J.D. Foley, A. Van Dam and Fundamentals of Computer Graphics, Addison

Wesley (1983).

52. J.D. Foley, *A User Interface Design Aid*, Department of EE and CS, George Washington University, USA (1985).

53. W.. Freeman, M. Baslington and R. Pack, "A Model Lift System as a Test-bed for Students' Real-time Programming Experiments", YCS.52, Department of Computer Science, University of York (May 1982).

54. F. Gallo, R. Minot and I. Thomas, "The Object Management System of PCTE as a Software Engineering Database Management System", *Proceedings of 2nd SIGSOFT/SIGPLAN Symposium on Practical Software Development Environments*, pp. 12-15 (December 1986).

55. N. Habermann, R. Ellison, R. Medina-Mora, P. Feiler, D. S. Notkin, G. E. Kaiser, D. B. Garlan and S. Popovich, *The second Compendium of Gandalf Documentation*, CMU Computer Science Department, Carnegie Mellon University (May 1982).

56. P. A. Hall, P. Hitchcock and S. J Todd, "An Algebra of Relations for Machine Computation", *Proceedings of the 23rd ACM Symposium on Principles of Programming Languages*, pp. 225-232 (1975).

57. P.A. Hall, J. Owlett and S.J.P. Todd, "Concepts for Modelling Information", pp. 95-110 in *Modelling in Database Management Systems*, ed. G.M. Nijssen, North Holland (1976).

58. K.G. Hamilton, "A Remote Procedure Call System", TR.70, University of Cambridge Computer Laboratory (1984).

59. M.D. Harrison, "Monitoring a Target Network to support Subsequent Host Simulation", *Journals of Microcomputer Applications* 8, pp. 75-85 (1985).

60. P. Hibbard, A. Hisgen, J. Rosemberg and M. Sheiman, "Programming in Ada: examples", in *Studies in Ada Style*, Spinger-Verlag (1981).

61. P. Hitchcock, "A Database View of the PCTE and ASPECT", pp. 37-49 in *Software Engineering Environments*, ed. P. Brereton, Ellis Horwood (1987).

62. P. Hitchcock and A.W. Brown, "A Comparison of Databases for Software Engineering", *Proceedings of Software Engineering '90*, Brighton, England (July 1990).

63. S.J. Holmes, "Overview and User Manual for Doubleview", YCS.109, Department of Computer Science, University of York (January 1989).

64. F.R.A. Hopgood et al., *Introduction to the Graphical Kernel System,*, Academic Press (1983).

65. A.D. Hutcheon and A.J. Wellings, "Elaboration and Termination of Distributed Ada Programs", pp. 195-204 in *Ada: The Design Choice, Proceedings Ada-Europe Conference, Madrid*, ed. A. Alvarez, Cambridge University Press (1989).

66. A.D. Hutcheon and A.J. Wellings, "Specifying Restrictions on Imperative Programming Languages for Use in a Distributed Environment", *Software Engineering Journal* 5(2), pp. 93-104 (1990).

67. A. F. Hutchings, R. W. McGuffin, A. E. Elliston, B. R. Tranter and P. N.

Westmacott, "CADES - Software Engineering in Practice", pp. 136-144 in *Proceedings of 4th International Conference on Software Engineering, Munich*, ICL, Kidsgrove (September 1979).

68. K. Jackson, "Tightly Controlled Project Support Environments", pp. 147-180 in *Proceedings Joint IBM/University of Newcastle upon Tyne Seminar* (2nd-5th September 1986).

69. W. H. Jessop, "Ada Packages and Distributed Systems", *SIGPLAN Notices* **17**(2), pp. 28-36 (February 1982).

70. J. Katzenelson, "AEDNET: a Simulator for Non-linear Networks", *Proc IEEE* **54**, pp. 1536-1552 (1966).

71. D. Keeffe, G.M. Tomlinson, I.C. Wand and A.J. Wellings, *PULSE: An Ada-based Distributed Operating System*, APIC Studies in Data Processing Series, Academic Press (1985).

72. A. M. Keller, "Updating Relational Databases Through Views", Ph.D Thesis, Stanford University (Feb 1985).

73. W. Kent, "Limitations of Record-Based Information Models", *ACM Transactions on Database Management Systems* **4**(1), pp. 107-131 (March 1979).

74. L. Lamport, "Time, Clocks, and the Ordering of Events in a Distributed System", *CACM* **21**(7), pp. 558-565 (July 1978).

75. B. Liskov and R. Scheifler, "Guardians and Actions: Linguistic Support for Robust, Distributed Programs", *ACM Transactions on Programming Languages and Systems* **5**(3), pp. 381-404 (July 1983).

76. J. McCormack and P. Asente, "Using the X Toolkit or, How to Write a Widget", *USENIX Association Conference Proceedings*, pp. 1-13 (Summer 1988).

77. A. Meier and R.A. Lorie, "A Surrogate Concept for Engineering Databases", *Proceedings of Int. Conf on Very Large Databases*, pp. 30-32 (1983).

78. R.W. Mitze, "The UNIX system as a Software Engineering Environment", pp. 345-357 in *Software Engineering Environments*, ed. H. Hunke (1981).

79. J. Mylopoulos and H. K. T. Wong, "Some Features of the TAXIS data model", pp. 399-410 in *Proc. 6th Int. Conf. Very Large Data Bases* (1980).

80. B. J. Nelson, "Remote Procedure Call", CMU-CS-81-119, Department of Computer Science, Carnegie-Mellon University (May 1981).

81. P.A. Oberndorf, "The Common Ada Programming Support Environment (APSE) Interface Set (CAIS)", *IEEE Transactions on Software Engineering* **14**(6), pp. 742-748 (June 1988).

82. Laguna Beach Participants, "Future Directions in DBMS Research", *ACM SIGMOD Record* **18**(1), pp. 17-26 (March 1989).

83. V. Quint and I. Vatton, "An Abstract Model for Interactive Pictures", pp. 643-647 in *Human-Computer Interaction - INTERACT '87 (Participants' Edition)*, ed. H. -J. Bullinger and B. Shackel, North-Holland (1987).

84. D.S. Robinson(ed.), "Aspect - Specification of the Public Tool Interface", aspect/wb/pub/pti/Zspec3.1, Systems Designers PLC. (August 1987).

85. M. J. Rochkind, "The Source Code Control System", *IEEE Transactions on Software Engineering* **SE-1**(4), pp. 364-370 (December 1975).

86. B. R. Rowland and R. J. Welsch, "Software Development System", *Bell Systems Technical Journal* **62**(1) (January 1983).

87. R. W. Scheifler and J. Gettys, "The X Window System", *ACM Transactions on Graphics* **5**(2), pp. 79-109 (April 1986).

88. M. Shaw, "Abstraction Techniques in Modern Programming Languages", *IEEE Software*, pp. 10-26 (October 1984).

89. S.K. Shrivastava, "On the Treatment of Orphans in a Distributed System", *Proceedings of the 3rd Symposium on Reliability in Distributed Software and Database Systems*, Florida, pp. 155-162 (October 1983).

90. M. Sloman, J. Magee and J. Kramer, "Building Flexible Distributed Systems in Conic", pp. 86-105 in *Distributed Computing Systems Programme*, ed. D. A. Duce, Peter Peregrinus Ltd. (1984).

91. J. M. Smith and D. C. P. Smith, "Database Abstractions: Aggregation and Generalization", *ACM TODS* **2**(2) (June 1977).

92. D.S. Snowden, "Specification of a Trace-Replay System for Ada Programs", Aspect Document wb/pub/dds/dss1, Department of Computer Science, University of York (January 1987).

93. R.A. Snowdon, "An Introduction to the IPSE2.5 Project", *ICL Technical Journal*, pp. 467-475 (May 1989).

94. B.L. Somberg, "A Comparison of Rule Based and Positionally Constant Arrangements of Computer Menu Items", *Proceedings of HI and GI Conference*, pp. 255-260 (April 1987).

95. M. Spivey, *The Z Notation: A Reference Manual*, Prentice Hall (1989).

96. M. Stonebraker, *The INGRES Papers*, Addison-Wesley (1986).

97. B. Sufrin, C. Morgan, I. Sorensen and I. Hayes, *Notes for a Z Handbook Part 1 -- Mathematical Language*, Oxford University Computing Laboratory, PRG, July 1985.

98. A. Sutcliffe, *Jackson Systems Development*, Prentice-Hall (1988).

99. I. Sutherland, "SKETCHPAD: a Man-machine Graphical Communication System", *AFIPS, SJCC* **23**, pp. 329-346 (1963).

100. Systems_Designers, *DEC/VAX Perspective Technical Overview*, November 1984.

101. P. Szekely, "Separating the User Interface from the Functionality of Application Programs", *ACM SIGCHI Bulletin* **18**(2), pp. 45-46 (April 1987).

102. G. Szwillus, "GEGS - A System for Generating Graphical Editors", pp. 135-141 in *Human-Computer Interaction - INTERACT '87 (Participants' Edition)*, ed. H. -J. Bullinger and B. Shackel, North-Holland (1987).

103. Atherton Technology, *Atherton Tools Integration Services (ATIS) - Phase 2 (ATIS01.03)*, June 1988.

104. W. Teiltelman, "Ten Years of Window Systems - A Retrospective View", pp. 35-46 in *Methodology of Window Management*, ed. F.R.A. Hopgood,

Springer-Verlag (1986).

105. R. Took, "The Presenter - a Formal Design for an Autonomous Display Manager for an IPSE", pp. 151-169 in *Software Engineering Environments*, ed. I. Sommerville, Peter Peregrinus Ltd. (1986).

106. R.K. Took, *Presenter Programmer/User Manual*, Department of Computer Science, University of York, UK (1989).

107. C. Tully, "Software Process Models and Programs: Observations on their Nature and Context", *Proceedings of the 4th International Software Process Workshop*, Devon, UK., pp. 100-103 (11-13 May 1988).

108. A.O. Ward, "Good Software Engineering: The Only Guarantee to Meet Tight Scales and Limited Budgets", *Proceedings of MILCOMP'86*, Microwave Exhibitions and Publishers Ltd. (1986).

109. J. Warnock and D. K. Wyatt, "A Device Independent Graphics Imaging Model for Use with Raster Devices", *ACM Conference of the Special Interest Group for Graphics*, pp. 313-320 (July 1982).

110. W. B. Warren, J. Kickenson and R. Snodgrass, "A Tutorial Introduction to Using IDL", *ACM SIGPLAN Notices* **22**(11), pp. 18-34 (November 1987).

111. A.J. Wellings, D. Keeffe and G.M. Tomlinson, "A Problem with Ada and Resource Allocation", *Ada Letters* **3**(4), pp. 112-123 (January/February 1984).

Index

The A.P.I.C. Series
General Editors: M. J. R. Shave and I. C. Wand

* Out of print.
† Now published in the Computer Science Classics Series.